HOW TO DANCE FOREVER

DANIEL NAGRIN

HOW TO DANCE FOREVER

FOREVER

Surviving Against the Odds

QUILL · WILLIAM MORROW
NEW YORK

Title page photo:
JAZZ Three Ways (1958–67)
Music: Yancey, Cole and Monk
Photographer: Marcus Blechman

Grateful acknowledgment is made to Alfred A. Knopf, Inc., for permission to reprint an excerpt from *The Rebel* by Albert Camus, translated by Anthony Bower.

Excerpts from "Wiest and Langella Play Complex Roles in 'Fall' " by Samuel G. Freedman, 11/5/84; "Relaxation: Surprising Benefits Detected," by Daniel Goleman, 5/13/86, copyright © 1984/1986 by The New York Times Company; and "Older Dancers Should Have a Place in the Theatre" by Jack Anderson, 3/3/86, copyright © 1986 by The New York Times Company. Reprinted by permission.

"Dennis the Menace"® (cartoon of 4/22/87) used by permission of Hank Ketcham and copyright © by North America Syndicate.

Permission to quote from *Arnold: The Education of a Bodybuilder* by Arnold Schwarzenegger with Douglas Kent Hall, Simon and Schuster (1977), page 192, is gratefully acknowledged.

Thankful acknowledgment is made to George Allen & Unwin Ltd, London, for permission to reprint a stage direction from the Gilbert Murray translation; Euripides, *The Bacchae* (1961).

Permission to quote from Aleksandr Nekrich, *Renounce Fear: Memoirs of an Historian*, Overseas Publication Interchange, Ltd, London, is gratefully acknowledged.

An excerpt from an essay by Lewis Thomas is reprinted with permission from *The New York Review of Books*. Copyright © 1987 Nyrev, Inc.

Library of Congress Cataloging-in-Publication Data

Nagrin, Daniel.
    How to dance forever.
    Includes index.
    1. Dancing—Vocational guidance. I. Title.
GV1597.N34 1988b   793.3'023'73   88-1421
ISBN 0-688-07799-4
ISBN 0-688-07479-0 (pbk)

Printed in the United States of America

First Quill Edition

1 2 3 4 5 6 7 8 9 10

BOOK DESIGN BY MARIE-HÉLÈNE FREDERICKS

dedicated to
ALICIA ALONSO,
a great artist and an inspiring survivor

Acknowledgments

To recognize here in print who it was who helped me as I wrote this book is an impossible task. I have long felt that I am the complex accretion of all whom I have met. Having seen Charlie Chaplin, I am that much different than I might have been. Accepting the futility of a comprehensive acknowledgment, I will start off with Mrs. Shapiro, who in the third grade revealed the · architectural glories of the English language. I had first encountered communication as a porridge of gems from Russian, Yiddish and newly acquired English. Her syntactical diagrams on the blackboard revealed the elegant bones of the English sentence: subject and predicate with its attendant verb, object, clauses, and modifiers. Writing and speaking became a gymnastic delight. Leaping across half a century, I will pause to give thanks to the chair of the Dance Department at Arizona State University, Dr. Elizabeth Lessard, who cleared a space for me at A.S.U., giving me the time and the wherewithal to write this.

Between these two names, listed in alphabetical order, without clarification or emphasis, are all those who in one fashion or another played a vital role and to whom I am deeply beholden. Though their support, information, assistance and advice were invaluable, I alone am responsible for the opinions and interpretations that fill these pages.

Whitney Alexander
Morris Axelrod, Ph.D.
Howard Bay
Suzanne R. Bias, M.B.A.
Lisa Booth
Suzanne Cheung
Xenia Chlistowa
Shirley Clark
Alyson Colwell, M.F.A.
Irene Dowd
Michael Engel
Irene Feigenheimer
Ara Fitzgerald
Meghan Found
Annabelle Gamson

Acknowledgments

Gary Harris
Edith Heavenrich
Jules Heller, Ph.D.
Harold B. Hunnicutt, Ed.D.
Sybil Huskey, M.F.A.
Marion Jones, M.A.
Sylvia Dick Karas
Keith J. King
Connie Kreemer
Richard V. Lee, M.D.
Jacques Levy, Ph.D.
Ann Ludwig, M.S.
Melinda M. Manore, Ph.D.
Sheila Marion, M.A.
Pamela Matt, M.A.
Ellen Mayer
Kathleen W. Milbrandt
Michael J. Miller, Ph.D.
Woodrow C. Monte, Ph.D.
Timothy Moore, M.F.A.
The National Endowment for the Arts
   (a collection of gracious individuals)
Shane O'Hara, M.F.A.
Madelyn O'Neal
Michelle Piette
Joan C. Randall
Nigel Redden
Joseph H. Reno, M.D.
David Romney, M.D.
Bernice Rosen, M.A.
Dean Seymour Rosen
Mel Rosenthal, Ph.D.
Eric Salzman
Ben Shaktman
Stanford University Dance Division
Sheila Sullivan
Gail Teton
Eugenia Y. Tu, M.S.
Larry Tucker
Stephen A. Vanpelt, M.D.

Acknowledgments

Linda Vaughan, Ph.D.
Julia Weldon, M.F.A.
Jennifer Williams

To all, thank you.

Tempe, AZ
1987

Contents

Contents

Contents

Contents

INTRODUCTION

To choose to be a dancer is a lovely act of defiance. "Common sense" often tries to dissuade us. We are told from early on, "But your life will be so limited." The belief, the assumption, and I say the myth, is that dancers must retire from professional life as performers in their early forties. This is precisely the time when artists and professionals in other fields are building up steam, often *beginning* to do their best work, and riding high with the prospect of at least another twenty or thirty years of productive work.

The premise of this book dubs the pessimism of a forty-year barrier for dancers as sheer nonsense. History dubs it nonsense. Too many great dancers have, late in their lives, filled stages with that special exaltation that only dancers can bring to an audience. With wisdom, knowledge of the body, a zest for life, canniness and a good dollop of luck, a dancer can and should be able to perform beautifully, dancing joyously into his/her sixties.

Galina Ulanova, Dame Alicia Markova, Dame Margo Fonteyn, Alicia Alonso, Maya Plisetskaya, all fine artists of a most demanding art, went on to perform to the joy of audiences everywhere while simultaneously defying the myth of early retirement. In the modern field, Merce Cunningham, Annabelle Gamson, Erick Hawkins, Pearl Lang and Murray Louis have danced into their fifties, and some beyond that. Kazuo Ohno, at seventy-eight, had a successful concert in Tokyo in 1985. The author's most recent performance took place half a year after his sixty-sixth birthday.

I salute all of you who reject "common sense" for good sense. Not to do what you love is neither common sense nor good sense. Still, there's no way out of it; dancing *is* difficult, hard on the body and often dangerous, but to repeat: With wisdom, knowledge of the body, a zest for life and canniness, one can "dance forever."

This book is for all who dance: for the teachers of that wild and beautiful art, for the young people while they are still undamaged and particularly for mature dancers who suddenly become aware of the finite limits of the dancer's time. To the latter, there may be more time than you imagine. This book hopes to help you.

For those of you out there who do not dance, feel free to browse among these pages and learn how we steer past Scylla and Charybdis in order to dance for you.

Finally, at no point in this book am I pretending to give hard answers. From beginning to end I am uttering guesses and assumptions that are based on years of accumulated empirical evidence plus a grounding in biology, nutrition, anatomy and kinesiology. I seriously doubt whether anyone, from medical doctors to witch doctors, can do anything but guess and make assumptions about the mysteries of the human body. More than anything, this book is a *call for an exchange of thoughts from all of us in the field,* not only to the doctors and the other healers but to the dancers, the teachers and the choreographers. Separately we all know but bare bits of what wants to be known. *All together we know a great deal.*

Yes, there are more questions than answers in this book, and nothing would make me prouder than to know that it provoked serious exploration and research into what we need to know in order to be able to "dance forever."

CHAPTER I

THE DANCER'S DAY

Every profession has its own peculiar rhythms, rigors, hazards and joys as its members proceed from dawn to night to bed to rise again. Dancers are a breed apart. This first section will examine the dancer's day.

Rising

I recall my amazement at witnessing a dance student coming down from her room at a recent workshop in Maine; sweetly greeting me as I was preparing my breakfast; going through the door and then making a blur across the two windows facing the road as she was off and running. That afternoon I learned that she had awakened only fifteen minutes earlier. This was incredible to me. I require a minimum of an hour and a half from the moment of waking before I am willing to assume any responsible act in this world, whether it be dancing or business. I wake fragile. This woman woke ready. Neither of us is wrong, only different.

Rising, we are returning from strange places, known to no other human and barely known to ourselves. Rising from that personal sea, we are shedding shadows and objects invisible to others. Even though awake and moving about, many of us are not quite present. All of us should learn to wait until the others truly open their eyes and say, "Good morning."

HOW TO DANCE FOREVER

Here, at the beginning of the day, you are faced with a matter of choice. You have to decide what is right for you. You may as well face it: Throughout life you will be dealing with people who will tell you what is *the* correct way not only for this but for that and for every other thing. I knew a teacher who demanded that her students get up from the floor in one "correct way." This was entirely apart from dancing. It happened to be a good suggestion but also a suffocating command. I think the role of a teacher is to open doors, not shove people through them.

It is a vital premise of this book that there are a significant number of choices that are crucial not only to your longevity and your health but to your entire career as an artist. Some of these allow for an infinite number of choices, one of which is not only right for you but is your responsibility to discover for yourself. You unearth these answers, not leaving them to some health guru or to an authoritative, dogmatic teacher or to the most subtle power of all, the style and customs of your peers. In Chapter VI, The Heart-Mind of the Dancer, precisely this matter of style and choices is gone into more fully.

Decide these things in the privacy of your own mind, with your own research, your own experience and your own sensitivity. The rhythm, time and style of your rising is one of these. It's easy to be cowed by the heroics of fast risers. They can sleep later or get up earlier and "get more done." Let them. If you find that you need two hours to get going, take it. It's vital that you are not channeled into a style that is imposed from the outside and doesn't suit you.

You may be touring with a group in which everyone gets up early. Let them and make them let you get up late and running. In this matter, listen to your own body and learn whether you need a big breakfast or a small breakfast, a hot bath or a cold shower, time to dawdle or the exhilarating crunch of no time at all. Rising is as personal as how you like your eggs cooked.

Strange to me, who eats a minimum of six times a day, are those who have no breakfast and eat nothing until midmorning or even wait until lunch. There are quite a few experiments that indicate the importance of a well-balanced breakfast of about five hundred calories. A portion of protein, a complex carbohydrate and a fruit at breakfast seem to raise the efficiency and alertness compared with no breakfast at all. Yet some very efficient people can't stand early food. Food choices will be discussed in the next section.

Out

The dancer leaves home or hotel, for school, studio, rehearsal hall or the theatre—burdened. You can spot us anywhere in the world. We are the glamorous "schleppers" of the world. A schlepper is one who has hanging from a shoulder a beautiful sack of leather or colorful canvas containing sweat pants, tights, two or three pairs of dance shoes, a T-shirt, towel, dance belt, cologne, lunch, a book, etc. And it is heavy. Choreographers add to this by schlepping a tape recorder and tapes.

So often the shoulder bag is an extravagant gift; nevertheless a shoulder bag is bad for your spine. It is particularly bad if you always carry it on the same shoulder. A better way would be to shift shoulders and switch to hand-carrying, right and left.

During the summer of 1987, I ran a practice-bag survey of dance students and teachers at the American Dance Festival, held at Duke University in Durham, North Carolina. More than half of the ninety who responded used shoulder bags, about a fifth used backpacks and a few hand-carried. More than 63 percent had mild to moderate back problems, with the backpackers having the least and claiming that in their experience it felt better for their bodies.

To my eye, backpacks appear clumsy, tedious to put on and take off and they do force the spine to tilt forward to counterbalance the weight. Suggestion: Invest in a good, solid luggage carrier. The cheap models are a bother. Schlep it all behind you, not on you. Steps are awkward, but you'll walk freely and probably last longer.

The Daily Class

Having just discussed two matters requiring a personal choice, we now come to one that allows for little or no personal choice. After making the most personal decision of your life, to be a dancer, you are committed to the ritual of the daily class for the duration.

The rules are remorseless. If you are a fully grown student— two classes a day. If a professional in rehearsal—at least one class a day or a thorough self-conducted workout of at least an hour

HOW TO DANCE FOREVER

in length before rehearsal. If you are on a prolonged vacation—after the first week a solid daily workout becomes a necessity.

Novelists, painters and poets can take off for a few months and even come back to work refreshed. A week's rest after a long, intensive spell of work never hurt any dancer. From then on, each day not dancing is like a ball of wool unraveling. Little by little, you are ceasing to be a dancer.

I once read something by Merce Cunningham on this matter of the daily class. For years I quoted it to my classes, and then when I went to work on this chapter I wrote him asking where it could be found. To identify the passage, I sent the following paragraph to give him some sense of what I had always attributed to him:

> The daily class is an act and a ritual that defines the dancer. The daily confrontation with the limitations and the possibilities of the body constantly challenges the dancer to renew her/his reasons for dancing. Not to go through the class each day is to loosen the structure, the authority and the honesty of the dance gesture when one is finally onstage. All the thinking and studying makes it possible, finally, to think less and dance more.

Merce graciously answered quickly. It was a paragraph from an essay entitled "The Function of a Technique for Dance," which he had written for a book titled *Dance Has Many Faces*.

> The dancer spends his life learning, because he finds the process of dance to be, like life, continually in process. That is, the effort of controlling the body is not learned and then ignored as something safely learned, but must go on, as breathing does, renewing daily the old experiences and daily finding new ones. Each new movement experience, engendered by a previous one, or an initial impression of the action of the body upon time, must be discovered, felt and made meaningful to its fullest in order to enrich the dance memory.*

If you are well but don't "feel" like taking class—tough. You don't have a choice. If you feel rotten or unslept—go. Go and

*From Walter Sorell, *Dance Has Many Faces* (New York: Columbia University Press, 1966), p. 252. As a side note, my memory of what Merce said is a classic example of the way that most of us learn from each other. I reveal more of myself by my "quote" of Merce than I do of him.

The Dancer's Day

work within your limits, but work. On occasion, I have an eerie experience. Feeling just dreadful but moral, I force myself to go to the studio.* I work twenty minutes and decide to give up, but stay because the two hours were paid for or because I think I should. After forty-five minutes I say, "The hell with it," start to leave but don't make it to the door. "I'll do a few battements and then leave." I put on a record to give me a little energy. Fifteen minutes later I realize I'm dancing up a storm and in touch with my body in a way I haven't felt for weeks and I can't figure out how I got there. Mysteriously, fatigue and even depression often bring us to some profound energy source.

But, then, there are those signals that do say, "No. Don't dance today." It may be actual pain, injury, a cold, a stomachache or an inexplicable indisposition. A day missed is certainly not the end of the world, but a pattern of days missed is a matter begging to be understood. Are your body and your secret insides saying, "Dancing is wonderful, but I don't really like to do it?" If that is the hidden song, you'd better listen to it, for the chances of injury are multiplied and misery is guaranteed. Nobody should be a dancer who doesn't need to dance—every day—from their bone marrow out to their sweaty skin.

The Class Structure

For a short while I studied aikido, a Japanese form of unarmed self-defense, both beautiful and moral. The teacher was called Yamada Sensei.† He had a suggested preclass ritual: to be in the workspace fifteen minutes or more before class to meditate, warm up and/or review earlier material.

Punctually, at seven P.M., he would walk onto the mats and kneel with his back to us, facing a framed photograph of Morihei Ueshiba, the man who created aikido. We, upon his entrance, would form a kneeling line behind him facing similarly. We all bowed to the photograph. Yamada Sensei would then pivot on his knees and bow to us as we bowed to him. Then he would smile graciously and we would all rise to our feet to begin the class. This ritual never failed to move me. I wish we dancers had something comparable each time we started a class, a rehearsal

---

*I rarely take class. In the parlance of the trade, I give myself a class.

†Yamada is his surname and *sensei* means teacher or, literally, "One who goes before."

HOW TO DANCE FOREVER

or a performance—a moment to reflect upon those who nourished us in our beginnings. Even rebels should never forget where they came from.

Sometimes this book is going to sound like your mother. It can't be helped. Some things have to be said. Don't come on time to a dance class or a rehearsal. "On time" is already late. Come early. True, there are people who are always early, others who are always late, and then there are the punctual ones. Dancers have no choice. They have to come early. It is a form of insurance. Lining up your mind releases and directs the complexity and wealth of energies contained in the body.

Most mature dancers and many young dancers become aware of specific personal weaknesses that are materially strengthened by a little extra attention before class. Further, it is rare that a teacher's work touches all the bases for each dancer. Some very good teachers don't go into sufficient footwork for some dancers. Others move too quickly, too soon, for some. A little personal preparation helps to cope.

Nothing is so delicious as getting started with a few slow, sensuous stretches, but bitterly coiled up inside almost all delicious things is the snake of danger. Too many dancers use this time to stretch for limberness. Serious stretching before a class or at the beginning of a class is the worst time of all, while "cat" stretching or "yawn" stretching actually allows the antagonist muscles to play against each other. You're playacting at waking up to the class to come. That's fine and even organic. Hard stretching at this time is a case of miscalculated eagerness.

In a December 1980 article in *Dance Magazine,* Dr. Ben Benjamin presents the thought that stretching is for muscles only. The safety and integrity of the body's bony structure rests on the power and tone of the ligaments. They hold the bones together. Stretch them or loosen them in any way and connections that should be firm begin to wobble. Backs "go out." Ankles give way easily. Knee joints shift in ways that make cartilage injury or tearing probable. Tendons, which attach muscles to bones, are not designed to be elastic. If you stretch them, they won't spring back to their original length. On the contrary, a stretched tendon is an injured tendon. These injuries range from microtears that can cause tendinitis to separations that demand surgery. Dr. Benjamin notes, "Tendon and ligament injuries . . . take much longer to heal than muscle injuries because of their limited blood supply." Similarly, a stretched

The Dancer's Day

ligament is not only injured but will not return to its original strength.

So, you ask, what should we stretch? Muscles, but *only warm muscles*. Cold muscles resist stretching. Stretching doesn't warm them up. Only activity—only contraction, release, contraction, release—over a significant period of time will bring a rich, generous supply of blood to muscle tissue, thus permitting extension of limberness. Stretch a cold body and some tissue—muscle, tendon or ligament—will give but it won't stretch.

Dr. Benjamin's stretching rules are neither few nor simple. They can be summarized with a positive for every negative:

BAD: Stretching a cold muscle
GOOD: Stretching a warm, well-worked muscle

BAD: Feeling the stretch sensation primarily near the joints
GOOD: Feeling the stretch sensation primarily in the belly of the muscle*

BAD: Forcing or bouncing a stretch
GOOD: Holding a stretch for 30 to 60 seconds

BAD: Stretching into pain
GOOD: Stretching no further than mild discomfort

BAD: Stretching a weight-bearing muscle. Example: Stretching the hamstrings while standing.
GOOD: Try sitting or lying down for stretches

One almost funny note. Have you ever observed very young female students before a ballet class? They are usually found on the floor, rolling about from outrageously effortless splits to lying with legs sticking out in second and resting their unbloomed bosoms on the ground as they murmur and gossip quietly with each other. They can probably get away with it for a few years since they are often extravagantly limber. Witness teenage female gymnasts. The blood supply is so much more generous in the

---

*An eminent neuromuscular theoretician and trainer questioned this, claiming the location of the stretch sensation in a warm, well-worked muscle will vary with the individual.

growing young body, thus keeping it warmer and more easily pliable.

It's worth noting that in the structure of the traditional ballet class, stretches are not the focus until the end of the barre, i.e., thirty to forty-five minutes into a class, by which time the dancers' muscles have been well worked and warmed. I suggest that modern dance teachers who give stretches early, or even before anything else, reconsider that timing.

The structural design of a class is as variable as the number of people who teach dance. Beyond the point about stretching, I wouldn't for a moment venture to say which was the "best," or the "healthiest," or the "safest."

Finding the technique and the teacher that are best for you are two of your critical choices. And yet, there are times when you can't choose: if you live in an isolated area with only one or a few teachers available, or if you are enrolled in a college where choices are limited. Nonetheless, nothing should stop you from realizing your talent. Who taught Isadora Duncan? Pablo Picasso's teacher was his father. Who ever heard of Pablo Picasso's father?

In respect to the central concern of this book, survival, i.e., being able to dance fully and joyously, with few or no injuries and for a long time, there are two conflicting points that could be made about the dance class, about the study and teaching of dance technique.

1. To Teachers: In the passion for giving exciting classes, attracting many students and making a lot of money, please don't get to the challenging sweaty stuff before the bodies of your students are ready. By ready, I mean two different time frames: First, that time in the class when their bodies are warm and ready; and second, that time in their training when they have the fundamental skills to deal with "the really interesting stuff." Both take time.

2. To Teachers and Students: Along with the understandable wish not to hurt or get hurt, don't teach or learn to dance with caution in the center of the room. At the core of our art is the physical adventure. The risks—the dangers—are encapsulated by one word: *virtuosity*. It's one of the reasons we go to look at dance. Those brave bodies go further than we thought possible or safe. Virtuosity is a metaphor for human courage.

The Dancer's Day

My best explanation of this contradiction between caution and the challenge of taking risks is the image of that most daring of performers, the bullfighter. How pathetic if at each charge of the bull he jumped back. No. The game is to draw the bull close to the body. That is bullfighting. But it is equally important to be so schooled and skilled that you *don't get gored by the bull*. A great dance technique uses courage and skill in equal proportions.

A note to students: If you're "off" or have an injury but you're still taking class, you help yourself and your teacher by finding a moment before class to let the teacher know and then finding an inconspicuous spot to work.

One time, in an "advanced" class in suburbia, a woman enrolled in the middle of a term. She said she'd been in a dance company and sure enough, she was rather marvelous. Exquisite feet, limber, well-placed extensions—but her stomach jutted out. A few times as I passed her I gave her a gentle finger poke, saying, "Pull it in!" After class she told me, "Oh, by the way, I'm pregnant," whereupon I offered to cut off my hand.

Teachers appreciate and need to know if you're in trouble or limited in some way. Knowing that the teacher knows will relieve some of the pressure when you're in difficulty.

Finally, the general style of ending classes tends to be theatrical. To repeat: Teachers want to be loved for giving exciting, sweaty classes. Students want to experience "the real thing." Almost invariably, the last part of classes are filled with fast, strenuous sequences, including elevation. Then there is applause, enthusiastic or dutiful. And the class is over. The trouble is that, technically speaking, the class is not, or rather should not be, over. Organically, at least another ten to fifteen minutes of warm-down and stretching are a must.

The profoundest ground rule of all physical training is that strength must be complemented by limberness. Heavy, fast and prolonged intense periods of muscle contractions must be followed by the slow, easy stretching of these same muscle groups.

All physical activity that adds strength increases muscle tone. Muscle tone is a residual tension that exists in a relaxed muscle. It is precisely that which endows such subtle excitement to the sight of dancers at ease. Degas's lovely drawings of ballet dancers at rest attest to this. But, the more tone, the more contracted the muscle, and consequently, the shorter its length. Keep that up and you arrive at what is known as muscle-bound, i.e., very strong but with little range of motion. Bad for dancers and bad for everybody. That great apostle of body building and twice Mr. Universe, Arnold Schwarzenegger, writes in his book *Arnold:*

> Stretching the muscles, making them long and limber, is one of the things that sets off the champion from the guy who is as big as the champion but who doesn't look as good. As soon as I started doing the stretching exercises, my muscles started flowing together. . . . My body had more flexibility. It felt better. You can imagine what your body goes through when you . . . never allow the muscles to straighten out. I've seen musclemen who couldn't bend over and touch their toes. . . . I started to stretch right after an exercise. I devised some stretching exercises I could do after every workout, and it helped me tremendously.*

Stretching also decreases the possibility of cramping. It restores symmetry of alignment, which is particularly necessary after rehearsing or performing a sequence that heavily emphasizes one side or part of the body. Muscular asymmetry in the body almost certainly leads to profound injury in the future. More of that later.

What all of this comes to is that the classic length of a dance class, ninety minutes, is too short. Add another thirty minutes and there is time to explain things more carefully, give more individual corrections, and still allow for cool-down and stretch time. Unfortunately, the economy of dance schools and the schedules of universities make two-hour classes all too rare.

The Rehearsal

Though the wild vortex of performance has justified my existence and presence in this world more than anything else, some of the juiciest and richest times of my dance life have been in rehearsal. The sweet messy sweats that cool the hot body, the privilege of being able to dance your heart out without the terror of making a mistake, the explorations, the unexpected discoveries, the constant learning and unlearning and, best of all, the give and take with fellow artists, be they dancers, musicians or designers, make that time almost equal the rigorous balance beam of performance.

There's a perennial division among dancers about how much

---

*From Arnold Schwarzenegger and Douglas K. Hall, *Arnold: The Education of a Bodybuilder* (New York: Simon & Schuster, 1977), p. 192.

to put out in rehearsal. The classic injunction is to give no less than you would in performance. Some claim they need an audience to turn up that full head of energy. I imagine there are some very good performers who work precisely on this assumption. Theoretically, one can justify both points of view. I lean toward full-out rehearsing and bet that most choreographers do too. They want to *see* what it will really look like. To the dancer entering the profession, a cool and low-key rehearsal style is probably a risky choice that will earn the hostility of choreographers.

Rehearsal strategy is critical. For example, what do you do in rehearsal when you're "doing nothing"? You watch and you watch and you watch and you learn. Martha Graham tells of how she watched as a nobody with nothing or near nothing to do in the Denishawn company. One day someone took ill, and immediately Martha not only let it be known that she was there and available but that she *knew* the material. She stepped right into the role and the company.

And while you watch, you move, subtly and incessantly—feet, fingers, torso, delicate demi-pliés and everything else, but inconspicuously. The company heavies will destroy you if you stand in their visual range doing brilliant battements up to your ear while they are rehearsing. When you feel the need for doing conspicuous, broad-ranging movement, disappear to another room or a hallway or wait for a break. It is rude to practice highly visible movement while another dancer is rehearsing or performing. I have known dancers in the wings to practice pirouettes, jumps and violent swings in full view of fellow dancers onstage. Indirect aggression of this order is unspeakable. Summation: In rehearsal, unless you're on, be invisible and never do nothing for long.

Here we touch upon something that all dancers, as well as other humans, have to contend with—the others. Some will be supportive of your ambition and continual activity, but then there are the competitive ones, and on the other side the cynical downbeat ones who have all sorts of snob and "sophisticated" ways of trying to slow up a fanatical worker.

The problem is not complicated. If being loved by all your workmates is most important to you, you'll probably be loved by most of your workmates and have a good chance of evolving into an ordinary dancer. If dance is what you're about, whatever talent you've got will probably flower and everyone may love you—or not. Bending to peer pressure and peer style is not the road to becoming an artist, nor to becoming a strong, exquisitely coordinated dancer.

In the rehearsal, aside from the glory of it, the physically safest role is the one where you are dancing all the time. A cold body is infinitely more vulnerable than a fatigued one. On the one hand, if your fatigue is such that you fear your coordination is going, speak up. If your choreographer doesn't care or respond to your implicit plea for a break, you have a problem. The world has a problem. There are some terrible people out there, and if it is at all within the range of your power, try to arrange your life so that you work with and for life-enhancing people.

I am continually awed and mystified by the number of people (including dancers) who are attracted to manipulative and sadistic leaders, teachers and choreographers. That ambience must be meaningful and enriching on some level for some people, but they have no right to be surprised when they find themselves abused and/or injured. All the yogurt, wheat germ and pliés are not going to protect you if you place yourself in the hands of a bastard.

Still, it must be noted that some of these unattractive human beings are extraordinary and even great artists, and there are dancers who will knowingly risk and suffer the association, feeling that the gain is worth the risk and the occasional humiliation.

Noise

The most rudimentary talent of a performer is simply to execute the movements as given by the choreographer. Many teachers are patient and slow down for the slow learner. (They make their living from students.) But, few choreographers are patient or understanding of slow learners. There are too many good dancers out there looking for work, and there is always too much to do in too little time. This is a given in our present world.

Slow learning, uncertain learning and insecure execution of new material are ideal for losing coordination and sustaining a nasty disability. Also, spending four times as much energy simply learning dance material is pathetic when the most significant and difficult work begins precisely when you "know" how to do it. Bringing the dance phrases to life with your own personal creative contribution is what it is all about.

The Dancer's Day

What follows is an address to slow learners that I have found particularly helpful when I teach a class called Jazz Dance Styles, a very concentrated lexicon of jazz dance steps extending over a century, including five dances—a cakewalk, a Charleston, a lindy hop, a lindy couple dance, and a blues. In a short space of time, many steps, complex weight shifts and unusual uses of the feet and torso are presented and hopefully not merely learned but performed with the correct inner spirit and intelligence.

Good and swift learners can now skip to page 33. This lecture for slow learners is entitled NOISE.

1. *"I just made a MISTAKE!"* Thinking this in terms of horror is NOISE in the head and interferes with learning. ALL GOOD LEARNERS MAKE MISTAKES. THEY ASSUME THAT THEY WILL MAKE MISTAKES IN THE PROCESS OF LEARNING AND THINK NOTHING OF IT. Bad learners are aghast at their failure, giving more attention to that than to what they are supposed to be learning.

Assume learning involves mistakes. An error is only a sign to ascertain quickly the correct move and to start over again, leaving horror behind. Ask what questions or demonstrations you need to understand what is being given. Above all, be certain you learn as quickly as possible what happens on count 1. If you don't know count 1, count 2 will be ridiculous.

2. *"Oh, I'm so slow [or dumb] learning this!"* Observations such as these have nothing to do with the fact that to start this particular phrase correctly, the little half air turn to the left must land on the right foot and not the left. The latter is the only proper observation. The former is NOISE.

3. *"Jackie learns so quickly!"* All observations and thinking about "Jackie" or any other quick learner will do nothing to clarify the phrase for you and will only qualify as NOISE. It is ironic that there are some extraordinarily quick learners who are not particularly good dancers. Learning is their talent and actually the extent of their interest. Simply being able to do what is given, without then drawing up out of themselves a deeper personal poem that gives the movement life, leaves them ordinary, dull dancers. Forget "Jackie," and put your entire mind to the phrase at hand.

4. *"Oh, that's such a hard phrase to do!"* The good learner is challenged and juiced up by difficulty. A Bad Learner becomes a Good Learner by looking for the tough dance step, hoping to be given the chance to work on something substantial that will qualify her/him as a "hotshot."

5. *"Everyone is watching me and notices how slow, stupid and dumb I am."* Everyone is much too preoccupied with their own problems to more than merely note, at most in a passing glance, that you are having difficulty. NOISE like this is actually extraordinarily vain.

6. There are high-class neurotic bad learners who are doing something so complex that no silly quote will serve. Unfortunately, they are not as rare as they should be. These are the people who feel right when they are wrong. It is only then that they feel like themselves. They're not happy about it, but being unhappy feels natural to them. Being wrong and failing gives them the perfect excuse to go into their act—punishing and severely scolding themselves. It's a schizoid game wherein part of them achieves a moral purity and stature by being able to reproach themselves, as if it is more important to let themselves and the world know that they know what is right and wrong, rather than to do what is right. Weird, but all too common.

Come on, how many times in class have you made an error and, while still dancing, visibly frowned and sternly shook your head as if you were scolding some stupid recalcitrant student, i.e., yourself, and incidentally letting the teacher or the choreographer know that you knew? Knowing that you are wrong when you are wrong is necessary to becoming right, but bathing in it is NOISE in your head and has nothing to do with learning the dance step before you. It has more to do with unresolved problems that obviously need attention, BUT NOT IN THE CLASSROOM AND NEVER, EVER IN REHEARSAL. Even worse, this mannerism of self-disapproval can slip into your neuromuscular system and, horrors, you'll do it onstage, in performance, and YOU WON'T REALIZE YOU'RE DOING IT.

7. There is another class of poor learners who, unlike the guilt-ridden just described, feel utterly innocent. *"Why is the choreographer giving us such terrible movement?"* *"What awful choreography!"*

The Dancer's Day

"That's old hat." "I'm going to look terrible doing that." "It's all being taught so badly and in such a confused manner. How can I learn it?" As fast as you can, you had better face up to the possibility that in your career you will probably have to work with ordinary talents, or even untalented choreographers and fellow performers. Your task, your skill and your claim to being a professional is not to be a critic but to make every move given you turn into shimmering, breathtaking beauty. Even if the choreography stinks, your performance of it should make the choreographer look like a genius. Being critical of what is being given you is NOISE in your head and will make you a slow and bad learner. If it's intolerably bad, there's always the door. But if you choose to be in that class or that studio rehearsing, make it all sing and learning will not be a problem.

8. Another unhappy learner comes to mind: THE WATCHER. This one is locked into the conviction that learning is impossible for her/him and the only solution is to follow. Usually THE WATCHER focuses on a bright, quick one who knows everything immediately. Chronic following is the statement of one who accepts the designation of hopeless learner and leans on the fantasy that somehow all the sequences can be danced by picking up cues and hints out of the corner of the eye.

A whole chain of disastrous results flows from this gambit. THE WATCHER is *always behind the beat,* inasmuch as nothing can be done until the smart one does it first. If THE WATCHER ever makes it to the stage, the eye of the audience will always go to the person on or before the beat, since she/he is bringing the news first. THE WATCHER rarely achieves what every dancer needs, personal authority, since that has tacitly been given over to the watched hotshot. Inevitably, THE WATCHER assumes what can only be described as a sneaky expression, since she/he is really stealing someone else's hard work by glancing surreptitiously out of the corner of the eye. The style of THE WATCHER can best be described as "Dancing out of the corner of my eye." Finally, always looming on the horizon is the dread probability that sooner or later THE WATCHER will be watched dancing alone, with no one to follow. Ironically, they often manage but at a cost: a mild case of suppressed hysterics.

The advice is the same one would give to any addict: QUIT! Stand in the front row and start learning to learn by making your own mistakes. A mistake is not the end of the world, it is merely one step in the process of learning.

9. There is also the case of the premature artist. This one has a beguiling innocence, some very good dancing and bad timing. This dancer is trying to be too good, too beautiful, too soon. Give such a one a movement, and immediately it is turned into a work of art ready to be performed at full tilt. This dancer applies the correct impulse too soon. We are nothing as artists unless each of us ultimately does something to the movements given us, but we can't do anything to a movement until we can do it. To this eager one the injunction is, "Save the poetry until you know the steps." Good learners who are fine dancer artists know enough to approach all new movement with an objective detachment until execution requires little thought. Then they pour it on.

10. Finally, we come to the most difficult of all slow learners. These, and some of them are good dancers, say quite calmly, *"Oh, me? I'm a slow learner,"* as if they were describing their Roman nose or that their cat has six toes. Not only is it a given with them but if you listen closely there is a faint note of pride. Worse, they are saying, "This is immutable." I will venture to say that this thought is quite possibly nonsense. If you're human, you can change. If you lock yourself into a position, that's where you'll be. If you have a passion to change and you don't stand smugly on the pedestal of your sacred self-image but concentrate on the phrase of movement that is given you, *whoosh*, you may master it in no time at all—and won't you be surprised?

Easily said and hard to do. What to do? All the variations of NOISE are really forms of self-focus. A colleague here at Arizona State University, Pamela Matt, calls it ego-static. She asks the slow learner to turn full attention to the static, the NOISE—to name it, know it, analyze it, even give it its due—and hopefully by that focus and understanding, its potency will be diminished.

Good point. In order for them to learn fully, I tell my students to imagine being a clear, sensitive piece of photography paper, or a blank sheet of paper, or a white untouched canvas—to receive what is given from the outside with innocence and no preoccupation with self.

Confession: I myself was a terrible learner, a past master at some of the ploys just mentioned. I did have one talent. Whenever I saw another student do something breathtakingly beautiful, I would manage to get behind that person, and without being quite conscious of what I was doing, I would blot up what I was seeing with my body. I would *become* that person dancing that exquisite motion. Acting is becoming someone else, a game at which I have a facility and which I love to do.

It was in a ballet class of Edward Caton's. I can still see those arrow-elegant legs of Leon Danielian thrusting the floor away to shoot up into the air effortlessly. I worked behind him whenever I could. I gleaned some things about elevation from Leon, which to this day I cannot articulate, but they did enter my body and became a part of my craft.

This would succeed only when I already knew the movements. I was not following to learn but to absorb his timing and his inner impulse. Many times I have charged up a class by letting one firebrand of a dancer demonstrate and then challenging the others to *become* what they are seeing—and they do! End of lecture on NOISE.

Other People's Movement

The title of this section is awkward and strange but very much to the next point. The problem of learning and performing "other people's movement" is one upon which I cannot speak with great authority. Most of my readers, if they are deep in the study of dance or are already professionals, dance largely what is given them by teachers and/or choreographers.

For the major portion of my early concert and Broadway career I worked with Helen Tamiris,* who always encouraged me to evolve my own phrases which she would accept, reject, change and/or edit. Thus, though it was all clearly her choreography, most of the movement phrases were spun out of my own body. Then later I went on to develop solo programs, completely choreographed by me.

Likewise, in my study of dance technique from the time of becoming a professional, I rarely took modern dance technique

---

*Too many young dancers today are unfamiliar with her name and her role in the creation of the modern dance in America. Since I will be referring to her several times in this book, I have included a brief summary of her career on page 267.

classes, concentrating on ballet technique for the first few years and then very quickly learning to work by myself on technical problems. Finally, I stopped taking technique classes of any kind, giving myself a class instead and mixing modern and ballet material. At this point I will not venture to evaluate that course of action. I mention it not to recommend it but merely to make clear who is writing this, and to make the observation that in all probability one of the factors in my personal survival has been the fact that most of the dance problems I encountered came from my own body and my own particular coordination.

This is a radically different life from most of yours out there. Almost all of your dance language is learned and absorbed from other people. Profoundly, that is one of the cornerstones of your craft. The more interesting the choreographer, the weirder, more difficult, more unexpected and more demanding will be the movement. You have to lend yourself to the work rhythms and metabolism of another. The choreographer may have a freaky freedom with the left leg while your free flyer is the right. Until another's movement becomes your movement, I would say there's an element of hazard.

Sometimes, and unhappily, you will find yourself working with an inconsiderate, or unskilled, and/or dangerous choreographer. I recall a Broadway show that broke some kind of record in sending young men to the doctor and even to the hospital. This particular schlock choreographer was terribly impressed with the sensational knee slides introduced by the great show choreographer Jack Cole. He was going to outdo Jack. He demanded knee drops out of double air turns, air turns coming up from the knees, jumping into knee drops and enough knee slides to wear holes in pants overnight, and all at a brutal, blinding speed. There isn't all that much work out there. If you should find yourself engaged by a beast such as just described, you have a tough decision to make.

The wonderful thing about the present generation of dancers is the range and depth of their technical training. Many ballet dancers have had some modern training and most modern dancers study ballet. Many of you have had some gymnastic work and almost all have had some form of jazz, be it show jazz or the authentic material. There are now many schools and universities with teaching staffs of wide-ranging differences who teach the techniques and repertory of a variety of choreographers and styles.

Thus, the rarest phenomenon today is a dancer schooled in only one technique. More and more dancers who reach the point of seeking a professional position have had a rich variety of training. I know that there is a whole school of thinking that believes a dancer who is profoundly schooled in one technique will be better able to cope with a variety of dance experiences than, as they would put it, "one who has had a smattering of this and that." I don't really know. I've simply observed some startlingly beautiful movers who can shift with great ease from one technique to another, having had training in a multiplicity of styles.

As an aside, I will throw out a speculation: Since many injuries and accidents are the results of errors of coordination, and since tap dance demands and teaches extraordinarily subtle and quick weight shifts, is it possible that tap dancers or dancers who have had early training in tap sustain fewer injuries than other people?*

The Audition

Having just discussed Other People's Movement makes this the time to touch upon the audition, the tremulous and narrow bridge to getting hired. Here, learning another's movements quickly and performing them with style on the spot, is what it's about. The audition is the cross of our profession, not only for the dancers but usually for the choreographers as well. For them, the audition is their biggest gamble. All too frequently the dancer who indicated the most promise turns out to be just so-so, while the one who just squeaked through may become a star. All directors are fully aware that the whole process is guesswork and almost all accept the truism that 50 percent of success is in the casting. Therefore, dancers: Know the odds are that that cold person passing judgment upon you *is every bit as nervous as you.*

I warrant that all sensitive choreographers are aware of the breath-robbing tension that auditioning dancers experience and many will do everything they can to get you to relax. In my career, I auditioned others much more frequently than I myself auditioned. Thus, whatever is noted here is from that vantage point. There is no magic to circumvent the wobbly feeling that threatens your coordination and performance in an audition. Be prepared in the sense that your body is hot and ready to go; that your work

---

*As part of the work of this book, I conducted research into dancers' injuries that included this question. See pages 285–286.

clothes set you off to your best advantage—as a person of exquisite taste. Never give anyone auditioning you the responsibility of imagining how good you can look if you were *really dressed*. If you have the skill to make meditation work for you, find a moment ahead of time to allay impending hysteria and fear. Coming in and working with a relaxed authority is impressive in itself.

There is a rough contradiction in dealing with the new movement that you will be expected to learn and perform very quickly. Learning requires a cool attitude and performing asks for the heat of involvement. Try to "read" the choreographer. If precision appears to be a very high priority, be sure to learn accurately before you tear loose. If your guess is that high performance style is being sought, risk a few errors and go for it.

If you get the job, congratulations. If you don't, *don't buttonhole the choreographer to try to find out why you didn't get hired.* You're confronting someone who is loaded with awesome problems that do not include you, who may have hated the audition process as much as you, and *who does not owe you the truth.* Chances are you will get an evasive reply, and if you do get a direct answer you may earn resentment to boot.

A failed audition shouldn't make you feel hopeless and ripe for getting the next ticket out of town. If audition after audition delivers nothing, you then have good reason to back off and assess what is going on.

The Performance

For the most serious and deeply involved practitioners of our crazy art—this is what it is all about. The astronomical numbers of pliés, the classes, the rehearsals, the weariness, the sacrifices, all point to performance.

In a sense, all of my "wisdom" stops here. What can my experience mean to another performer? The very act of performance, from the moment of entering the theatre, the elaborate (or cursory) preparations and finally arriving at that strange shift from offstage to *onstage*, is as personally expressive as how one makes love. It *is* an act of love, or it should be, and for that who needs a book? Only my grossest vanity would allow me to say that my way is the way for anyone else. The only unforgivably dumb thing is for a performer to know what he/she needs as preparation and proceed, because of so-called "obligations," laziness or whatever, to skimp on that preparation. The Bible is loaded with proverbs to

The Dancer's Day

the effect that wisdom for a fool is pouring wine into a bottomless jug. In Yiddish we would dub a woman or man who risks his/her body in the rigors and glories of dance performance without adequate preparation a "schmuck." A schmuck is a smart person who makes a self-destructive choice out of vanity, laziness or not thinking.

I was working on and around Broadway from 1940 to 1956. In all that time I rarely performed without having been in the theatre for at least an hour and a half before curtain time, though the call was always a half hour. Usually, I was somewhere backstage warming up at least an hour before going on. There is a strange group of people who are made uneasy and, yes, jealous by the sight of hard workers, particularly fanatics. For whatever reason, I was/am one of the latter.

I can recall one stagehand in *Plain and Fancy* who would observe me with a sardonic eye as I time and again would run through a phrase of movement that was troubling me. At least once a week the lids of his sleepy lizard eyes would flicker and in a grave voice he would observe: "I worked a lot of shows with Jack Donohue. You know, the great hoofer. Always come into the theatre way ahead of time. Always rehearsing. Died of a heart attack at forty-two. Always rehearsing." Having been taunted by experts from my earliest job in the theatre, this went right by me.

I didn't start to work intensively and professionally until I was twenty-three, though my first dance class was at nineteen. From 1940 to 1942, each summer I worked at Unity House, a resort owned and operated by the International Ladies' Garment Workers' Union. I "never" left the casino (a dance hall with a stage at one end for our performances). I would get to meals late and leave early, having eaten enough for three, and then rush back to the casino to practice the elusive pirouette or to solve the mystery of turnout. Starting late in life makes everything in dance doubly mysterious and elusive.

In the second summer, Helen Tamiris was the choreographer, and I recall complaining bitterly to her about the snide digs I would garner from some members of the cast as they passed me on their way to lunch or dinner while I was doing some frantic exercise. Tamiris opened my eyes. "Daniel, you frighten them. You are a reproach to them. You're like a firecracker going off in the middle of their conscience."

Plainly put, if it's survival you're interested in, you absolutely must do all you consider necessary to do a fully expressive and personally authoritative performance. Anything less is not only inviting your own self-disapproval but also physical injury. A poorly prepared, uncertain body called upon to perform for the public is wide open to disaster. An artist does not live out of the corner of her/his eye, i.e., waiting to see what the "others" think before proceeding with her/his own inclination and understanding of what is necessary.

My Pre-performance Ritual

For the sake of younger dancers and students who have had comparatively little performance experience, I will describe my own ritual. Mature performers will have already structured one for themselves and can easily ignore this section. Young performers may find this helpful in developing their own ritual.

If a performance is at 8 P.M., I have to finish eating no later than 5:30 P.M. since I require a rest or a nap after eating. By 6 P.M., I am in a dressing gown and at the makeup table, aiming to be made up and changed into practice clothes and onstage by 6:30 P.M. For a variety of reasons I ask each sponsor to supply me with a backstage assistant from 6 P.M. until I leave the theatre. There are the obvious needs of costume changes, keeping me apprised of the time, getting me some coffee, etc. A more devious need is revealed by an almost unvaried pattern. Since I tour in universities primarily, my assistant is usually a student and I find myself asking many questions about his/her major, career intentions, etc. Canny-cat Daniel is finding a way not to think about himself, the coming performance, and all the attendant concerns that so easily turn into a flood of anxiety. In addition, I'm perennially interested in people, and what better time to learn about one of them?

Being a soloist, I have the good fortune to have the stage to myself and I generally pick a spot upstage center to start my warm-up and workout, wearing eyeglasses. Since I am quite nearsighted and almost always dancing on a stage that is new to me, it is critical that I fix a sense of the new space deeply into my consciousness. The routine of the warm-up is a slimmed-down version of a full "class," that is, I do most everything very deeply and fully but with fewer repetitions. I'm always keeping an eye on the clock. By 7 P.M. I am ready to go through specific phrases

The Dancer's Day

that have been troubling me. If I work on them now, there is less chance that I will worry about them in a performance.

That done, I am ready to run through a couple of dances. Early in my career as a concert soloist, I learned that an evening of dancing alone is not as difficult as I feared it would be. In fact, in a performance I get stronger with each dance and, contrary to expectations, the most difficult dance is the first one. The answer to that one? Do at least two dances before the curtain and so by 7:15 P.M. I am ready to run through a couple of dances, preferably a slow dance and then a faster, "dancier" dance. I never do them full out, though I might dig into a phrase or two. My body then feels oiled and ready to go. The concert will start with the "third" dance.

By 7:25 or 7:30 P.M. I'm back in the dressing room and refreshing the makeup. The light sweat and heat of the preperformance workout helps the makeup set into the face and look less "made-up." I get into costume and am onstage by 7:45 or 7:50 P.M. From this moment on until curtain, I never stop moving, twisting, stretching, flexing my feet, unlimbering wild battements, little darting leaps, relevés, balancés, tiny phrases from the first dance, or suddenly freezing to a stillness and breathing deeply. There is neither a rationale nor an order to what I am doing. Why should there be? I'm nervous as hell. Moving stops me from exploding and keeps me oiled for that first mysterious moment. And it is mysterious. I don't know about anyone else, but the most unpredictable thing in the world for me is the state of my body when the curtain rises. Feeling wonderful and strong in the warm-up and finally exposed to the viewers, my body may go dry and elusive. Feeling rotten, depressed, and achy in the warm-up, the flooding of the lights and the music may rev up the wildest motors within me and I am off and flying.

What if you're not in this simpler world of a soloist? I have on occasion shared programs with other artists and companies where there were twenty to thirty people backstage and onstage. Knowing that it is going to be awkward, I come earlier, find the best corners for me to do my workout, and make certain that I get a reservation for seven to ten minutes when I will have the stage to myself for my little run-through. Well-disciplined dance companies usually give a brief company class before the curtain and sometimes the director will do a last-minute rehearsal of some item that wants a bit more attention. If there's no one to decide for you, then design and schedule your own sequence with every minute accounted for and leave a little extra allowance of time for the unexpected, which is guaranteed to happen.

What about injury during performance? The show must go on? Impossible to answer. The heat of performance, the shame of stopping and tearing the fabric of illusion and the professional sense of responsibility all tend to make most of us continue in spite of injury and sometimes in spite of serious injury. The complexity is complicated by the body's response to injury during performance. With prolonged intense physical activity, we produce endorphins, which are chemically almost identical with morphine. Thus, in performance, our bloodstream carries a painkiller all over the body. An injury would also release the panic hormone, adrenaline. This also blocks awareness of pain. Thus, during performance we often are unaware of injury.

Through the welter of all these surges, if your instinct tells you that more dancing will seriously compound the injury, would you stop? I've injured myself badly at least five times during performance: three ankles, one back, and one knee. I never stopped a performance. Would I have had less of an injury if I had? I don't know and I'm not giving anybody any advice.

Once in rehearsal I experienced a bad hit. I was assisting Helen Tamiris on our first show that made it to Broadway, *Up in Central Park*. In the role of assistant, as well as being lead dancer in the chorus, I had just done a first-thing-in-the morning chore and arrived at rehearsal after it had started. Without a warm-up (what can I tell you? I was very young), I stepped into the Rip Van Winkle number in which, surrounded by two clogging men, I jumped up into an arch, pretending that they had kicked me in the rump. At the peak of the leap, my sacrum was "slammed by a twelve-pound steel hammer," and before I returned to earth I knew I was on my way to the hospital. My body went limp to land on hands and feet and as the dancers continued, I crawled parallel with the apron offstage, out the stage left exit, into the house and found a dark space under the iron steps leading to the boxes. I doubled up and cradled the worst pain I'd ever known and lay there quietly for ten to fifteen minutes while everyone was scouring the theatre calling, "Daniel! Daniel!"

Finally found, I was laid out on a stretcher and shipped off to a hospital for a two-day bout with a cruel spasm. If that had happened in performance, what would I have done? There's no way of telling, because human metabolism in performance can't be the same as in rehearsal, and beyond that there is the old magician, the human mind. How would I have handled that hit? There are so many factors involved, all the way from metabolism to professionalism and pride, any one of which would have saved me or wrecked me.

After the Performance

Here I believe there are two immutable rules. Rule one is clear, obvious and difficult to follow. All through my career, particularly when the performing demands became intense, there would be those terrifying nights when I would wake with a vicious leg cramp. Since they were rare, I simply regarded them with regret and a little horror. A few years ago, they began to pick up steam, becoming frequent, and I decided that I would have to impose a strict rule upon myself: Following every performance, no one was allowed backstage for at least ten minutes which were to be devoted solely to stretching. It worked!

A few months after instituting this practice, I went backstage to congratulate Bella Lewitzky and her magnificent company after one of their brilliant evenings. Being an old colleague, I was permitted backstage while the rest of the fans had to wait. Surprise! The wily Bella was giving notes to her company stretched out on the floor, stretching. Upon congratulating her for using this strategy, she said she had been doing this for longer than she could remember and the company had not suffered a single serious injury in the past eighteen months. If you've ever been privileged to see the intense involvement and the virtuosity of Lewitzky's company, you would appreciate how remarkable this was.

Our vanity thrives on the tangible accolades of devoted fans and unknown members of the audience who feel impelled to delay their return home in order to come backstage and gaze upon us just once more and tell us in person how unworldly and beautiful we are. If we keep them waiting, won't they go away? As a matter of fact, many of them will. You can't have it both ways. Intensely used muscles must be stretched immediately after use. Exactly this was said earlier and one could write a whole chapter and say nothing else, over and over again, and it would be justified. So choose: cramps, knots and spasms, or disappointing a few fans and giving fewer autographs and kisses.

The last point brings up the second "immutable" rule and I feel awkward. Once more, I must sound like your mother. If you are so fortunate as to have a loving lover, giving and receiving kisses upon the mouth is probably one of the joys and signs of your shared love. If it's survival you're interested in, that's it. Kissing anyone else on the mouth is out. As performers touring the country and the world, we are sometimes magical targets to members of the audience, particularly those who know us and have much affection for us. In the postperformance excitement and exultation, you probably will be offered admiring and sometimes passionate mouths, each one of which is rich in an alien life you need like a hole in the head. Graciously handshake, embrace, hug, but, above all, duck that kiss.

Sleep

The most mysterious part of the day. Among scientists studying sleep there is still much that is puzzling or unknown. I am convinced that sleep is a function of a specific chemical or combination of chemicals. I myself am a napper. During my ideal day, I take ten-minute naps after lunch and after dinner. I get sleepy after eating. My head is foggy. I set my wristwatch alarm for precisely ten minutes, stretch out, and in anywhere from one minute to three minutes, I clock out. In the best naps (all are not equal), the alarm terrifies me awake. I gasp, open my eyes and my skull is clear. My mind feels as if it has been washed, completely alert and ready to go. The difference between my state of mind before and after the nap is radical. It feels as if before it was muddy waters and after, a crystal-clear substance. If, on the other hand, I nap any longer than twenty minutes, I wake leaden, groggy and useless for at least thirty minutes to an hour. I think these changes are both mysterious and chemical.

I suspect that most of us do not sleep enough. Almost everyone I know in dance is usually overcommitted. Between making a living, getting the laundry done, the performing, the rigors of the profession, dealing with friends, foes and lovers, keeping up with the culture and having a little fun, when is there time for a good night's sleep?

For me, sleeping myself out has been a rare achievement. If I had more often, would I have worked better? Performed better? I think so, and I think there's something radically wrong with the contemporary structure of our lives. Most of us do too much too quickly. How I ache for a simpler way of life, taking all the time it takes to do something fully rather than almost always delivering under pressure. I'm sure this overcommitment is partly me, my excitement and involvement with almost everything; but it is also true that in the scramble for existence as an artist in our society, there will always be too much to do. How are you other professions out there doing?

So many times upon retiring for what I know must be an unfortunately short night of sleep, I will fantasize that I will "sleep faster." A pathetic wish and it brings up what appears to be a theory upon which most sleep scientists seem to agree. They think that each of us has a built-in rigidity: Whether we like it or not, everyone has a personal optimum sleep time. They further indicate that once you have found the amount of sleep time you need to feel good and ready for the day, you should accept it and make every effort to build your life around that fact. Any radical change in sleep patterns could be a sign of either emotional or physical trouble and should be understood and analyzed, with professional help if necessary.

Jane Brody, whose very useful column, "Personal Health," appears in *The New York Times*, wrote about changing sleep patterns on August 20, 1986.

> A newborn sleeps 10 to 18 hours. . . . By age 4, the average night is 10 hours; in the teens, 9 hours, and by young adulthood, 7 to 8 hours. But for the elderly, 4½ to 6½ . . . are both typical and normal. . . . And quite a number . . . function very well on just 3 to 4 hours. . . .
>
> . . . As people get older, the amount of deep sleep is reduced by 60 percent.
>
> Also, the number of times people wake during the night doubles . . . sleep becomes lighter and more fitful with age. . . . This is neither good nor bad; it is simply normal.

The big question: Is what is "normal" for the general aging population "normal" for older dancers? I'm getting and enjoying longer sleep as I get older.

Also in *The New York Times* there appeared an article about some successful and highly productive people who discovered that they are happiest and work most efficiently with ten hours or even more a night. For a long time, most of them fought this unseemly and apparently self-indulgent amount of sleep. Our puritanical work ethic pats early risers on the head and frowns at the late risers. It took these people years to accept their need and take the ten hours or more of sleep not only with a clear conscience but with relish.

My fantasy is that I will take a week or two and arrange my life so that each day I will sleep myself out to find out what my body-mind will do when there is no alarm to tell me the "right" time to get up. Perhaps I will do that as a bit of research, but I really don't know when I will find the time to do it.

On the other hand, I recall a conversation with Meredith Monk, who complained of insomnia. Upon questioning her I learned that upon waking she was usually refreshed and ready to go. Is it possible that those few hours of sleep accomplished what seven or eight do for most of us?

So again, there are no general rules, except two:

1. Find out how much sleep you need.

2. Be a genius and arrange your life so that you get what you need.

Oh, yes, and if you succeed, please write a book on how you did it and remember to send me a copy.

In the hype of our business and our time, some people often find it difficult to ease off and get to sleep. As a youngster, I had some occasions when I could not fall asleep for hours. For some reason the experience was devastating and I learned to dread it. Thus, I deliberately set about developing techniques for falling asleep so that I would never find myself tossing and wide awake at four A.M. As a consequence, I discovered and invented for myself one method after another. They either wore out or got uninteresting. Some of these techniques of breathing and relaxation, I later learned, were variants of Eastern meditation. The earliest came about from staying up late at night reading while my parents were out. Knowing that they would be upset if they found me up, when I heard them at the door I would pretend to be asleep. I was very interested in acting and loved to attempt a verisimo version of sleep. Surprise! While pretending to sleep, I would fall asleep very quickly. Later on, if I would have difficulty sleeping, I would try this trick on myself, with great success.

The next method that I recall developed when I had just entered

The Dancer's Day

college. I had a bedroom that faced a street with trolleys running on it. In the quiet of the night, they could be heard at a great distance away. I would listen in the silence for the first sound as if that were very important, and when the faintest rumble became audible, my attention would cling to the sound and hold on to it to the exclusion of all other thoughts all the way through the arc of its rumbling past my window and slowly disappearing into silence. Guessing from which direction it came was also part of the game.

Then there was a method I learned from Dr. Albert E. Wiggam, a psychologist who had a popular Sunday radio program. Listening to it was a family ritual. His technique relied on deep breathing combined with an image of the various parts of your body becoming hollow tubes. You started with the toes of your right foot, imagining their hollowness and inhaling and exhaling slowly ''through'' the toes. Then you shifted your attention to the left foot, then to the lower right leg, etc. There's a sweet and sexy joke about this process that would be totally inappropriate in the context of this book. If you're curious, ask some older person who is good at that forgotten art of telling funny stories, or if we should meet, I'll tell it to you.

Then I developed and put to use a really powerful sleep inducer based on a comment from a high school health-education teacher. He claimed that slowing down the breath was very good for relaxation. It is. I went one step further with it, developing a technique that has lasted me for years: Find a comfortable position in bed, take an easy deep breath and let it flow out just as easily. Then lie there in that nonbreathing moment of a completed exhalation and use any image of relaxation—melting, floating or falling—*and do not inhale until your breath monitor says, ''Hey, you need some more oxygen.''* You'll find that this inhalation is longer and deeper than ordinary. Make the following exhalation a part of that falling-melting-floating image all the way through the nonbreathing stage, up to the moment when you feel the slightest need to inhale. Then do so easily and as deeply as your breathing monitor dictates. The consistent effectiveness of this method also convinces me that sleep is a chemical alteration of the body's state.

Observation: Yawning is an accepted sign of the onset of a sleepy state. It is a profound and deep intake of breath, which increases the body's supply of oxygen. It is probable that when the body-mind is fatigued, breathing becomes slower and shallower, thus decreasing the amount of oxygen in the bloodstream, so much so that there is an insufficient amount of oxygen, which triggers the yawn. With the sudden intake of all that oxygen upon yawning, the rhythm of breathing slows down and there is more carbon dioxide and less oxygen in the blood than when the body-mind is more alert and active. My guess is that this off-balance way of breathing, which I call The Quiet Pool, subtly increases the amount of carbon dioxide in the blood and thus creates part of the chemistry of the state of sleep. It has worked for me for years. I fall asleep very quickly. In time, I added the hypnotists' device of counting backward. On the bottom of each exhalation I would count 100–99–98, etc. Then I started a game of beginning with the lowest number I dared, hoping to fall asleep before I reached zero.

I learned later that this was the reverse of the yogic *pra-nayama* technique called *sukha purvaka,* or "retention of breath," wherein the peak of the inhalation is held for a longer period than usual, rather than the method I had evolved where the end of the exhalation is prolonged. Each produces a very different result, one energizing, the other giving a quieting effect. The peak of my skill came when I could begin with the number 12 and be asleep before I reached 9; less than a minute! I added one little twist: If I discovered that my mind had wandered away from counting, I would have to start up again at 12 or whatever number I had picked as the starting point.

Meditation

This moment at the end of the day is as good a place as any to talk of meditation—what it is and what it is good for. What is it? Again, as in the case of sleep, we have a state of mind that I suspect cannot be described with any degree of certainty or precision. It's easier to describe how to get there than what it is that you find when you arrive.

The human mind has the capacity to be aware of and deal with a tremendous variety of stimuli. Witness the cartoonists' delight: the adolescent talking on the phone and doing homework while both the radio and TV are on. It's not merely funny; it can be and is done. I myself can be deeply involved in my dance workout, be listening to and feeling concerned about the disturbing news coming out of the radio and find my mind shift to 1941 and that theatre on Thirty-ninth Street in New York City where I learned

The Dancer's Day

from Tamiris the exercise I am doing at that moment. "What was the name of the theatre?" I will ask myself while all the other thoughts run parallel in the stream of my mind.

In any social situation, be it a meeting with one or ten people, your mind contains the people there, what you think of them, what they think of you, what you think they think of you, and all the while you're balancing a canapé in one hand, a drink in the other *and somehow you take it all in and don't spill a drop*. It is quite an amazing and necessary skill and sometimes it is unbearable. Sometimes it's all just too much and a nap, a rest or going to sleep doesn't take care of that sense of being overwhelmed. You have to be awake and somehow what your mind needs most is exactly what the teacher would sometimes ask you to do: "Please clean the blackboard." Sometimes your mind cries to be cleared of the plethora of things and details if you are to move on to the next step. Meditation can do just this.

All forms of meditation do basically one thing: They ask that powerhouse that can be aware of and deal with so many different things simultaneously to focus on but *one* thing. Almost always that thing is not complex, and almost always repetition is involved. Meditation techniques, depending on the culture and the person, will focus on breathing in a prescribed way (yoga) or the making of a sound (the Buddhist "om") or the repeating of several syllables (a Transcendental Meditation mantra) or counting from 1 to 9 over and over again (Zen) or turning in one place for a very long time (Sufi dervishes) or looking at a light or even twiddling the thumbs. The methods are many more than mentioned here,* but *all ask the most complex organ on this planet to focus upon a simple task, performed over and over again.*

The effects of this are as various as the techniques, the cultures and the individuals practicing it; but for all of them, meditation makes it possible for the conscious mind to ease off and arrive at thoughts, states of being, degrees of clarity and a relaxation not at all easily found any other way. Not to have at your command a meditation technique that serves your needs and temperament is to be lacking a vital tool for relaxation, creativeness and unexpected insights that could change your life and give you those

---

*There is more on meditation in this book on pages 321–330. Some of the techniques are specifically designed for dancers.

occasional islands of serenity that make it possible to survive the very evident madness of much of our lives.

Out of my own experience, the experiences of friends and an untold number of accounts from cultures of all times and countries, the values of meditation are such that it behooves everyone to at least make a stab at it. As a way to relieve stress, attain clarity and open creative doors, it can be practiced at any time of the day, night or even in the middle of the night.

CHAPTER II

DIET

31 pages of The Dancer's Day and not a bite to eat! Ridiculous! Everybody knows that dancers eat like horses, or rather that they are skinny and eat nothing. Actually, the complexities of human nutrition and particularly the needs of that passionate animal, the dancer, require more than a passing comment. In truth, it calls for a comprehensive book to do it justice and I challenge some nutritional wunderkind out there to do just that, and soon. At the very least it deserves a chapter. Here it is:

David's Diet

My diet was determined way back at the beginning of my career by an incidental conversation that occurred at my first breakfast on a job in the theatre, high in the Pennsylvania Poconos. It was at the summer resort owned by the International Ladies' Garment Workers' Union mentioned earlier. For entertainment, the management engaged a rather good company of dancers, singers and actors.

The dining room was in the style of a massive airplane hangar and it had a menu to match. At the time, 1941, most of the union members were Jewish and Italian, notoriously hearty eaters. On this first morning, I had come early, as I always do when food is in question. Two people were ahead of me: an actor who years

HOW TO DANCE FOREVER

later became one of the best-known teachers of acting in New York, and a dancer who at the time was his wife or sweetie, too long ago to be sure which.

After the good-mornings I picked up the gargantuan menu and sighed, "Here I go again. I was here last summer and finished the three months of work five pounds heavier, in spite of dancing my head off day and night."

I must tell you that the table was laden with heaping baskets of fragrant rolls, slices of moist rye and corn bread, large pitchers of milk, sour cream and heavy sweet cream, half a dozen jars of marmalade and every kind of preserve, plus miniature mountains of butterpats. The printed menu continued the fantasy, offering every kind of omelette, cereal, pancake, sweet roll, fruit, etc. If anyone had ever eaten it for breakfast at anytime, anywhere, it was on that menu.

At this time, David, the actor, was lean, blond, blue-eyed and sinfully handsome. Sinful because he was a Jewish man and looked like nothing less than a Nordic god. (Recall, this was Nazi time, 1941.) To my concern about gaining weight, he snorted in his superior and contemptuous manner, "Daniel, it's simple. You can eat a full meal, have room for dessert and still not gain. You merely have to follow a few rules." And without asking me whether I wanted them, he continued, laying down the dietary laws that roughly have governed my eating ever since.

"No more than one slice of bread a meal. No butter at any time, neither on bread nor on any vegetable. No gravy on any food, either meat, fish or poultry. Little or no oily dressing on salad. Use vinegar or lemon and, if you must, a bare touch of oil. No sour cream or sweet cream, at all. Skim milk rather than whole milk. No potatoes, no lima beans and easy with the corn. NEVER ANY FRIED FOOD. NEVER. NEVER. NEVER. Cut away all fat from meat and remove all skin from poultry. Follow these rules and you can eat well and still enjoy your dessert with no fear at all of gaining weight."

I have listened to David all of these years and have at every meal enjoyed my penchant for sweet cake or a mess of cookies and still maintain a fairly good weight for dancing and for living in general.

As a footnote I should add that David, aside from becoming one of the most successful teachers of acting in all of New York

City, also grew to be one of the fattest. I don't know quite what to make of that except to misquote Confucius: "Knowing right way easy, but doing it . . . ?"

Also a footnote about the potato: David was right only insofar as the reality that potatoes are hardly ever eaten except in a form that doubles their calories—with butter, sour cream, bacon bits or fried. He was wrong in assuming that it is itself high in calories. Actually it is not. It has a good mix of carbohydrates, some protein, vitamin C and some useful minerals. I have since learned to enjoy a baked or boiled potato with a pinch of salt and nothing else.

One more note: David stated this diet almost completely in the negative. The only thing he tells one to eat is the dessert. Which creates still another footnote: I've since learned to discriminate among desserts, avoiding anything deep-fried or heavily creamed and pies whose crust is half shortening. If you must have pie, leave the bottom and the heavy edge untouched. Baked goods have fewer calories. Oh, the wonder of these strategies, to substitute a little wrong for a greater one. We are quite silly, aren't we?

Introduction to a Balanced Diet

In no section of this book do I feel quite so vulnerable as in this one. The nutritional experts specialize in pouring scorn upon each other. Now along comes Daniel, Dancer and Eater of Cookies, who writes a lengthy discourse on DIET! ! ! Yiddish has slang expressions to cover almost anything. For this the word *chutzpah* will do nicely. To boot, I'm actually going to discuss my personal diet and shopping list!

I can just see it at all the supermarket check-out counters across the land, a headline on the cover of the latest edition of *The National Enquirer:* SURVIVAL DIET KEEPS AGING DANCER ON HIS TOES! And right next to it, a *Reader's Digest* wrapper reading "The Only Shopping List You Will Ever Need!" Since caution is not one of my virtues, I will persist, but not out of vanity. I have found that in any discussion, a specific reference point grounds generalizations. What ensues might help you take sharper note of what goes into your shopping cart and perhaps gain a perspective on the specifics of your diet. Finally, I believe my diet is on the whole quite sound, though flawed in some aspects.

HOW TO DANCE FOREVER

Here is a shopping list that includes stuff bought over a period of two to two and a half weeks:

Frozen fruit juices, assorted: orange, grapefruit, apple, cranberry (unless my backyard orange, grapefruit and tangerine trees are bearing)

Whole-grain breads: wheat, rye or mixed grain. I avoid buying bread that has "enriched wheat flour." That means white flour with some vitamins added. To me it means a nutritional rip-off (no bran, no wheat germ, etc.).

Eggs: I avoid the monster-size eggs, assuming that their mommies had even more antibiotics and female hormones than the other mommies.*

Milk products: skim milk, yogurt, low-fat cottage cheese and hard cheese, preferably made with skim milk

Coffee, tea and herb teas

Fruit preserves

Oats or four-grain cereals for cooking and Shredded Wheat, the simplest of dry cereals

Canned soups: They have too much salt, oil and monosodium glutamate, yet I buy them—the "chunky" ones. Ideally, I should make my own soups, but the time!

Lettuce, tomatoes, scallions, celery, peppers

Bananas and one or two fruits in season

---

*This is what I have believed and still do. Abnormally large animal produce makes me nervous and suspicious. Yet here is the note Dr. Woodrow Monte made on the first draft of this chapter: "All mommies get the same diet. Larger eggs probably have more egg white, which is higher in protein than yolk and contains no fat or cholesterol." Dr. Monte is a leading nutritionist here at Arizona State University and has a national reputation. A hunch versus a scientist.

Diet

Chicken parts: usually dark meat, which I prefer, even though white meat has less fat

Fish: usually frozen since I now live in Arizona; also tinned shrimp, sardines and salmon. Trick: If packed in oil, drain and blot up the oil; or find fish packed in water.

Beef: Since my teeth are in a precarious state, I'm into chopped beef, *but* I'm careful. I look through the trays of meat for the leanest and the toughest cuts, i.e., those with the least amount of marbling. Marbling, as you gourmets know, indicates the most tender cuts of steak. Marbling, as you gourmets may not know, means more of the particular kind of fat that not only is fattening but is rumored to clog up your arteries, i.e., kill you slowly or suddenly. Trick: I find a chunk of beef with a fresh color and little or no marbling and then I ring for the butcher. Very solemnly I intone, "Please cut off all the fat and grind it once. If it's a choice of leaving a little fat or losing a little meat, please, cut away the meat. My doctor . . ." I don't finish the sentence. They do a great job—like surgeons.

Vegetables: Really, the works. I love all of them, green, yellow, red, leafy and roots.

Cookies and cakes: This is a little awesome and a little silly, but I consume at least three and a half pounds of this stuff a week. But, then, David showed me how.

At the health-food store, the Co-op: I avoid all raw dairy products and raw nuts. They could too easily be a long time away from "home." I do get brown rice, sea salt,* tempeh, tofu, wheat germ, bran, brewers' yeast flakes (never have learned to handle brewers' yeast), lecithin,† and cold-pressed safflower oil.

---

*No more. My nutrition experts say that unpurified sea salt may contain arsenic and mercury.

†I've stopped using lecithin on learning that it is essentially a fat (I try to keep my intake of fats to a minimum). The health-food characters hold it to be helpful as a diet supplement. Professional nutritionists express doubt.

Margarine and sugar: purchased for guests only. I never use them.

Dried fruits and nuts

Wet stuff: dry red wine, dry white wine, dark beer and rye whiskey. Occasionally club soda or champagne. Regular or diet soda for guests only.

Oddments: various kinds of crackers, some salty and tasty, some rye and unsalted. Also couscous, a North African micro-pasta that is basically a white flour (against my principles but I use it as a tranquilizer. When I'm agitated and I have to eat, the blandness of this starchy food coats my stomach in a way that eases me. Part of the survival game is learning what you want, eliminating what is going to kill you even if you want it, indulging those hungers that aren't that harmful, and encouraging the "good" ones. So, a little occasional couscous is okay.)

Not for one moment am I hustling this shopping list as the foundation for a miracle diet. For one thing, it is in a constant state of flux. Example: A glass of warm milk before bedtime is an item associated with children or very young people. For years into my maturity, I had a glass of warm milk every night before retiring. Sometime around thirty-eight or thirty-nine, I stopped wanting it, and stopped having it. My body spoke up and that was it.* Occasionally, there will be weeks when my system says, "No coffee," and tea takes over. As long as the structure of one's diet conforms to some basic principles that we think are correct, the individual patterning and eccentricities make sense.

Taking another tack, this time I'll go through another list, a typical day's eating. This is not projected as a model diet for anyone. Again, this is simply a point of departure to give a perspective on this matter of diet. It is only to make you think of what *you* eat.

---

*This is a bit uncanny. Dr. Woodrow Monte noted in the margin, "This is about the time that milk in New York State was being contaminated with significant amounts of iodine." It was being used carelessly as a disinfectant in milk production. Recently, I have begun to drink milk again.

Diet

BREAKFAST: juice, more often than not a citrus fruit from my yard; otherwise frozen, which retains vitamins better than bottled or canned and is the best buy

Each morning I alternate a hot or cold whole-grain cereal with one egg. To the egg or the cereal I add a tablespoon each of wheat germ, brewers' yeast flakes and a bit of bran. There's brown sugar and milk with the cereal and fruit preserve with the egg. The egg minus a teaspoon of the yolk is "fried" with barely any safflower oil in the pan.

A slice of whole-grain bread, usually wheat, and if I'm into losing weight I forgo the bread and mix in with that reduced-yolk egg a little cooked brown rice or one-minute oatmeal. The logic? Baked bread contains shortening, sweetening and salt. Cooked rice and oatmeal do not.

Coffee, tea or herb tea; no milk or sugar

An hour later: coffee or tea and a little sweet—a few cookies or a small portion of coffee cake

Lunch: one of the thick chunky commercial soups—chicken, fish chowder or vegetable—riched up with cut-up lettuce, wheat germ, brewers' yeast and cottage cheese if I think it needs more protein. All are heated and stirred together with seasoning but no added salt. These canned soups usually have too much salt, sugar, oil and MSG.

An unbuttered slice of whole-wheat bread. A banana almost every day

Coffee and a little sweet—cookies or cake

AFTERNOON: a bit of fruit or some green tea or a good British tea with honey and lime

DINNER: fish or chicken or beef, in that order of frequency. If I use any oil in the cooking of these,* it is the barest minimum

*Since the advent of my microwave, I use even less or no oil in cooking.

in the fish marinade, or, if I'm using a pan, I'll heat up the oil and then tip the pan over a grease can, letting all the excess oil pour off before frying or lightly sautéing. Two hot vegetables or one portion of brown rice or whole-wheat noodles, and some mixed vegetables, green, yellow, red and orange. *My ground rule with all of this is variety.* I don't get hooked on any one or two foods. I keep changing.

Tea or coffee and some sweet cookies or cake.

Before or during dinner, a bottle of beer or a glass of dry wine, red or white.

Supper (about an hour and a half before retiring): a chunk of cheese, unsalted Norwegian rye crackers, a beer or wine or rye whiskey and some sweet—cookies or cake. It rocks me as I list all these sweets, but since I barely use any sugar in my diet, and eat no candy or ice cream and the barest minimum of fats, I get my required fats and tolerable amounts of sugar in my modest but frequent sweets.

My guess is that this totals not quite three thousand calories, which for an active man is not bad. When I was younger and danced harder and longer than I do now, I probably approached five thousand calories a day, but I also weighed ten pounds more. In addition to a thin coat of fat, I probably had more muscle mass than I now have.

The Balanced Diet

I hope for your sake that what follows is not news. I hope the next few pages are boring because you "know all of that." If you don't, you're literally gambling every time you sit down to eat. In that crazy wish and need to dance with power and joy and freedom and for a long time, perhaps you're hoping that what's going in not only tastes good but is going to support that wish. Good luck. You'll need it, because not knowing about food stacks all the odds against you.

There are several ways of classifying nutrients. Chemically, the broad categories are:

Proteins

Carbohydrates

Fats

Vitamins

Minerals

Water

As foods the categories are:

Seeds

Vegetables

Fruits

Milk products

Muscles and organs

Most of the second list contains some or all of the six chemical categories listed, but in different proportions. Seeds include grains and nuts; grains have a rich supply of everything with a larger proportion of carbohydrates, and nuts have a high percentage of fat and some protein. Vegetables vary so much, no such generalizations can be made. Fruits are high in carbohydrates, vitamins and water. Milk products are high in all six. Muscles and organs, which include meats, poultry and fish, are all high in protein, vitamins and minerals, and some are high in fat.

The complexities of each of these categories are so great that the combinations that make for this elusive Balanced Diet are infinite, all the way from a strict vegetarian diet to one that includes the entire list of foods. I would venture to guess that your body performs more chemical operations during the ingestion of one peanut butter and cucumber sandwich than take place in all the chemical transmutations by all the chemists and chemical factories of the entire world in one day. This includes everything from Dupont's Wilmington plant creating electric plastic wires to the Chinese acupuncturist in a remote village burning herbs on a pin stuck in a patient's back. Conclusion: Never try to simplify your diet by living on yogurt or brown rice all day or, if you're trying to save money, by living only on pasta, cheese and tomato paste. If you do, *your* factory may have to close down. Variety. Variety. Variety.

To me, three critical aspects determine a good diet:

1. Variety

2. You love what you eat.

3. You eat what you need.

I suppose we should add one more: You're smart enough to shun the junk you desire.

A few comments before attempting to give the design of The Balanced Diet. Nutritional thinking is changing continually. Take the matter of protein: Someplace in my last year in college, when it had become apparent that I was going to make a stab at becoming a dancer, I had to go to our family physician with an infection from a floor burn. After dealing skillfully with the nasty swelling, she pulled a terrible ploy on me, probably in collusion with my mother, to the effect that my choice of dance was ill suited to me. Her reasons: My neural responses were slow and one kneecap was higher than the other. I was badly shaken for three moments and then said, "That may be but I seem to move faster than anyone in my classes and further, your right eye is higher than your left and Charles Weidman always does an attitude turn on his right leg, and I don't know anyone who is completely symmetrical." With a sigh she said, "Well, if you persist, be sure to eat a lot of meat since dancers require extra protein." I followed this advice for years, but now I learn that in place of five big daily portions of protein, about half that amount is more than adequate. Today's thinking says that regardless of the extent of your physical activity, two or three modest portions are sufficient. It's carbohydrates in the form of complex, unrefined grains and fruits and vegetables that should make up the bulk of your diet.

Diet

Fats are necessary but insidious and everywhere. It is a given that we need them, but the American diet is drenched in fat. We are inundated with video double-talk about "crisp," "low cholesterol," "not greasy," "only vegetable fats used," "natural polyunsaturates" and "lean pork." Vegetables are inevitably buttered, salads swim in oily dressings, potatoes are fried or mashed with gobs of butter or baked and decorated with sour cream, bacon bits and the inevitable butter or margarine. Fat, fat and more fat. Hamburgers are advertised as lean but legally can contain 30 percent fat and probably most of them do, since fat is cheaper than red meat. Chicken comes dressed in a deep-fried batter, as do fish sticks, shrimp, etc. Then there are veal cutlets and that midwest masterpiece of tempting yuck, the chicken fried steak. Gourmet cooking means sauces that may have more calories than the foods they adorn. We need fat, but only a fraction of the oily sea in which much of our food swims and often drowns. Quick-food service stations float in a sea of fat.

Well here it is, The Balanced Diet, as of this moment. Each day you should have:

2 to 3 portions of *protein*-loaded foods: Meat, fish, poultry, eggs, milk, cheese or beans*

2 to 3 servings of *vegetables:* changing constantly from leafy green to yellow to red to starchy (potatoes, lima beans)

4 to 5 servings of *carbohydrates:* unrefined grains (wheat, rye, oats, brown rice). If flour is white, at least be sure it's enriched.

1 to 2 servings of *fruit:* any and all of them are good, with citrus and bananas leading the pack for value

1 to 2 servings of *milk* and its permutations: yogurt, buttermilk, skim milk and cheeses—low-fat cottage cheese and part-skim mozzarella (go easy with the others, which are loaded with fat)

You may note a crossover between protein-loaded foods and milk products. Both are protein-loaded, but the milk products

---

*On the suggestion of Dr. Monte, I eliminated nuts from this list of proteins on the grounds that their fat component far outweighs their protein content.

have the extra dimension of much calcium and a wider range of vitamins. Together they shouldn't total more than three modest portions a day. The heavy no-no's cover salt, sugar, alcohol, saturated fat and animal fat; all should be used sparingly.

Putting it another way, a *New York Times* article on March 23, 1983, discussing an optimum diet for athletes, calls for 55 to 60 percent carbohydrates, 30 to 35 percent *or even less* of fats, and 10 to 12 percent protein. Dancers are included in this category.*

Vitamins and Minerals

Few things add as much to the confusion, complexity and debate about diet as this subject. Stating my predilection: I'd sooner eat a delicious meal created out of the myriad of possibilities that comes under the heading The Balanced Diet than a handful of megavitamins. There is a whole class of "little things that go a long way" in our bodies. These include vitamins, minerals and hormones, each of which is potent in very small quantities. The first two we can get without a prescription—in any amount! What are the right ones to take? And how much? They give me the uncertainties, otherwise known as the willies.

I have great resistance to miracles and panaceas of any kind. If I need magic, let it be a piece of fresh fruit, the flower of foods. Or let it be a bowl of romaine lettuce, red lettuce, avocados, tomatoes, scallions, cucumbers, sweet green pepper, dry-curd cottage cheese, tempeh and a handful of crisp apple chunks, topped with a pungent dressing of rice vinegar, a bit of tamari, cayenne pepper, marjoram, minced garlic, dry English mustard and a teaspoon of white horseradish to give it a wild twist. I can always pretend this carefully concocted concoction cleanses my blood— or is it the formula guaranteed to improve my memory? I forget which. In any event, it tastes great and much better than a fistful of pills, which may do more than I want, or even need.

That said, I do take a small handful of pills each night before retiring: 1,000 milligrams of vitamin C, 800 I.U. of vitamin E, 500 milligrams of calcium, a buffered aspirin and a garlic capsule. More than thirty years ago, I had a brilliant and good internist as my G.P. He was part of a gang of hotshot endocrine researchers. Some of them took off each year to ski in Switzerland. They

---

*These proportions are constantly being changed by leading nutritionists. Try to keep abreast of the latest thinking.

discovered that if they dosed up on vitamin C a month ahead, they wouldn't get the sore muscles and charley horses one would expect from sudden intense physical activity after a year-long layoff. So my doctor recommended 1,000 milligrams of vitamin C every day, claiming that it facilitated muscle recovery and thus was ideal for me, being a dancer. In the last fifteen years, the belief has surfaced that large doses of vitamin C are a must and the solution to many health problems. Forgive me if I got that special heady lift that comes with being years ahead of most people.

Now recent research indicates that megadoses of vitamin C can cause kidney damage to some people and may even provoke the destruction of vitamin C that is in the body. Something tells me it has helped me over the years and that one gram is within a safe parameter, so I continue even though the debate about vitamin C is far from over. The vitamin E and the calcium were prescribed for a devastating series of nightly leg cramps. It worked, and when I slowed down on the pills the cramps resumed. The aspirin is to reduce the kind of joint inflammation that comes from a dancer's daily bruising and intense use of the joints. Recently I heard that a little aspirin every day may reduce heart complications. The garlic is for magic.*

It is possible that some of you who knowingly eat badly out of supposed necessity imagine you're covered by taking a daily massive all-encompassing vitamin-mineral pill. It won't work. Complete nourishment demands three radically different things, not two: vitamins, minerals *and nutrients*. Your body is built out of the nutrients and minerals. Vitamins are the facilitators of nourishment, not nutrients in and of themselves. Incomplete nourishment equals malnutrition, which in time will shamble some part of your body as surely as you are reading this sentence.

Conservative medical opinion has it that a proper diet will supply all the vitamins and minerals that the body requires. Personally, I lean in that direction. When I see health-food stores plumping

*From *The New York Times* article of October 3, 1984, "Garlic May Be Good Against a Variety of Ills," by Jane E. Brody: ". . . Recent scientific evidence indicates that . . . garlic may have distinctive health benefits, including protective value against heart disease, stroke, cancer and diabetes, as well as antibiotic properties." The article goes on to cite instances of its being used successfully against the plague, to control wound infections, prevent gangrene, prevent traveler's diarrhea, as a pesticide and as a mosquito repellent. Masses of it could be a person repellent, but, then, everything costs.

for massive doses of zinc or selenium, I worry. These are called trace elements, which implies that a small quantity will do it. The chemistry of the human organism is an exquisite balancing of a dazzling number of reactions that subtly and precisely alter each other every moment of our existence, sometimes for more than a hundred years! I suspect that stuffing yourself with trace elements without clear evidence of a deficiency has an element of risk. At best it gets eliminated and at worst it knocks that marvelously balanced system off-balance. On the other hand, I can easily imagine that if your system is seriously off-balance, some prescribed form of megadose therapy may not merely be helpful but necessary.

We are swimming in a sea of conflicting opinions. Nutritionists, medical researchers, "holistic" healers, brown-rice fanatics, fasters, all shout each other down, never once hearing what any of the others are saying. I particularly fault the medicals and orthodox "scientific" nutritionists in how they react to the "crazies," the monomaniacs, who have a single or monistic solution to everything.

Has anyone truly researched the premises of the macrobiotic people? Is there some truth to their claim? There are polarity people who deal with food as if they were discussing the zodiac. You eat this but must take two teaspoons of apple cider but never eat it with that. Eat the Indian root essence and face north for five minutes, etc. Who knows? They may have a point. I doubt whether they have THE ANSWER, but I wouldn't be surprised if their single-mindedness did contain elements of value—to all of us, including the honchos of the American Medical Association. Many of those lords of the medical profession could do worse than, say, reading *Diet for a Small Planet*.*

To carry the point a little further and call things by their rightful names, a difficult task in a world of politesse and evasion, there is the simple, ugly matter of greed. If someone goes to a homeopathic physician, he/she is not spending his/her dollar with a member of the M.D. club. Gentlemen, could that play a role in your decision of what to research and what to pretend does not even exist?

What are we to do in this babel of conflicting opinions? Listen.

*Frances Moore Lappé, *Diet for a Small Planet* (New York: Ballantine Books, 1982).

Listen to all of them. Also learn to listen to our own bodies. Then go with our hunches as to whose way or ways are best for us.

The "Right" Weight

If you think this area of vitamins and minerals is loaded with uncertainty, what about the business of gaining and losing weight? Could it be that books on losing weight keep half the publishing houses of America financially solvent? Was there ever an edition of *Reader's Digest* that did not carry "5 Ways to Lose 10 Pounds in 2 Weeks Without Even Trying" or a copy of the *National Enquirer* that did not scream ANCIENT ROMAN SECRET FOR WEIGHT LOSS!? Actually, the Romans did have one: the same self-destructive secret of the bulimics.

Well, here goes. I will wade into the waters of confusion and make my waves. My position will probably be considered conservative by many. To lose weight successfully, these are my principles:

1. Eat a balanced diet; meaning go to no extremes of eating only steak and water or only grapefruit and yogurt or spending any significant amount of time fasting.

2. Enjoy what you eat.

3. But eat less of it than you do normally.

4. Never work for a swift, radical weight loss.

5. Significantly increase your physical activity.

To discuss the above list, point by point. *Eat a balanced diet.* Since you live in a complex organism with complex needs, if you ignore that complexity by fasting for more than a day or restricting your food intake to just a few foods, some part of that organism will literally starve, atrophy and/or malfunction, and with us, if a part goes, then the whole is in trouble.

Enjoy what you eat. The most dismaying thing about most dieting is that after months of abstinence, watching and controlling every calorie and being successful at losing weight, most people when they go back to eating "normally" proceed to gain back what they lost. Some difficult-to-define beast within us seems to have its own concept of the right way to live and eat. Go on a stringent and unappetizing diet and by sheer willpower you will hold it at bay, but sooner or later it will break through the barriers of your discipline and you'll find yourself sitting there helplessly and guiltily drowning in the joy of a rich sundae and once more being thrown for a loss, *regaining the lost pounds.* I think the one way to mollify the greedy glutton beast that most of us seem to be harboring is to keep it happy by eating delicious, well-prepared foods and by learning to deny it only one thing, large quantities. Which leads to the next point.

Eat less than you do normally. This seems quite obvious and yet human nutrition is not that simple. It seems that there are people who upon passing a pastry shop put on pounds. There is so much more to be understood before these unfortunates can easily lose weight. I haven't an inkling of what to say to them.

Even that well-intentioned ploy of keeping down the calories by the use of artificial sweeteners is in question. A human study by Dr. Richard Wurtman, professor of neuroendocrinology at the Massachusetts Institute of Technology, indicates that the consumption of aspartame with carbohydrates may encourage the hunger for more carbohydrates.

A rat study by Dr. William Bennet, editor of the Harvard Medical School health letter supports the belief that the ingestion of aspartame and other artificial sweeteners stimulates the hunger for more sweets.

Even a study conducted by the G.D. Searle Company, the manufacturer of aspartame, commonly known as Nutrasweet, found that people who used aspartame complained of weight gain more often than those who didn't use the artificial sweetener. Can it be that the body can't be fooled by nonnutritive sweets and is simultaneously provoked to hunger even more for the real thing? Time to sing that old spiritual, "There's No Hidin' Place Down There."

Never work for a swift, radical weight loss. Eating less is probably the foundation for any weight-loss program, but starvation diets, or any radical reduction of food intake, pose two hazards. First, when the harsh regimen succeeds and the rigorous dieting ceases, the odds are that the greedy glutton beast will take over and every pound lost will return. Second, the staggering complexity of human chemistry demands a staggering complexity of nutrients. Unless your total diet is under the supervision of a superskilled nutritionist, eating a spoonful rather than a bowlful will take away pounds and give you malnutrition instead. Malnutrition is not simply bad nutrition, it can be life threatening.

Dehydration is one of the oldest ways of losing weight. It is also ineffective in the long run, uncomfortable and sometimes downright dangerous. Plastic airtight dance clothes overheat the body and cause water loss but not true weight loss of fat. Also futile are all attempts and prescriptions for spot reducing.

Significantly increase your physical activity. Addressing such a remark to overweight dancers is adding insult to suffering, and yet there may be something to be said here. Despite the fact that all of us—fat, normal and skinny—expend vast quantities of sweat charging up and down those dance studios and stages, there are great differences in how we all move. Take any group of dancers and give them exactly the same choreography and then measure their expenditure of energy. I venture to guess the variance will be great. Some dancers are generally behind the beat, just as some tend to be ahead. The style of some leans toward a low-keyed dynamic while others are highly charged. Is it possible that those overweight dancers who tend to the slow and light touch would lose pounds if they were to reorient their timing and their dynamic in the direction of greater speed and greater force? There's a research project here for some physiologist interested in weight and exercise. Another research project could pursue the question, Are slow-moving, soft-touch dancers heavier than up-tempo, forceful dancers?

My hypothesis is that they are, and on the basis of that assumption I have evolved a regimen that may help some people lose weight. Call this process UP-TEMPO. It needs research to prove its worth. My guess is that it would be an inappropriate way to lose weight for people who generally are of the quick, high-dynamic and forceful type and also a negative for nervous individuals, those prone to intense anxiety and probably bad for anyone with hypertension. That said, here goes:

UP-TEMPO

FIRST WEEK

Monday: Observe your walk without altering it, particularly taking note of its tempo.

HOW TO DANCE FOREVER

Tuesday: Wherever and whenever you walk, walk just a bit faster than you did on Monday.

Wednesday: Wherever and whenever you walk, walk a bit faster than Tuesday.

Thursday: Exercise no attempt to control the tempo of your walk, except to be observant of it.

Friday: Walk a little faster than you did on Thursday. (*All increments of speed should be small, not radically faster.*)

Saturday: Walk a little faster than you did on Friday.

Sunday: Forget all about it. It's Sunday.

SECOND WEEK

Monday: Observe the rhythm and tempo of your motions as you move about your home doing your chores, such as rising, dressing, preparing your meals, bathing, etc.

Tuesday: Perform everything you do in your home just a bit faster than you did on Monday. By "faster," I do not mean doing any less of a task in order to finish quicker. I simply mean moving faster. One exception: Don't speed up in the bathtub. A broken neck would put any weight problem in the background.

Wednesday: Do everything in the confines of your home a little faster than you did on Tuesday.

Thursday: Exercising no control over the tempo of your household activity, simply observe how quickly you are doing things.

Friday: Do everything in your home a little faster than you did on Thursday.

Diet

Saturday: Within your house do everything a little faster than you did on Friday.

Sunday: Let it go. Go to a movie.

THIRD WEEK

Monday: Observe the rhythm and tempo at which you do your work—rehearsing, performing, teaching, taking classes or holding down a job-job.

Tuesday: Yes, do your work just a bit faster than you did on Monday. This may be inapplicable in some activities or it may gain you a raise.

Wednesday: Do everything a bit faster than you did on Tuesday.

Thursday: Simply observe the tempo at which you are working without trying to control it. Is it faster, slower or the same as it was on Monday?

Friday: Do your work a bit faster than you did on Thursday.

Saturday: Do your work a little faster than you did on Friday.

Sunday: Take a holiday from all of this. (Hidden within the work of this third week could be the key for some dancers not only to lose weight but to add crispness, bite and life to their dance style. Everyone who inter-acts with music, be they dancers or musicians, at every moment is faced with a choice: to be directly on the beat, a little ahead of it or behind it. For this week, the dancer who drags the beat should, wherever pos-sible, in class, rehearsal or yes—performance—cut in a bit before the beat. Aside from adding brilliance and zest to movement, it will burn up more energy and calories. Of course, don't try, as with the other tasks, to get faster and faster each day.)

HOW TO DANCE FOREVER

FOURTH WEEK

Observe the tempo and rhythm of your speech and then apply the same structure over the course of the week as you did with the other activities. I suspect speaking even a little faster would have a profound though subtle effect upon your internal rhythm and, yes, upon your metabolism, in time. Also, this could drive you crazy. If it does, forget it and go back to the focus of the first week—walking, second week—chores in the house, then your work the week afterward, and so on for at least three full cycles, making a sequence of nine or twelve weeks.

If at any time you develop a case of the jitters, drop the whole proceeding. UP-TEMPO may not be for you and it may create more problems than you are trying to solve. If you do attempt this regimen, you will be pursued by the very special madness that characterizes us, our perennial self-dissatisfaction. Pussycats don't have it, but for us it's the source of our greatness and misery. This hunger for perfection drives us to the theatre, to films, to wonder at and vicariously live the exquisite metaphor of the perfect line and ease of great ballet dancers or to soar away on chords of some romantic symphony in its hunt for the absolute, for perfection. In my youth, Fred Astaire served up that vision of a human who had everything, did what he wanted, couldn't be faulted, and he was skinny in the bargain. So read on, do your pliés and lose weight, or gain, for the odds are you're not at all satisfied with what the scale told you this morning.

If you are truly serious about changing your weight, gaining or losing, there are five actions that would indicate that this is the real thing:

1. Buy a book or chart that has a fairly complete listing of the foods we eat, their calories *and nutritional content*. Both are critical for successful and healthy dieting.*

---

*The best are *Composition of Foods*, Agriculture Handbook No. 8, and *Nutritive Value of American Foods*, Agriculture Handbook No. 456, both from U.S. Government Printing Office, Washington, DC, 20402. They cost about $7.50 each. Most easily available is *Nutrition Almanac*, which can be found in health-food stores, but it cites all the Rodale and Adelle Davis beliefs as proven facts. Look out. *Laurel's Kitchen*, by Robertson, Flinders and Godfrey, is good but best suited for lactovegetarians.

2. Buy a fairly precise food scale to measure weight in grams as well as ounces.

3. Get a little calculator so that you can quickly discover that a serving of avocado listed as 2.5 ounces has 118 calories, or 47 calories an ounce. Thus the portion of avocado you have on the scale weighing 3 ounces will stuff 141 calories into your rump. Cut half away and wrap it in plastic. Save that for tomorrow's salad and you'll be eating only 71 calories.

4. Have a pad and pencil with this handy dieter's kit to be able to note all the calculations. You need to *know* what you are doing, and, most important of all, to be able to make a master total of the day's sins or noble accomplishments in the joy of eating coupled with enlightened restraint.

5. If you own a computer there are software programs that can answer many questions on diet and dieting.*

One bit of good news: Do this for a couple of weeks and you'll probably get the hang of it all and won't need to constantly consult the chart and weigh the food. Once the knowledge sets, you'll know that covering the bread with butter is going to add sixty calories to a sixty-calorie slice of bread, or that one little Fig Newton is fifty calories.

However, before launching into this profound revamping of your image, you should ask the question, Does your weight need changing?

As I remarked earlier, most of us live with some sort of dissatisfaction with ourselves and quite often about our weight. In the general population, this applies mostly to women. According to the March 1985 issue of the *Journal of Abnormal Psychology*, women tend to think negatively of their bodies while men tend to think they look pretty good. How dancers compare to "other people" we don't know. Generally, we want to lose. Rare is the dancer who feels the need to gain weight, and we all know those bony ones who would like to lose "just a little more."

---

*Here at Arizona State University, they have been using in their health and nutrition courses the NUDEAL SYSTEM and also the MONI-DEM SYSTEM.

What I am getting at is the rarely examined question, What is correct weight? On the one hand there is definite disagreement among health experts, and on the other is the savage role played all too frequently by some dance teachers.

Once, in the middle of teaching a jazz class way upstate in Brockport, New York, I found myself saying, apropos of nothing at all, "If any of you happens to be a confirmed sadist, there is a profession that is perfect for you. Become a teacher. You can play at smashing egos, torturing people and creating dependents all under the umbrella of doing it 'for their own good.' If you're really artistic about it, you can play your game in the name of *love*. Best of all, society will pay you to do this and not a few of your victims will welcome your ministrations." No one said anything. We went on with the lindy hop and I never learned what they thought of all that.

Relentless pressure on a young person who the teacher decides is too heavy can be damaging. Our culture, certainly our profession, and much of our audience demands, particularly of women, the Russian wolfhound look. Who says there is an ideal body? Do you have the faintest idea of how many different ideal bodies exist in the world, let alone in any audience? Who says that the only people who can grace a stage must conform to one preconceived ideal? I have witnessed ravishingly beautiful dancing by people of all shapes. I shudder at the almighty power of those doyens of dance who stand at the portals of some schools forbidding even *entrance* to some whose "bones" are not right.

A few years back, the North Carolina Dance Theatre, affiliated with the North Carolina School of the Arts, appeared at the American Dance Festival. They were doing a ballet based on *Dark of the Moon*. Within a minute of the curtain rising, a small young woman appeared in what was unmistakably the entrance of the principal woman. Surprise! Not only was she small but large-breasted, quite large-breasted. Neither I nor anyone in that audience had ever seen a figure like that on a ballet stage. Within a few moments some more entered, among them a tall woman, also deep-breasted. It was a fine performance, and within thirty seconds, those two lovely dancers demolished several shibboleths about what a woman must look like to perform ballet, at least for that audience.

No way out of it. We are dealing with aesthetics and, yes, ethics. Personally, I see beauty everywhere, and not in some circumscribed "aristocratic" hothouse. So much for my prejudices. I can understand a choreographer choosing dancers of a specific physical type as expressive of her/his artistic sensibility. I can see the re-creators of certain traditional dance forms seeking out definite physical types because the ideal inherent in their repertoire is romantic otherworldly creatures. Personally, when I see a stage full of women or men all of one physical type, I do not see an "ideal" but rather a banal convention, while the sight of human multiplicity and variety electrifies me.

Teachers, please do not discourage the tiny man or the six-foot-two woman or the woman with the delicate top and large thighs or the square chunky man with the big head and short legs. It's the passion to dance that makes dancers, not the right physical type. Some dancers feel right with a heavy frame. They shouldn't be made to feel like freaks or automatic failures.

They should have the realities of the dance field made known to them, i.e., that looking a certain way is a prerequisite to being employed by some choreographers and dance companies. Likewise, that there are choreographers who seek out all shapes and sizes. In addition, there is that challenge for some individuals to create their own stage, their own company or even a solo career. As long as we teachers give our students a realistic picture of the dance field as it is, we should allow them the adult choice of radically altering their weight or not. I knew a teacher who kept a scale permanently on the threshold to the studio. You couldn't enter without her standing by as you paused on the scale for the two of you to know the worst. Does being in the right give anyone the license to be insensitive, cruel and intoxicated with power—and all in the name of the good?

Of course there is weight that threatens health and interferes with dance, whether it be too much or too little. Each has its particular hazards and problems and it is a responsibility of the teacher to point this out, preferably privately, in a sensitive and respectful manner and not like a prosecutor relentlessly and publicly pursuing the guilty and always for their own good.

Without looking at those elaborate charts drawn up by insurance companies telling you the correct and healthy weight for your age, height and sex, and without modeling yourself after some choreographer's dream-man or -woman, and even without looking in the mirror, by thinking another way you may arrive at a surprising conclusion about yourself.

HOW TO DANCE FOREVER

If I am dancing-dancing, and I do not know I'm wearing shoes even though I am wearing shoes, those are perfect shoes. If I am dancing-dancing, and I do not know I am wearing a costume, that is the right costume. Awareness is often a sign that something is wrong.

Here is what may be the key for you. Ask yourself, When I am moving in the dance, do I carry a consciousness of my weight? Of my heft? Is there a little *umph!* I have to add when I perform a quick maneuver, or in a sudden change of direction is the effort a little much? To my way of thinking, your weight is organically correct when you feel right and you are aware only of the totality of yourself acting and doing in space without the sense that you are dragging something extra along. If you're heavily dressed and booted in the winter and you run with difficulty to catch a bus, that explains itself. If you're speeding through space in light-weight form-fitting dance clothes and you sense a drag on your motion, no matter how little, you're probably carrying fat you do not need.

Personally, I am highly prejudiced in the matter of eating. As noted earlier, I'm at it at least six times a day and no matter how depressed and miserable I might be, six times a day I have a fine flying high. As to total quantity, I have of course backed off from the staggering amount that I used to ingest daily. In my early time I was considered a phenomenon when it came to eating.

In fact, there is a period of life for not a few dancers, quite often young men, who can devour gargantuan portions of food, all day long, with no weight gain. Though they may feel lucky, they had better anticipate the probability that this privilege usually doesn't last into maturity. There is much that is not understood about who does and who does not gain weight easily. Still, when growing stops, the food needs of the body decrease quantitatively, and not only because of the onset of physical maturity. A mature, skilled dancer is just that, skilled, and by that token significantly more efficient than she/he was as a young dancer. To achieve the same results, warming up, taking class and performing, all simply take less energy. A "fully grown-up dancer" is neuromuscularly smarter and consequently needs less fuel—I mean food. Pity the dancer who does not go with this change. He/she becomes any-thing from sleek to chubby to (horrors) *fat!* And nothing will age

Diet

the psyche of a once-slender dancer more than daily facing that slightly familiar but klutzy-looking creature who dances along in the mirror and refuses to go away.

Being narrow-minded about the joys of eating, I look askance at anyone who doesn't live to that tune. Many years ago, when I was on Broadway and dancing in *Annie Get Your Gun*, I had dashed into the coffee shop across from our stage door for a quick lunch. It was a matinee day and an early rehearsal had run over into my usual eat time. In a state of mild panic, I ordered a ham and cheese on rye with lettuce, tomato, a little mustard and "Hold the butter!" Waiting impatiently for what was the only way I could conceivably get through the next five hours until dinnertime, I glanced across the counter and noticed, sitting at right angles to me, one of the singers in the chorus of *Annie Get Your Gun*. She had before her a large salad plate with what appeared to be a mound of tuna in the middle. We began to chat and as she spoke she gesticulated with her fork while I bounced my right foot nervously on the footrest. My sandwich arrived and I launched an immediate attack into the heart of it while continuing to mumble my share of the conversation. In short order, the ham and cheese sandwich disappeared and I managed to catch the attention of the flying counterman to order a cup of coffee and a piece of toasted pound cake. It arrived in a flash. New York deli countermen are possibly the most efficient human beings on earth. As I chased the last crumb of pound cake across my plate, my eyes spread wide in disbelief. The singer's tuna salad was intact. She had waved her fork but hadn't used it!

"Aren't you eating?" I asked. "Half hour is just ten minutes away!"

"Oh, I'm not hungry. To tell the truth, I'm never hungry. I have to look at the clock to know when I'm supposed to eat, and then I sort of make myself do it."

To my ears, this was the most incredible remark I had ever heard. Not interested in food! In the ensuing weeks, because of that conversation, I began to observe her a little more closely. Two things emerged: one, that she was an extraordinary blond beauty on the order of the French movie actress Jeanne Moreau, and two, that she carried around a constantly subdued depression. She seemed to be holding her breath most of the time, waiting for the moment when something would really happen, but somehow never did. The subdued manner acted as a cloak, hiding her beauty.

All of which introduces the contemporary matter of anorexia and bulimia, neither of which I will bother to define since they are so much in our consciousness and in the news these days. I have little knowledge of or experience with individuals caught in that mind-set. I have been given to understand that some ano-rectic and bulimic dancers actually feel fat even though their bones are more apparent than their muscles.

I am fantasizing: I am seeing a reader, a woman with harsh hollows at her temples and sunken cheeks, reclining in a chair reading this book while munching on an apple. It is nine P.M. and the last time she ate was seven-thirty A.M. Her breakfast was a half glass of orange juice, a piece of dry toast and some hot tea with artificial sweetener. Not for one moment does she imagine this passage applies to her! How does one reach someone like this?

Assuming you, the reader, are a dancer, and assuming that quite frequently friends, teachers and choreographers express concern to you about how thin you are, perhaps you should doubt how you feel about yourself and at least consult a physician or nutritionist whom you can trust. Even more, you might consider talking to a professional who can help you deal with what's going on with your head and your emotions—they're rarely separate from this matter of deviant weight, fat or skinny.

Meat Eaters versus Vegetarians

On now to the challenge of the vegetarians. Some of them put us meat eaters on the defensive on moral grounds even while wearing leather shoes, belts and carrying split-hide luggage. Let's not deal with that. Here we are talking about health and specif-ically about what it takes to keep a dancer flying for a long, long time. I doubt whether anyone has taken a survey of how many dancers and athletes have lived well or badly for a significant number of years on a vegetarian diet. More has been discussed in relation to competitive athletes, but mostly on an empirical basis, nothing definitive. Personally, I have met many vegetarians who use their bodies to the limit and are thriving. In my mind there is no question that one can leap just as far and as long eating meat as not eating meat. My guess is that the clue lies in that overused but still useful phrase, The Balanced Diet.

The only problem that must be pointed out is that if your diet does not include meat, fish, poultry, eggs, milk and/or milk products, you had better know an awful lot about nutrition, particularly protein. There are twenty-three amino acids involved in the synthesis of protein. Most of them can be made by the body from various kinds of food, but nine of them cannot. These nine can only be obtained from the foods we eat. To live, and I mean to survive, not merely to live well, these nine amino acids in the proper proportions are the essential building blocks that make up protein. Deprive yourself of one or more of them and you will get sick, and then, after a while, you die. If any of the above, from meat to eggs, is present in your diet in a sufficient amount, you get the nine amino acids.*

Of course, with too much meat you get too much fat and other negatives, and too many eggs give you too much cholesterol.† It is tricky. But it's not half as tricky as a puristic vegetarian diet. One egg contains the whole range of twenty-three amino acids, including the essential eight in their proper proportions, though milk has the balance of proteins that is best for humans. With the single exception of soybeans, not one vegetable contains all the twenty-three and the essential eight in the proper portion to supply us with the protein we need. Beans and other vegetables, grains and nuts deliver all you need *only in certain combinations.* If you know what you are doing, fine. If you don't, you may be a vegetarian but chances are you'll be a sick one very soon.

Suggestion: Find *Laurel's Kitchen*, by Robertson, Flinders and Godfrey, and study it. It's clear, passionate, well written and has the kind of information a vegetarian must be aware of.‡ One reason, having nothing to do with morals, for seriously consid-

*This represents a vital complexity which does not have to be probed by eaters of meat, eggs and milk, but *has to be studied by vegetarians.*

†It should be noted that the cholesterol and fatty content of eggs are found only in the yolk. The perfect protein content is in the white of the egg. Since learning this, I've been lifting out a teaspoon of yolk from the morning egg.

‡The pioneer book in this area was *Diet for a Small Planet*, by Frances M. Lappé, and it still has material of interest. *Laurel's Kitchen*, according to the nutritionist Dr. Woodrow Monte, is more up to date and has less-fattening recipes.

ering switching to such a diet is that today's major suppliers of beef, poultry and pork load their feed with questionable quantities of hormones and antibiotics. Is anyone out there asking how much, and more significantly, what all that stuff is doing to us?

While we're on the subject of books, the most common-sense one available is *Jane Brody's Nutrition Book* by Jane E. Brody, who writes for *The New York Times.* It has a good chapter on athletes, which includes us. Good stuff on unnecessary overloading of protein and demolishes other myths.

Bad! Bad! Bad!

Now let us leave the angels and turn our attention to the sinners. A muncher of a whole-wheat pita stuffed with raw peanut butter and bean sprouts feels like a good person. Oppositely, those who delight in carving up a chocolate sundae or dropping a generous gob of butter on the baked potato or downing a cocktail, bear the uneasy aura of being bad. Indulgences in sugar, fats and alcohol make many of us feel vaguely sinful. For the sake of clarity, let's leave morals out of this and only talk about health, for it is possible to be a human monster and still be healthy, or, conversely, a sick saint.

SUGAR, FIRST!

If you never ate any sugar or honey in your entire life, you wouldn't be missing anything except pleasure, as long as you had sufficient carbohydrates from grains, vegetables and fruits. Your personal factory, your body, has the capacity to convert carbohydrates (starches) into the only sugar used by the body, glucose. Most of the delicious temptees we eat are loaded with sugars that have neither vitamin nor mineral nor any nutritive value except calories. Brown sugar, maple sugar and blackstrap molasses have some potassium and calcium, and thus as sweeteners are preferable to honey. Yes, honey comes from busy bees, is natural and tastes good, but it is almost as impoverished nutritionally as purified cane or beet sugar.

Fiercely negative opinions about sugar are expressed by some. To them, a handful of M & M's may not soil your hands but will certainly mess up your soul. Everything from criminal behavior, hyperactive children, violent mood swings and fluctuations of energy is ascribed to sugar ingestion. I really don't know the validity or inaccuracy of these assertions. Personally, I'm a passive victim of a modest hunger for sweet baked goods.

FATS

You know how careful you are not to pour bacon drippings or rendered beef or chicken fat down the sink drain? You're smart, you know it will clog the works. Well, eat too much of the stuff and that's exactly what will happen to *your* pipes in addition to accumulating more body fat than you need. Your body converts excess fat into a sludge that sticks to your arteries. Nothing gets through a clogged sink and sooner or later clogged arteries starve your heart or your leg or your brain, and that's that.

What to do? Cut them down to a minimum. Tricks: Recall the bit about eating a pie? Have only the upper crust and the filling. No edge and no bottom. Pancakes? Eat only two. The first one with a light sprinkle of salt, the second with a thin artistic smear of butter and a little spill of maple syrup. It'll taste even sweeter after the first one. Try a baked potato with a bit of salt and pepper and no butter at all. You might be surprised at how good an unadorned potato tastes. Steam your vegetables and, if you like, salt them lightly just before eating, with no butter. The first time you might feel poor. The third time you might taste a flavor that was buried by the butter. Make your favorite salad dressing, leaving out the oil altogether, or at most use a quarter of your usual quantity. You may get to taste lettuce for the first time.

In preparing food, I have adopted the principle that all seasoning and taste-enhancers have only one function: to bring out the taste of the food, not the enhancers. Potato salad is all about mayonnaise, not potatoes.

This is a good time to ask a question of the gourmet gurus of *The New York Times*. These influential writers on food often suggest in their recipes that you might use little or no salt, implying a certain caution against its overuse. On the other hand, they consistently describe a cuisine calling for large portions of butter or the ubiquitous cup of *heavy sweet cream*! The question: Why do you gurus recommend such caution with salt and such an extravagant use of cholesterol-weighted sauces? Of course this tastes wonderful, but one can just as easily develop a taste where emphasis is on the food and not on the overwhelming sauce: a way of eating of an entirely different sensibility and a damn sight healthier.

HOW TO DANCE FOREVER

ALCOHOL

Torrents of words have been poured over this matter of drinking. I'll add but three thoughts:

1. If you drink a little, I think you are lucky. Some of it tastes great, feels great to drink and, even better, is said by some medical researchers to actually have a positive effect on health.

2. If you don't drink at all, that's great. Alcohol is like purified sugar. Neither has any nutritional value beyond pure carbohydrate.

3. If you drink a lot, you're in serious trouble, or on your way to serious trouble. If you think you're not in serious trouble, then you're really in serious trouble. That's my belief and I think you'd better get help—now.

In summation, sugar, fats and alcohol are insidiously seductive. They make most of us glow and feel good, and when there's not even a glimmer at the end of the tunnel, a chocolate sundae or a hit of bourbon or a rich food binge seems to solve something, for the moment at least.

The Saga of the Salt Pill

In the early fifties I went on a well-booked July–August tour for eight weeks. My fellow artists were a percussionist and a pianist, each a soloist in his own right. I appeared in every other number, often having to underdress in order to get onstage in time. The first two weeks were in the South, and the moment we hit Washington, DC, the thermometer rose to 90 degrees and stayed there. As we swung up to the Midwest, the challenge grew. It never fell below 100. In Pittsburg, Kansas, we lived through a record 125 degrees. On the Friday of the sixth week, we did a nine A.M. performance at Northwestern State College in Alva, Oklahoma. (Is there anything more obscene than performing at nine A.M.? I've adapted to innumerable difficulties in my life, but my flexibility gives out when called upon to glitter before lunch.)

As usual, I sweated gallons (I never learned to do easy dances). Following the performance, we hurried to a nearby luncheonette. I felt strangely wild and asked for hot soup despite the unbearable heat of the day. Had that and still felt dissatisfied. The percussionist was digging into one of those ice-cold thick midwestern frosteds. I ordered one, going through it with an inexplicable urgency. We went outside and suddenly I sagged against the side of our station wagon.

There was an ice pick in my stomach. A large rock lodged inside my head. The jitters were crawling up my arms. I had never experienced such diverse misery all at once. My fellow artists got me to the hotel and phoned the college for a doctor. Within fifteen minutes the phone rang and a gentle, weary voice asked me to describe my condition. I did. He asked, "Have you been taking salt pills?" "No." "Well sit tight and I'll have something sent up to your room." In twenty minutes or so, a young man arrived with a little envelope. To this day I can see those pills. They were quite beautiful. Oval and turquoise in color with white flecks. I was lucky that we had three days off.

I never again want to know that mess of violent stomachache, headache and inner trembling, all in a steaming-hot hotel room. This was before the advent of air conditioning. I kept the tub filled with water constantly, and whenever one of those symptoms became too much I soaked for a while. Between that, the rest and the beautiful pills, I was in good enough shape to finish the two weeks of the tour, but I was always armed from then on with a supply of salt pills. On Broadway, and later when concertizing and touring, as an invariable rule I took a salt pill at intermission and at the end of every performance. My doctor even suggested taking a salt pill before performances.

This was my sacred routine for years. Naturally, whenever I conducted a summer workshop I preached the doctrine of the salt pill. With great authority I would enunciate the infallible signs— an insatiable thirst, a furry mouth, a nervousness—and suggest hurrying to the nearest fountain armed with a salt pill. If you also had a stomachache and/or headache, you were on the edge of a nasty condition. All the students listened to me, of course, until sometime in the late seventies at an American Dance Festival in New London, when I was contradicted in a faculty session by a very knowledgeable colleague. Checking her out, I learned that the then-current medical opinion claimed that plenty of water and a normal diet would supply all the body needed to cope with copious sweating. I was also told at that time that salt retains water in the body and thus adds weight. I listened and in time stopped taking salt pills when I performed, with no ill effects. Surprise!

Then, a couple of years ago, I began to get frequent muscle cramps in the middle of the night. A doctor informed me that I needed to drink a solution of electrolytes, which include a little salt, potassium and calcium. They helped, and at the next summer dance workshop, in Minneapolis this time, I recommended to my students—electrolytes! What else? Whereupon one of the students, a teacher in a small Minnesota college, let me know that she read an article in *Runner's World* saying it's a mistake to dose up on electrolytes.

I'm relating this Saga of the Salt Pill because it proves how little we know about some very fundamental things that affect and control our work capacity and health.

A short paragraph to finish up this uncertain business of salt and "science." Several years ago I read an article by Jane Brody, who as I mentioned earlier writes the "Personal Health" column for *The New York Times*. It flat out said that everybody, not only people suffering from high blood pressure, should add little or no salt to their food and that all those tasty goodies, such as pickles, capers, feta cheese, herrings, etc., were no-no's. In the January 1984 issue of *Consumer Reports* I read, "The Food and Nutrition Board of the National Academy of Sciences/National Research Council estimates that an 'adequate and safe' intake of sodium for healthy adults is 1,100 to 3,300 milligrams a day, the equivalent of approximately ½ to 1½ teaspoons of salt." The claim: If you don't have high blood pressure, adding more than these amounts of salt may give you high blood pressure. Sending the article to my doctor, I wrote, "Say it isn't so." He wrote back, "It is so." Since then I rarely indulge in my penchant for generously salting my food and eating pickled herring and feta cheese. Who am I to contradict the authorities?

A few months ago I read that one group of medical researchers is convinced that salt is not involved in adding to the probability of getting high blood pressure. Others claim that only some people get high blood pressure from eating excessive amounts of salt. I wish I knew what to do, or say. I still go easy on salt, but the other day I bought a little jar of pickled herring and one night, with my evening beer, I'm going to risk a few bits of it.

Talking of salt of course brings up water. No one disagrees here. Drink lots of it. What you don't need will wend its way back to the waters of the earth. If you do our type of work with insufficient water, you're damaging the machinery. Never, ever, try any weight-loss program that involves limiting the amount of water you drink. When touring in strange cities and countries, check out the water with a knowledgeable local. Bottled and/or distilled water may be the way to go.

Eating In. Eating Out. Eating on Tour.

The only time many of us get to eat in is when we're unemployed! For the dancers in ballet companies, modern dance companies, industrial shows and touring musical shows, it's far from home that we often are. A few, working in New York or Los Angeles, can go home for dinner. To me, they're the lucky ones.

Many of my college summers were spent working in kitchens as a busboy or a waiter and I know what too often happens there. Even in the honest, conscientious restaurants, the pressure of speed, the turnover in help and the occasional need to cut corners put questionable food into the guts of their customers. And how many servers and purveyors of public foods are indifferent, ignorant, sick or even unscrupulous? I don't know and I don't want to know. Whenever I can, I eat in, where I know what I'm eating.

I'm going to make a guess. I think most dancers lose a week or two every year from some mysterious something, and that mysterious something is tied in with how they eat. For clarity's sake, I'm going to start with the home, then brown-bag it at rehearsal, go out to dinner and finally go on tour—all to observe the boners that are really not easy to avoid, considering the kind of life we lead.

As I said, I think we do best eating at home. We know for sure what's in the stew and when all its ingredients were bought. This brings up one flaw. The story of my life is about leaving home, doing concert tours, residencies, extended workshops, and then finally returning home to New York. Problem: Few of us are rich. Economy is the order of the day. Each time I would return, I would go to the cupboard or the refrigerator for a snack or a meal and then hesitate. How long does a dry cereal last? Should I throw it out? Can't stand that. Is that mold on the strawberry preserve? When did I buy that frozen fish? The point is obvious. It's very easy to doubt almost all the food that's been waiting for you to return. Maybe it wasn't waiting. Maybe it was "maturing" all that time. The rule is simple: *When in doubt, don't.*

HOW TO DANCE FOREVER

Okay. Rehearsal and lunchtime. Four choices:

1. Too busy to eat.

2. Run out for lunch.

3. Order from a local deli.

4. Brown-bag it.

I don't think I have any French blood in me, but I can't bear one-hour lunches and I don't know how or why most of you do. Eating quickly, eating on the wing and running out to grab a bite are almost givens with most dancers, and I think it's awful. If ever you can control your midday schedule, open your eat time to at least an hour and a half. A little civilization, please! As for skipping lunch, that's equivalent to racing to a fall. Ordering from the deli, fast-food palace or local quick luncheonette: Unless you're lucky enough to be near a "health bar," it's going to be deep-fried, too much bread, the wrong bread, too much mayonnaise or butter, etc.

Brown bagging it. This could be perfect. No time wasted getting dressed, going out, ordering, eating, paying up, getting back and redressing. Also, you can select attractive, nutritious food. Only one "but." I often see dancers nibbling on a carrot or tearing apart a juicy navel orange—but with unwashed hands. When we work, we really get around: hands on the barre, lifting sweaty bodies, catching our weight on the floor with our hands, putting on and taking off dance shoes, and then rarely washing our hands. Every alien bug entering your system has to be taken care of. It's you or them. You're well armed with a fine defense system, but it is limited. Give it too much to do and a real nasty alien will slip by and take up residence, i.e., you get sick and there goes one of those weeks when a "mysterious something" laid you low. (While we're at it, the wearers of contact lenses can ill afford handling them with unwashed hands or lubricating them with spit!)

On tour: Eating is always a problem. Between being at the mercy of airline "chefs,"* airport restaurants, sending out for food from

*If you're smarter than I am, you can order special meals ahead of time from the major airlines which may be closer to your tastes, convictions and/or religious preference: seafood, Kosher, Hindu, salt-free, vegetarian, etc.

Diet

backstage during rehearsal and tech setup, I pretty much have to take what's available, which isn't much. What I miss most are vegetables. Quick food recognizes one vegetable—French fries. Actually, I get partially saved by three things:

1. The growing number of salad bars in restaurants.

2. Sometimes I get to eat college food and over the years Saga Food Service* has learned to allow a few ingenious food crazies to eke out a healthy meal not swimming in an oily sauce. Tricky but possible. In Saga or any public eating place, pick "naked foods," such as grilled, baked, roasted or lightly sautéed fish, chicken or beef. If it's fresh it'll be obvious, and if it isn't it'll be obvious and you can return it. Trouble is some of you are so nice, you think it isn't "nice" to complain and make trouble. Well . . .

On the other hand, in any public eating place avoid all masked foods, such as hamburgers, stews, chilies, hashes, heavily sauced foods, heavily breaded deep-fried foods, mixed meats of any kind (bologna, sausages, hot dogs, etc.). Of course, much of the Oriental diet (Chinese, Japanese and Thai) is a mix of many different foods, often highly seasoned, and yet the delicious cuisine is quite healthy and generally cheaper than in other restaurants. Still, I first seek out a local recommendation.

3. Finally, whenever the residency goes over a week, I try very hard to get a room with a refrigerator and a stove, dig out my famous shopping list, fill up a cart at the local market and make myself a "home away from home."

Addendum

On July 24, 1985, I received two striking pieces of information. The first: *Ballet News* arrived in the mail with an article on diet. The central story was about Kevin McKenzie, a dancer with Ballet Theatre who had been haunted by a continual series of injuries. The problem was finally tracked down to a shocking loss of calcium due to a medication that had been prescribed for an ulcerated colitis. Once the condition became known through an analysis by a nutritionist, a carefully designed diet gave Mr. McKenzie a sense of renewal and *freedom from further injuries.*

---

*This is a food service in many American universities and colleges.

Second item: The American Medical Association recommended that colleges of medicine significantly augment the study of nutrition in the training of all physicians because too many practicing doctors *are insufficiently versed in this crucial matter*.

Two items, two sides of the same coin. What is your defense? *Become knowledgeable yourself*. The information is out there. It isn't all that exotic or hard to find. This chapter is as good a beginning as any, and then go on to read more. If you sense something is wrong, find a trained nutritionist, have your diet and your lifestyle analyzed and have a specific diet designed for you. If you are taking a prescribed medication, with whatever means available to you discover all of its possible effects upon the rest of your system. Know also that everything is subject to change. The hard conclusions of nutritional scientists get shaken from year to year. Above all, keep in touch with the latest thinking.

There it is, the chapter on diet, a mere glance at a complexity that demands infinitely more attention, research and a genuine dialogue among all the experts.

CHAPTER III

DANGER

In a way, I am loath to lump the ensuing mess of dangers into one chapter. Read in a rush, they may discourage or frighten some young dancer or, even worse, give some reluctant parents the perfect excuse to oppose and/or refuse support for their child's choice of a dance career. Put all the hazards of, say, the medical profession in one chapter and that could be dismaying, but of course the average yearly income of doctors is around $100,000* while that of professional dancers is a bit more than $20,000.† Yes, but we're beautiful.

Still, the best way to wet the fuse of danger is to recognize it, describe it and build a fence around it with canniness and anticipation. Regard this chapter the way you would a road sign warning you of a steep hill: SHIFT INTO LOW.

Well, here goes.

The Hazard of Youth

Ironically; the greatest danger to a long life of dancing lies at the very beginning. It is there that we encounter a devilishly deceptive

---

*Occupational Outlook Handbook, U.S. Dept. of Labor, 1984.

†The American Almanac of Jobs and Salaries, by J. W. Wright, cautiously says, "The estimated annual range is $15,000 to $29,000." The dancers in the survey done for this book averaged $21,000.

condition, our youth. It is precisely then that most future professionals begin to study; some before the age of ten, and some even
perform as children.

One can debate an early start, but it does present advantages.
A young body is sweetly pliant, thereby easily achieving and
setting the stage for that freedom and wide range of movement
so necessary for expression and virtuosity. Also, with the exception of singing,* all movement skills, such as playing a musical
instrument, swimming, tennis, gymnastics, dance, etc., profit from
early development of highly complex neuromuscular patterns.
The most recent generation of American dancers is astonishing the
world with their virtuosity, and probably most of them entered the
dance studio as "babies," paralleling the Russian practice.

Young, our bodies are beautifully designed to fall down, to make
mistakes and even to cope with disaster. We heal quickly, our joints
are literally wetter, our blood supply to the muscles is more generous
and our bone and cartilage surfaces are shiny, slippery and un-
scarred. Walking infants fall down all day, harmlessly, and only if
they bop their little heads do they release a justifiable howl. Their
cute dimples are really quilting tacks to hold the skin in place while
the generous coats of baby fat bulge to protect the elbows, the wrists,
the knees, etc.

However, sometime in our mid-twenties, we start the long process
of drying up. The lubricant of our bones is called synovial fluid and
that of the muscles is called lymphatic fluid. As these thin out, as
the baby fat diminishes, and as the blood supply and the healing
hormones become proportionately less plentiful, all the errors of our
youth begin to surface. In our middle to late twenties we earn the
results of all the bad teaching, the accumulation of all the accidents,
all the risks we took that failed, the knee drops, those pliés rolling
over into the arches and, most devastating of all, the acquired asymmetrical alignment and asymmetrical motion patterns that are rarely
noticed by us and all too rarely noticed by our teachers. These
include the charming tilt of the head, always a little to the left, a
nervous hike of one shoulder, a barely perceptible lateral shift of
the torso to one side and, of course, the dreadful swayback. These
are the sins that usually do not affect us in our youth but promise
to play a major role in our lives later, just when we're getting somewhere.

---

*Voices trained in the bel canto style used in operas generally do not fully
blossom until the mid-thirties or even early forties.

Danger

Take something like cartilage, which is a shiny, slippery, semihard stuff that takes up much of the friction and shocks between the bones. You have probably nibbled on some when having a chicken leg and called it gristle. It is an off-white resilient substance not unlike plastic on the ends of the bones. It's designed to take friction and stress, protecting the harder, more brittle stuff we call bone. It is also designed to last a lifetime. However, if you scratch it, chip it, shred it or tear it, it is a scratch, a chip, a shred, a tear for life, because cartilage has no regenerative powers to speak of.

A slight exaggeration. Most cartilage has little or no blood supply and so healing and/or regeneration is occasionally possible but rare, i.e., don't count on it. Take care of what you've got. Cartilage is not like skin or bone or the tissues of internal organs, which all have the capacity to repair extensive damage. The materials of the body are beautiful, tough and strong enough to serve us for the duration. Bad teaching, ignorance of the body and functionless and lopsided gripping have little effect on the powerful resilience of a young body, but this very resilience deceives by absorbing the errors of bad moves. The body is betrayed by its own protective resources which can last a very long time. A young foot rolling inward on every plié can feel just great. A knee rotating inward on every landing doesn't hurt and it won't give way for at least another ten or fifteen years.

Bad Moves

This section is addressed to two groups of people: the young and the teachers of the young. Many teachers give good classes but with very little correction. In the desire to keep the class rolling, or because of personal inhibitions about the confrontation implicit in criticism, there is little attention paid to or note made of specific individual errors. Some teachers prefer a general correction given to the entire class. Some teachers get cued in to one or two students and ignore the rest.

Personally, I regard these ways of teaching faulty. Highly skilled, experienced dancers can gain much from some of these teachers, but young dancers are jeopardized by this style. What follows amounts to a checklist of bad moves that must be caught and changed early. Not to do this makes future disasters probable.

To the young who read this, the task is more complicated. Some of these bad moves are not easy to detect in your own dancing. Most wrong moves feel right. If, however, you take note of the following descriptions and then look for each possible error in

HOW TO DANCE FOREVER

your fellow students, you'll develop an eye and an awareness to catch good and bad moves in yourself.

And now, a heavy question: Does your teacher see and correct the errors you observed?

Some teachers will now become very angry at me for asking this. Well, I'd rather a few teachers suddenly decide this book is trash if it will open the eyes of some students to ways that will give them a long future. Put plainly, if you become aware that you are studying with a teacher of dance who either doesn't notice or doesn't point out your profound dance errors, you may have good reason to start looking for a teacher who does.

To work: What follows is not in order of importance. A painful little muscle in your big toe can make an entire performance a misery. It's all important.

I'll start with the funny and almost charming "sit of the innocent." I can recall seeing only one adult professional beyond thirty doing this, but many times I've seen young and very young dancers sit, rumps flat on the floor, legs bent at the knees and inverted, i.e., the thighs are rotated inward 90 degrees so that the inside of the thigh, knee and ankle are resting on the ground. They look so comfortable and at ease. Some can even rise to a stand from there or lower to it from standing by simply rolling forward over their arches with feet turned out. I have a guess that for some this will never have a negative effect—but why find out? I think the position has little effect on the powerful and exquisite ball-and-socket hip joint, but the knee—the poor knee!

From the point of view of human engineering, the knee leaves much to be desired. It's as if you balanced the round head of a hardball bat on the top of a thinner softball bat, carving a few grooves so that they can mesh a bit, *but only when your legs are straight!* On page 90 are X rays of the right knee of Michelle Vorbeck, a nineteen-year-old dance student. We are looking at a very strong, healthy knee in the various stages of plié. The deeper the plié, the less the big "bat"—the femur—rests on top of the softball "bat"—the tibia—which is tipping more and more to make an incline. If you are now suddenly panic-stricken and paranoid, who can blame you? What holds them together in grand plié? Answer: *ligaments, tendons and muscle tone,* all under great stress and unfavorable leverage. No matter how strong you are, the deeper the plié, the greater the vulnerability of the knee.

A 1985 study by Dr. James Garrick, of eight hundred injured

amateur and professional athletes and dancers treated at the Center for Sports Medicine at St. Francis Memorial Hospital in San Francisco, indicated that "The knee was the anatomic area most frequently injured in all nine sports." In his study, 29 percent of the dancers had knee injuries treated, compared with 10 percent who had spinal injuries.

Don't stretch those knee ligaments. Don't stretch those knee tendons. Stretch the thigh muscles only. Correct thigh stretching demands two conditions:

1. The muscles are warm, hot and fully worked.

2. You are putting *no weight on the leg you are stretching*.

Above all, the stabile knee joint needed by every professional dancer demands extraordinary thigh strength.*

The "sit of the innocent" is often performed before a class or a rehearsal starts by someone who is very limber and feels comfortable doing it. While being comfortable, the weight stress on the inside of the knee will in time probably stretch precisely those ligaments and tendons whose function it is to hold this precarious joint stabile. Stretch those ligaments and tendons and the ends of the "bat" begin to wobble about. A wobbling knee joint under stress tears cartilage and ligaments.

Next. The most obvious bad move—bad habit—is pronation of the foot, or rolling the arch inward—sending the downward thrust of the body's weight inward and away from the center of the foot. Why do we do it? Many reasons. Mostly due to forcing a turnout by exploiting the fluidity of the ankles. Our ankles have the fortunate capacity to adjust laterally to rough and uneven terrain. This flexibility can be abused in the interest of a full turnout. The feet are angled out more than the thighs. In the plié, the arches roll in. Also, structurally some people have poor arches, knock-knees or weak tensor fasciae latae and biceps femoris muscles (muscles that hold the knees from swinging in). The way the thighs are set in the hip socket and the way the shin bones articulate in the knee joint can also cause pronation.

Everyone knows it's bad and yet an awesome number of dancers, even professionals, pronate at least one foot. The strength or

*More on this in Chapter IV, Healers and Treatments.

1

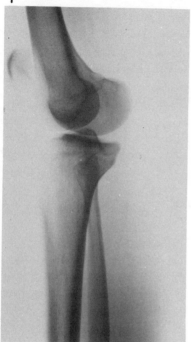

2

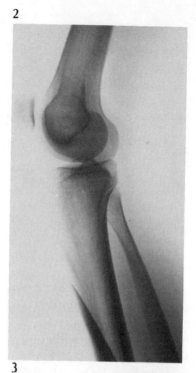

3

This is a rare set of x-rays, since it shows the right leg of a strong young female dancer in various stages of plie *while standing*. Practically all knee x-rays are taken while a person is lying down. For easier viewing on the printed page, the negative was developed into a positive.

1 Standing on a straightened leg. One odd note: In this x-ray, the dancer's leg appears to be hyperextended when in fact it is not.

2 Demi-plie

3 Her deepest demi-plie, while leaving the heel on the ground

4 Grand plie

5 Haunces resting on the heels with feet in first position

4

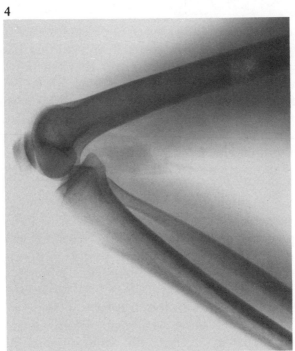

5

weakness of an arch and the degree of pronation can most clearly be seen from behind. Check yourself by standing barefoot and barelegged with your back to a mirror that reaches low to the ground. At a foot away, bend down far enough to look between your legs and observe your Achilles tendons. Ideally they should rise up straight out of the heels. If one or both of them curve inward, even a bit, you're pronated, indicating a structural weakness and wrong habits. Even if there is no pain or sense of weakness, you have work to do, strengthening the muscles that lift the arch.

The foot is a better piece of engineering than the knee, but it too has a structural vulnerability. Basically it is a triangle with direct support or ground contact on only two sides, the front and the outside. The inside is an exquisite bridge, supported by only two things: muscles and the intelligent use not merely of the foot alone but of the entire leg and ultimately of the entire body.

The key, of course, lies in the direction of the knee, or, more precisely, of the thigh bone. Wherever, whenever, however, it must always thrust in precisely the same direction as the foot. The image I give my students is to regard the foot as an arrowhead and the thigh as the shaft of the arrow.

However, it is possible to do this correctly and still pronate. The anklebone can slide inward even if the bent knee is correct. This is a subtle and not easily observed movement. Again there's an image that will help: Regard the two halves of the anklebone as having a notch or a gateway between them for the energy of the knee to pass through in line with the direction of the foot. Thus, the lower leg will move in one clean harmonic thrust with the thigh and send all your powers in one direction, whether it be down in a plié or up in a jump.

More knee notes: Early in my study of dance, I had the good fortune to get a year's scholarship with Martha Graham. When I acquired a bit of confidence, I would arrive early and sit down right in front of her. At this time, chiropractors were the new magicians and a popped joint was harp music to a dancer's heaven. I could get a pop in every joint of my body. One day, arriving early, I went to my place directly in Martha's line of vision, knelt, raised my body slightly, and slammed down hard on my heels, getting a magnificent triple pop out of both knees. Martha recoiled as if mortally wounded. I knew I had done a dummy and, though she said not a word, I never did it again.

Danger

I can't count the number of times I've interrupted young dancers as they were warming up or improvising because while in a full squat they were bouncing their rumps into their heels, thus violently stretching everything they needed to hold their knee joints together.

Another knee no-no is *any* kind of fall or kneel where the knee takes the body's weight with the *slightest* jar. Wherever possible, floor contact should be parallel with the outside of the knee with only a glancing impact and never on the inside and never head on. If there must be direct floor contact with the kneecap or high ridge of the shin, *fake it*. Stop the knee a fraction of an inch above the floor and then softly and secretly lower the weight to the floor. Also, for me, when I kneel I extend the foot with the instep touching the floor, rather than the ball of a flexed foot. The angle is flatter and more favorable to the kneecap. This could be because of my structure and not a useful generalization.

Regardless of how strong you are and how smoothly you kneel, I think no kneels or falls should ever be rehearsed or practiced without kneepads, and wherever the costume permits, they should be worn in performance if there is kneeling and/or falls. I strongly suspect that every knee impact causes some microdamage on the cushions of the knee—the cartilage. Enough micros will make a macro. Limit the number of kneels and/or knee falls in any one rehearsal. This allows for recovery time and obviates the fatigue factor causing a bad move.

It's been so long since I worked on Broadway that I almost neglected to bring up the matter of knee slides, but seeing an old Hollywood musical recently on TV, I caught an old competitor, David Lober, who brought it all back. I gasped with terror when on a high platform he swept the star into his arms at the same time that he went into a knee slide down the full length of a ramp. Back in the forties and fifties they were the thing for men in Broadway shows. "Thank you, Jack Cole." (He's the choreographer who introduced them.)

I even had a one-knee slide. In *Plain and Fancy* I would take a short fast run onto the right knee, extending the left leg in back, and sail in a lunge more than halfway across the stage. No way out of it. Knee slides are rough. Avoid them if you can. Give the choreographer a better and safer stunt. If you have to do them, kneepads. If you have to rehearse them, never many in one session.

Enough with knees. Now, the foot. The foot, like the hand, is a mass of bones with little muscle or soft tissue. Muscle mass and muscle control are primarily in the calf. Yet when we jump, leap, or run, our entire weight of over one hundred pounds crashes into the hard surface of a floor or lands like a whisper. The complex mass of responses and moves that make it possible for a trained dancer to land on this "bag of stones" without a sound or perceptible hit is one of the central miracles of good dance training and nowhere as common as it should be. A feather-soft land out of elevation should be a fundamental of every trained dancer, and too many do not have it. It's not merely an exquisite metaphor for flight, air, control, power, floating, etc., it's a life-saver when you have it and a destructive flaw when you don't. Consistent traumatic shocks will in all probability contribute to every structural weakness from your anklebone right up to your head bone.

If you have not solved this aspect of your craft, there are a few conceptions and images that might help. Most important to get rid of is the common formulation that a jump or a leap is *up and down*. No. It's *down and up*. If you think that an elevation is completed on the ground, the chances are you'll come crashing down, but if you reverse the thought process and think of the trip into the air as *starting on the ground and finishing in the air,* the landing becomes the beginning of the next step or leap. If the landing is a start, you will go/pass through it quickly to do something else and, in all probability, *spend less time* plunging into the floor. In teaching repeated leaps across the floor, I shout myself hoarse, "DOWN-UP! DOWN-UP! DOWN UP!" *From the height of a leap or jump, you should be on your way to creating the next move.*

Some dancers on landing release the heel too quickly, creating a bony smack on the floor. Try thinking of the foot as a pure, powerful muscle with no bones at all. This may help the landing and the takeoff be one continuous motion rather than a jerky one.

Finally, many women and a few men with beautifully extended feet make an error that guarantees a hard landing with little control. Instead of reaching for the floor with extended toes, their toes follow the lovely curve of their arched foot and curl under. The complexity of unconscious coordination that protects us uncurls the toes at the last moment before landing. They'd break otherwise, but in that motion of getting out of the way, they are moving from the very position needed to cushion the impact of the ball of the foot. Underuse of the toes in landing keeps them muscularly weak. This curling under of the toes is a difficult habit to break. Try extended reaching for the floor by the toes and practicing many slow extensions of the foot, many slow tilts into lunges in all directions, deliberately careful and focused small leaps, and jumps and big leaps ending in full, soft stops. The resilience and power of the toes will grow with these careful exercises and you'll be jumping higher as well as landing like a visitor from space.

Much of this entire examination revolves around the word *enough* and its permutations: *not enough*, and *too much*. Extending the body in all of its possibilities is one of the sweetnesses of the dance experience, and yet "too much" is a hazard.

"Too much" leads us into a touchy area where the characteristics of certain technical disciplines open the way to possible trouble. What follows is not an attack on any of the techniques mentioned. Every activity has its hazards. Swim and you might drown. Tennis is rough on the elbows, shoulders and wrists. So is conducting an orchestra. Basketball is hell on the ankles. Football is a threat to everything.

Returning to "extending too much": In his *Dictionary of Classical Ballet*, Gail Grant, in describing "Battement frappé," writes, ". . . the foot is thrust out to the second position striking the ball of the foot on the floor and rising off the floor in a strong point." The manner of expression easily gives the impression not merely of intense energy but of going all the way! Unfortunately, going all the way in any swift extension of the leg, or the arm for that matter, is not an extension but a nasty, *lateral* karate-like snap of the knee joint or elbow. Exhausted pitchers, off guard, may let the throwing arm all the way out, thus setting the stage for torn ligaments, tendinitis and even bone chips.

A frappé or any kicking extension of the leg is brilliant, beautiful and safe when met by an equally powerful check and pullback, stopping the leg just short of locking. Letting go all the way sets up shock waves of quivers in the thigh muscle and trauma in the joint. Letting go is a breaking action.

I learned this sadly from the opening move in one of my earliest solos, *Spanish Dance* (1948). Starting in profile, feet parallel and arms clasped behind, I very slowly pliéd on the left while drawing the right knee high with the foot extended. With a lightning thrust I straightened both legs with the free right leg kicking downward full force but just missing ground contact. A year of performing that and I developed a grape-sized lump on the adductor tendon just above the knee and possibly the beginning of my subsequent knee trouble. I did learn to stop that snapping extension and in a few years the grape (probably a calcification) disappeared.

In fact, slowly or quickly, every extension should be met by a pullback. When standing, the legs, visually straight though they appear extended, should not be fully extended but very slightly and imperceptibly bent. If this were taught early, many who are hyperextended at the knees wouldn't even get to know they have a problem.

Martha Graham's technique has a movement that opens the door to hyperextension if one is not careful. The beautiful and perky prances, having so much emphasis on lifting a fully extended foot, allow the body to settle its weight into the standing leg, thrusting the knee joint back in opposition to the forward foot motion. Pulling up on the weight-bearing leg will correct this.

More bad moves in ballet: There is a classic nervous gesture, not only at the beginning of a class but quite often preliminary to commencing a new sequence at the barre. Hand on the barre, with heavily rosined slippers, this dancer will dig both feet into a perfect fifth position and then straighten the legs. If there were a 180-degree ease in turnout, who could complain? If not—trouble. In demi-plié, the thighs of an unlimber person can turn out more. Straightened, the angle of the feet is unchanged while the thighs rotate inward, remorselessly grinding, stretching and ultimately tearing everything in its way. It's called torque. Torque is what you use to tear the greens from carrots. This turning, twisting force creates a shearing action at the knee, since that is the weakest of the three joints involved, the other two being the ankle and the hip. The ankle is designed to be twisted a bit, and the hip is too powerful to be budged, at least in this context.

I recall sharing a concert with José Limón at the American Dance Festival in New London, Connecticut. Standing in the wings, we were warming up before a matinee performance. While holding on to a light stand, José sighed heavily as he carefully placed his feet in a narrow-angled third position rather than a wide-open fifth and apologetically said, "I can't plié in fifth anymore. It wrecks my knee. I must have forced it too much." He was probably right. In recent years almost all good teachers of ballet have emphasized that the angle of turnout of the feet must be determined by the outward rotations of the thighs and not one jot more.

An unexpected and debatable note on the grand plié: Martha Myers, dean of the American Dance Festival, in the June 1978 issue of *Dance Magazine* quoted a large panel of medicals and physical therapists to the effect that it is a grievous error in the conventional structure of a ballet class to start with grand pliés within the first five to ten minutes. I mention this for what it is worth; I don't know whether they are correct.

Certainly one of the most magnificent techniques of dance training is the one devised by Martha Graham. Yet I can't help but think that, for certain bodies, one aspect holds a distinct hazard. She has created the amazing eloquence and variety of expression that takes place in a position that would apparently immobilize a human being, namely the sit in the fourth position. For those people who are not limber enough in the hip to sit easily with weight equally on both sit bones, the sharpest stress occurs on the medial, or inside, of the bent knee to the rear. Being bent, it is at its most vulnerable position, and worse, being weaker than the hip joint, it gets stretched more to bear half the weight of the upper body which cannot rest on the ground.

I did offer a suggestion to a graduate student who passionately wished to take a three-week course of study with a fine teacher of Graham technique who was visiting Arizona State University. He was concerned that a weakness in his right knee would be aggravated by the technique, with which he had some experience. I had a thick typewriter pad in my office. I lent it to him, suggesting that he slip it under the right buttock when sitting with the right leg in back, since that hip wasn't limber enough to let him rest its weight on the ground. He found it awkward in class but helpful when practicing.

I've always wondered about the life and longevity of the knees of those incredible male dancers of the Moiseyev dance company who perform Cossack dances with the most sensational moves into and out of a deep squat. Does anyone out there know what happens to these men? The ladies, of course, skitter by with their exquisitely twittering feet, never doing or being permitted to do those wildly hazardous stunts. In the long run, which is the greater hazard, being charmed or being charming?

Charles Weidman's technique class opens up with what many of us think is too much too soon. It consists of standing in a wide

HOW TO DANCE FOREVER

base and bouncing forward from the hips with straight legs and torso eight times, hanging back and bouncing from the hips eight times, side left eight times, side right eight times, and then, *whoosh*, four times in all these directions. Then, with remorselessly simple logic, two bounces in each direction, and then, unbelievably, a single rather violent bounce in each direction four times. Now, on its surface I would guess this to be a dangerous move, and yet I cannot honestly say that I know for a fact that it has been harmful to any significant number of dancers. I myself would never give a move like that in class, and yet many magnificent dancers, including the great José Limón, emerged from this training.

Take the matter of stretches. I'll state my negative convictions and you can remember all the exceptions that go against exactly what I say you shouldn't do:

1. No fast stretches

2. No forceful, violent stretches

3. No stretches until the muscles are warmed up

4. No repeated bounce stretches

5. No one stretches you.

The only exceptions to the last point are those who are very wise and very, very skilled. A fellow dancer sweetly and obligingly stretching you can easily push a bit too far. By the time you realize you're in danger, you speak, then you are heard, and then your colleague stops. That could be just enough time to tear a muscle loose from its roots, and I have heard of it happening.

If you do want help being stretched, there is a method with an element of safety. You must explain these ground rules to your helpmate very clearly:

1. Give the exact direction of the stretch.

2. Ask the stretcher to observe your breathing carefully. As you exhale, the stretcher can apply slow, careful, gradual pressure. When you inhale, that becomes his/her cue to slack off. The

Danger

longer you exhale, the longer and stronger the stretch. Every inhale is a sign to release pressure. Thus you are in control and, assuming you have a sensitive person helping you, this procedure might protect you.

Under the heading of BAD MOVES and "too much" is grabbing, the ultimate in "too much." I'm certain that as a young dance student I was often guilty of this. Starting to learn dance late and loving it so fiercely, everything had to be done full out. I don't think it was until I got my first leading role on Broadway that I really learned to shade and color my expression. Eight performances a week for two years teaches one a few things. Dancing ill, dancing blue, trying to dance with a stomach full of food because of poor service in a restaurant on a matinee day, all these school one in dynamics. Those nights I would just know that full out all the way was out of the question. I would never have made it through an evening.

In *Annie Get Your Gun,* which is the show in question, I learned after a bit when to deliver a blast and when to glide lightly through a move or a phrase. Best of all, I finally learned to do that even if I was feeling super with a full reservoir of energy.

The point is obvious but not necessarily easy to practice. Habitually applying more energy than a move or phrase requires nurtures bulky muscles, pulls the body out of kilter, tears tissues and, worst of all, exposes you as an artist lacking in taste and discrimination, and we mustn't let that happen.

For lazy or low-energy dancers, I have no advice. I don't understand them. Why do they go to the trouble to get into dance clothes? Why do they want to dance at all?

It is the eager, the passionate, the bearers of an insatiable love of moving, the beautiful crazies, that worry me on occasion. They often don't know when the body has had enough. I'm one of those for whom I worry. I have been hurt in the full flush of an excited, hot body.

A great moment in my career: Tamiris is choreographing a Bing Crosby film called *Just for You.* She has proposed a bullfight ballet and I'm hired to dance the lead. I arrive in Hollywood a week before rehearsals in early spring. The weather is a warm embrace. New York, which I have just left, has been raw, damp and mean. To keep in shape until the first day of rehearsal, I rent a studio space in the legendary Perry's Rehearsal Studios. The great and

HOW TO DANCE FOREVER

beautiful Carmen Maracci is teaching across the hall. I'm having a wonderful workout. My body feels like honey. By the time I get to working on elevation, due to the combination of the heavenly warmth, my excitement, and the fabulous workout, I'm flying. After an effortless jump sequence in place and tiny treads and skips across the floor, I pause at the far end of the studio to let loose a few big ones. A simple run, run, leap, and I take off first from my right and then off my power leg, the left. I can still feel the warm air brushing past my wet cheek as I hover higher than I have ever been. I come down, down, and my foot reaching for the ground from this unfamiliar height is not ahead of me where it always is but under me at the wrong angle, and my entire weight slides so deeply into a relaxed foot that I mash the top foot bones into each other. For years after that I had to be certain that I didn't plié too deeply on the right or I'd get an awful shot of pain. Could I have been smarter? I don't think so. There are outer reaches of space to which we aspire and by their very nature we don't know them until we get there. We study and prepare and hope that our skill can cope. Some surprises. Some victories. Some wounds.

Writing this chapter feels like composing a tunnel of terror. At each turn and twist I'm yelling, "Boo!" or "Look out!" or "Run for your life!" Read on. It'll be over soon.

Asymmetry

"Oh, I always do that." To my way of thinking, that kind of thinking is not thinking and, even worse, it's destructive. The awesome Grand Canyon occurred because the same thing kept happening in the same place and so the biggest ditch in the world was cut into Arizona. If you always do something, i.e., some movement pattern, say, sitting with your right leg curled up under you, some profound change will eventually cut into your body. These are habits we cannot afford. All asymmetrical physical habits will damage us. This applies to both our daily living and our dance choices. Members of the corps usually are called on to be more symmetrical. Soloists can more readily indulge in their own quirks to their ultimate disadvantage. I always knelt on the same knee until I tore a cartilage. My left leg was my workhorse. It always did the work of lowering the "aristocrat" right to the floor. The left kept getting stronger and the aristocrat got weaker. Do I have to tell you which one suffered the torn cartilage?

There is another kind of asymmetry that only recently has come to the attention of researchers. Dr. D. C. Reid, with others, compared thirty classical ballet students with thirty ". . . age-matched, active, non-ballet dancing females" in respect to knee and hip injuries and also inward and outward rotation of the leg. Of course the ballet dancers were much freer in turnout, but ". . . the dancers had significantly less passive hip adduction and internal rotation than the control group," and significantly more painful hip and knee problems.*

Professor Ruth Solomon and Dr. Lyle J. Micheli, in a wide-ranging study of injuries and dance techniques speculating on the ". . . low incidence of foot and ankle injuries in Graham-style dancers," write, "The preponderance of dorsiflexed footwork in this technique (compared with ballet or ballet-like dance)† may help maintain proper balance between the dorsiflexers and the plantar flexors." (Dorsiflexion is flexing the feet and plantar flexion is pointing the feet.)

A possible conclusion worth considering: Every set of muscles has its antagonist. Let one become much stronger and/or more limber than the other, and the resultant asymmetry becomes a threat to stability, harmonious motion and an injury-free body. To quote Professor Solomon, "The repetitive use of body mechanics that strengthen compensatory muscles and thereby produce musculoskeletal balance tends to reduce injuries, while the repetition of mechanics that create muscle imbalance encourages them."‡

Negative Emotions

Dancing while experiencing any strong negative emotion will probably throw you off coordination. Weighted by a heavy depression, movement may not be supported by sufficient force and/or mental concentration. Conversely, driven by strong anger, a dancer may apply unseemly force to a dance gesture. Speaking for myself, two of my worst injuries came from each of these opposites. I think anger helped tear a calf muscle that gave me a chronic weakness for years and lowered what had earlier been very strong elevation. Another moment, when a terrible sadness left me off guard, I tore a knee cartilage that required an operation.

*The American Journal of Sports Medicine, Vol. 15, No. 4, 1987.
†Emphasizing the pointed foot.
‡The Physician and Sports Medicine, Vol. 14, No. 8, August 1986.

HOW TO DANCE FOREVER

What to do? No easy answer. Buffeted about by a strong emotion is not conducive to the objectivity you need to say to yourself, "Cool it. You're dancing too close to the edge." And yet, who else will be there to warn you?

Dancing After Not Dancing

One of the most perilous moments facing a dancer is returning to dance after any prolonged rest, be it a pleasurable vacation or the unhappy business of recovery from injury. The rules of muscle strength and speed are not kind. Building is slow. Losing is fast. Those exquisitely chiseled calf muscles that launch you high into the air are the product of years of launching. Be sadly forced to immobilize a leg for ten days, say, in a cast, and chance to measure the circumference of the thigh and calf before and after those ten days, the result would bring a justifiable tear of self-pity. The loss would be staggering.

Leaving that dismal image, let's start with the more pleasant prospect of returning to class and/or work after a vacation of a week or more. The first day is the most dangerous. If you are a dancer who loves to dance, and not all do, you are infused with delight and eagerness. Your body feels great. You possess a neural mechanism that can easily recall and bring up all the same responses made when you last worked, i.e., when you were in shape. Problem. One thing is missing: the same muscle strength and, I suspect, the requisite speed you had before you stopped. Respond fully to the music and the demands of the dance sequence given and, at the very least, for the next few days you'll be miserably sore. At worst, you'll be resting all over again, only this time it will be for the need to heal something. I recall a lovely two weeks swimming-swimming for hours along the Connecticut shore and then returning to class, overjoyed to find again that tangible contact with the hard dance floor. The second day, jumping-jumping and snap went the plantaris on my right leg. I was out for six weeks.

I think that no matter how good you feel, the strategy for returning to work is to assume reduced muscle tone, strength and speed of response. Make minimal demands the first week and slightly increased demands the second week. Plow ahead the third and fly the fourth. The ground rule in returning: When in doubt—don't! Taking risks and extending our limits are givens in our profession. That's where the jazz lives, but not unless you're all there and in full command of the "equipment."

Now, to consider returning to work after the doubly perilous condition of recovering from an injury. Two stages should do it:

1. Don't go to class at first. Do your own careful workout. Work slower, shorter sequences and for less time than is your wont. A few days of this or even a week will tell you when you are ready for class. Going straight into class, you are prone to deliver when your body is not.

2. Returning to class, inform the teacher quite precisely as to where you are before the class begins, find an inconspicuous spot and work up to fatigue and no further. Let your body tell you when to start pushing the energy, and don't consult your ambition. You don't even have to finish those first classes. Above all, go supercautious with the fast work, complex phrases and particularly air work. Save them for the end of the first week, or better, the second week. Expect no quick gains. The body doesn't work that way.

One unhappy note: If ever you have the misfortune to have a major injury, you will have to live with the probability that whatever was damaged—torn, to be specific—*will never be quite the same*. Healing means replacing tissue at the juncture of the tear with scar tissue. Scar tissue is usually stronger than the tissue it replaces, *but it does not stretch*. This is not all that significant for healed ligaments* and tendons, for even healthy and uninjured they do not lengthen. It is our muscles that can and must elongate if we are to do our work, but if they suffer extensive tearing, in the healing process they acquire some unyielding scar tissue. Dance is a poem about physical freedom that depends on muscles that can release as easily as they contract. A scarred muscle "ain't what it used to be." It is not as elastic as it was. Thus, in the healing process stretching, carefully and never into real pain, must be a constant component to strengthening. However, once healed, that muscle will *always* need special attention. Never assume it's

---

*A torn ligament can heal in six weeks but will not recover full strength for twelve to eighteen months, thus limiting demands put on it.

all well. It can't be. It's not what it was. Never, ever, make any serious demand on it unless it is thoroughly warmed, toned and stretched. You can make it perform beautifully, getting all you wish from it, if you respect and remember its history. Once it is healed, what you want more than anything else is to forget its painful past. DON'T.

The Balance Beam of Teaching

We dancers can be divided into four groups. Many of us overlap from group to group. We are students, performers, choreographers and teachers (not listed in order of importance). Here too is the making of a study, a research that would be valuable. The question is: Are there particular hazards that are endemic to each of the groups? Do students generally have more trouble, say, with their calves and shins than do professionals? Do professionals have more trouble with the lower back? It is entirely possible that if a characteristic profile of injuries were the signature of each of the groups, they could learn to take precautions, strengthening and specific training to avoid living up to that profile of injury.

In my own experience, I divide my career into two parts: earning my keep on Broadway, in films and on TV from 1940 to 1956; and, from 1957 to the present, performing my own choreography in concert, touring and teaching. In the early segment, though I did concerts, they were not the center or the money earners; rather they cost money to do. Most of the hurts came while performing and/or rehearsing. This early period was when I was mostly doing the choreography of others. In the second half, since 1957, when I was doing almost exclusively my own choreography while performing, I had only one twisted ankle and one bone bruise. That was doing solo concerts and touring for twenty-five years. But while teaching in this same twenty-five years, there have been many more injuries. Teaching has been my hazard time.

There are as many styles of teaching as there are teachers. I have to dance. Still, I have to watch the students. Really-really watching while really-really dancing doesn't quite work, and so I'm torn on the cross of dancing and observing. In addition, there is the time out when an exercise is explained or a point is made verbally. For me, the lack of flow in doing either one thing or the other is what has made me vulnerable to muscle tears and strains. Spending a good twenty minutes observing and giving notes to students and then abruptly finding the need to demonstrate a point that can't be made verbally, my pride and passion to do well before my students and to make a point vivid demands my all when I don't have all at my command.

It's entirely possible that my vulnerability on this score can be ascribed to the fact that I started to dance late. I suspect that teachers who entered dance young may have fewer problems than I have had. I recall an arrogant Leon Fokine, teaching in street clothes and wearing heavy leather-soled cordovan shoes, coming up to Rem Olmstead, a giant who was dancing the role of Judd in *Oklahoma* on Broadway at the time. Leon, a small man, looked up at him, saying, "Look at the size of you and do you cover the ground? No! Look!" Whereupon he lifted into a sissone tombé, chassé, glissade jeté and assemblé, going the full length of the enormously long studio and almost out the window. This after having taught over an hour barely demonstrating, giving most sequences verbally with hand gestures, and all in street clothes.

Madame Xenia Chlistowa, the brilliant ballet teacher here at Arizona State University, gives beautiful brief demonstrations of all the work but doesn't do the work. Suddenly, she will demonstrate an allegro leaping/jumping phrase with height and abandon.

How do they do it? I ask.

What I'm describing of course applies also to choreographing. Helen Tamiris, with whom I worked for over twenty years, was a near miracle. In all the time I knew her, she had one physical problem. In one of her last public performances she suffered a foot cramp. She, who had never had any injuries, was so devastated by the experience, it convinced her to stop performing. True, at that turn in her career she was beginning to orient toward choreographing for Broadway. The cramp pushed her there.

I can recall Helen sitting and watching us rehearse a new piece, stopping us and restarting us innumerable times, catching every missed step. Then, suddenly, from the blue, leaping from her chair, taking her place on the floor, picking up the last choreographed moment as if she were a splice in a dance film, and dancing her way with a full-throated fury into a new phrase of dance, fully formed, often quite long and every bit as challenging as what had come before. I never understood how she could sit there five to ten minutes at a stretch, twirling a lock of hair, calling out critiques, and then, as it were, coming up from nowhere and dancing full out. It was utterly beyond me.

HOW TO DANCE FOREVER

This matter of teachers and choreographers is completely individual and I wouldn't dare make a suggestion. I can't even help myself out of my own dilemmas.

The Workplace

The workplace can work for us or against us. It is a truism that rigid floors are our enemy. Whenever you can, avoid them. If you cannot, you cannot afford to dance full out. To jump full out, do falls full out, do any kind of stamping full out, or any prolonged work on an unresilient floor is going to savage your body. You simply have to assume that. No way out of it. On tour you must not be deceived by a stage that has a wooden floor or a vinyl dance covering. Unbelievably, there are gymnasiums that have wood on concrete. Some of them have some kind of monstrous rubberish compound poured on top of concrete. How they expect their basketball players to survive is beyond me.

Upon arriving at a new stage, I may ask whether the floor is sprung, but I hardly listen. Not many know or even are concerned about my concern. Instead, I listen to my heels. I walk out to the dance area, usually in my street shoes since I can't wait to know. I simply swing myself lightly up to the tip of my toes and then slam my entire body weight into my heels, hard into the stage floor. If the stage is resilient—safe—the reverberations are easily felt through my feet. If it's dead, that's just what it feels like—dead. The shock runs right up into my head. Total nongiving response. Then I ask whether there's another performing space. That is usually not the case and I proceed to rearrange my mind on how I'm going to do the day's setup, rehearsal, warm-up and performance. In workout and rehearsal, I pay particular attention to pliés coming out of the air. Every land must be silken and slipped past like a kid's thrown stone skimming the water. No hard stamping allowed. All falls must be exactly like the plié, smooth and quickly flowing away from the point of impact, and I must be wary of fatigue. I can't afford it.

If you should unfortunately find yourself dancing, rehearsing or teaching on one of these surfaces in a dance studio, gym or stage, every move should be taken with the consciousness, not simply cautiousness, that a flesh, blood and bone creature is impacting on a totally ungiving, cruel surface. You simply have to dance differently. It can even be beautiful, but it can't be the same as if the floor were dancing with you.

Danger

The next problem probably can never be solved: Is there any dance surface that will make all dancers happy? I will never forget coming onstage at the American Dance Festival in New London, Connecticut, following the beautiful, entrancing, exquisite woman and dancer Pearl Lang. For that moment, she stopped being so beautiful, because the stage floor was covered with talcum powder. I'm an off-balance dancer and without some traction I'm skidding, not dancing. Her brilliance, her virtuosity and her beautiful dancing is done very much on top of her weight. Also, Pearl dances barefoot while I use shoes, and she's probably one of those wet-feet people.

It was a very long intermission as the crew swept up the talc and sloshed the stage with Coke and water. An awful solution, but the only quick one possible. I myself lose all personal authority as a dancer on a slippery floor. But even worse, I tend to develop strains and inflamed tendons from the frantic stress of my feet trying to keep a grip on the ground.

I would equate the perfect floor surface with the Holy Grail. Unattainable. Within the same dance there are moments when one needs traction and other moments when a bit of slide would be just right.

Vinyl floor coverings, now found on most stages and in many dance studios, are great for toe shoes and little else, but at least they have the virtue of safety due to their traction and freedom from splinters.

In my jazz work I need to slither a bit, and in other pieces I will tilt fiercely in order to change direction. The closest I've come to a solution is to travel with many, many different shoes. Some are leather-soled, some have smooth rubber and some have rubber of strong traction. When I did barefoot work, being one of the dry-footed ones I would step into a pool of glycerin just before entering the stage, which would serve me for at least five minutes.

Speaking of shoes, in my own experience a narrow shoe never felt too bad. A short shoe, on the contrary, felt like a crippling disaster.

More words on personal equipment: Where I'm coming from, I say, "Better you should sweat than you should shiver." I tend to overdress, to be very warm—to wear pants, ankle warmers, T-shirt and a sweater, even a bandanna around my neck—removing clothing only when I get hot. I think it's safer to be warm and yet I see any number of dancers who don't seem to be par-

HOW TO DANCE FOREVER

ticularly prone to injury working with sleeveless leotards that have deep and attractive scoops in the back and the front, and often just wearing thin tights or only trunks. I suspect this is a personal matter. I have friends who in the bitterest winter in New York will never wear an overcoat or even warm outer garments.

About a hundred years ago the natives of Tierra del Fuego, the southernmost tip of South America and one of the meanest, coldest spots on the earth, just across the way from Antarctica, ran around barefoot wearing nothing except a leather cape. How about that?

"Dancing in the Dark" may break your heart and dancing in the cold may break your leg. After my first sixteen years of professional life, on Broadway, in films, etc., my work shifted almost totally to institutions such as schools and community centers. Countless times I've groaned, "It's too cold in here to dance." Whereupon the reply was, as often as not, "Well, that's controlled somewhere else," or "The thermostat is locked," or "That's set by the computer." Dozens of variations, all coming down to the unacceptable—impotence. Unacceptable to me, at least.

I once found myself in one of the most brilliantly designed dual purpose buildings. It was a gymnasium, dance studio and theatre, all in one breathtaking hexagon, with ingenious ports for lighting high in the dome. In fact, I achieved some lovely lighting there. The college was West Coast prestigious and the long-established dance department was nationally recognized. All their large classes were held in this space. But, and a big *but*, it was cold. My complaint was met with an optimistic "It's usually like this. It'll warm up." An hour later, I realized my bones were banging into each other. This time I was told that the temperature was controlled by a computer. Nothing could be done.

I said, "Well, let me talk to the computer or anyone with building and grounds. Either one! Be assured, I am not going to dance in this nonsense." Half an hour later, a round-faced man appeared in a green-twill outfit with two hundred keys on a giant ring at his belt. Funny, he was sweating a little and I wondered where he had been working. Telling him my complaint, he brightly gave me the "We're all saving energy these days" business. My reply: "If getting from desk to desk was my problem I could manage, but I'm trying to get to the stars with this body. To dance in this temperature is a health hazard." Now, "health hazard" he probably understood better than "getting to the stars." "Oh, come here. I'll show you something." He led me to a dark corridor behind the bleachers and very briefly and clearly explained to me the workings of a somewhat tricky thermostat. "With this you can get whatever you need."

This building had been up twelve years and the dance department had suffered and accepted the cold days as unchangeable. I felt like Columbus as I led them to the thermostat. Docility is not safe. It is dangerous to your health. Being "nice" and "not making trouble" are poor excuses for not being assertive when it is necessary to speak up.

Pain

In weight-conditioning rooms across the country, you will read, high on the wall, NO PAIN, NO GAIN. In all my early modern-dance classes, I heard, "If it hurts, you're doing it right."

NO! NO! NO! A THOUSAND TIMES, NO!

This is a leftover from a sadistic, "heroic" sergeant mentality from World War I physical training that has no basis in good physiology, kinesiology and plain human decency. Good training, conditioning and dancing do not require pain.

On the other hand, pain can be the best friend a dancer ever had. It's our EWS (Early Warning System). Real danger can arise from a dysfunction that doesn't cause pain. It can become so deeply ingrained that by the time it does surface in the form of pain it has become chronic. Ignoring your EWS is not heroic. No generalization is possible about the proper response to pain. Learning to deal with all of its varieties is part of the canniness that goes into making a survivor in our field.

One kind of pain easily induces panic when it shouldn't. The body is an extraordinary precision instrument. Everything not only has a specific function but also a specific place. In the course of living, and quite easily in the course of dancing, some things do move out of their "appointed" places. One of the many tightly stretched tendons in the shoulder, or the powerful muscles deep in the groin, or a short ligament in the foot, will slip ever so slightly out of place, and *slam*, the pain can be not only shocking but immobilizing. Not only does it feel awful, but it is easy to jump to the conclusion that something terrible has happened.

I consider it one of my talents that I can almost always sense when there is a real injury, meaning something has been torn, or when it is just a kink. The word *kink* is perfect for this condition.

HOW TO DANCE FOREVER

The dictionary says, ". . . a sharp twist in a line or wire, typically caused by the tensing of a looped section." Some pains say "Stop," and I know I'm in trouble. Other times a pain asks me to wiggle, woggle and work my way out of it and I assume I have a kink. I follow those impulses by doing the following steps:

1. I slowly, gently and repetitively move precisely in the motion that hurts, with the intent of bringing more warmth (blood) to the problem area.

2. Then I begin to wiggle-woggle my way out of the tension that I am assuming is causing the kink.

3. I alternate step two with deep, slow stretches to realign what feels twisted or fouled.

4. When it's appropriate, as with a foot or an ankle, I firmly manipulate and twist the joint as if to force it back into place, though never with the swift, sudden move characteristic of chiropractors. I don't know enough to try that.

5. I search out the pain with my fingers and either use friction massage or prolonged pressure on the tender area.

One sign that a severe pain is a kink is that it comes on suddenly and usually without a traumatic impact or incident. Suddenly, it's there, and many times the flare-up will occur outside the work session. There won't be any significant swelling, but an intense irritation that can be temporarily alleviated by ice massage or submersion in iced water. If it clears up in a few days and you're back to normal as if nothing happened, it probably was a kink because tears do not heal in a few days. Ligamental tears usually take about six weeks. The healing rate of muscle-tissue tears is more variable but certainly not a few days.

One of the scariest kinks common to dancers is deep in the hip socket. My hunch is that once you are in the grip of one of these aberrations, you have to solve it before going back to serious full-out dancing. That may take an hour or even a day. I think that while the pain of a kink is still active, the odds are that your coordination will be thrown off sufficiently to raise the risk of another injury.

Remembrance of Things Past

The cause of the most subtle and elusive of all pains and physical limitations I call "Remembrance of Things Past."

There is that part of the brain that directs the major part of our muscular activity without our awareness. It is called the cerebellum. Many of the activities it directs can be raised to consciousness. For example, as you read this book you don't consciously tell your neck to hold your head at its present position. Now, if you wish, you can turn or straighten your neck deliberately and consciously.

Thus, this part of the brain is quite complex. It can work with or without your direction, within limits. It is the reservoir of most of your learned physical behavior. I use the word *reservoir* advisedly. The cerebellum is the "older" part of the brain and is located on top of the spinal column and under the brain mass. Almost everything in it was originally learned and consciously controlled in the higher brain center, the cortex. From infancy and throughout life, humans have the capacity to learn a skill that if practiced can become habitual. Here I am, more than fifty years since my first dance class, typing away using the touch system, which I learned only a couple of years ago. At first, every move was painfully conscious. Now I tap away with only a couple of errors per line. Most important of all, my fingers no longer consult my conscious mind. I think of what I want to say and my cerebellum takes care of the job of telling my fingers what to do. Or I can pause and deliberately peck out the date 3/2/85 because I never "learned" to touch-type the numbers. So, learning a physical activity means practicing it sufficiently to have it filed in the cerebellum, where the conscious mind is not.

Thus, if you had good training as a dancer, your unthinking reactions to weight shift, counterplay of the arms to legs, actual depth of plié, all make it possible for you to dance. In fact, aside from strength and endurance, the point of constant daily training is to implant and reinforce deeply and strongly into the cerebellum the most efficient, precise and unconscious adjustments to every conscious command you give to your body. No human being could give all the conscious orders to every muscle needed to perform the complex act of a triple pirouette or a spiral fall. Thus, all neuromuscular learning depends on the capacity of the cerebellum to remember past learning.

The child attempting his/her first ascent of a tiny hill in the park falls down until the day he or she makes it to the top and crows in triumph . . . and learns something. Something right was done and that was recorded, noted, remembered and planted deeply into the cerebellum. There may be another failure or two, but in time the ascent of Hill Number One is a given.

As a side note, the learning of complex and virtuosic neuromuscular skills is most efficient when started at an early age because the cerebellum may then be, as it were, a garden of limited size. Now, this is a Daniel Theory. Starting, say, piano study as a very young child, there is very little in this "garden." The ground is comparatively clear and all the learned actions have plenty of room to root deeply. However, in the early teens, the hands have already acquired an encyclopedia of digital skills: writing, throwing, handling tools, video games, sewing, etc. Every new learned activity has to go around, over, under, through what has already been learned. It's as if the new action is not only *to do* but *not to do* any of the other irrelevant actions. This all takes too much time, and I suspect at the root center of all virtuosity is speed. The great virtuosos have the fastest responses. Why? Because their skills were learned first and early. Acquiring the dexterity of a professional concert pianist by starting at age fifteen has probably rarely been achieved. There is too much already learned that is irrelevant and inefficient, and thus too much to unlearn. A paragraph of pure speculation, but probably correct.

This leads us, albeit indirectly, to the crux of what causes what I earlier called the most complex and elusive of all pain and muscular malfunctions: The cerebellum resists *unlearning*, particularly experiences of great pain and/or distress. In fact, as I understand it, much of the philosophy behind the therapeutic technique of Rolfing is based precisely upon this premise of the ghosts of old traumas persisting long past healing.

A personal example: Early in the run of *Plain and Fancy* (1954), an understudy for the ingenue lead had to go on. In the second act carnival ballet, I would pick her up and run stage right, see my pursuers, swing her down to the ground and, leaving her there, flee stage left. Rehearsal was tense, but okay. Come the performance, the poor terrified dear never released her grip on me as I released her and turned to run. Needless to say, a back that carries 110 pounds, assumes the lady has been deposited on the ground and turns to flee still with 110 pounds hanging on is going to get torn up. It was eight or more months before the pain was gone. The limberness returned and I was fine—but I wasn't. It took me fifteen years to realize—and probably too late—that I had unconsciously made a subtle weight shift that ultimately damaged one or more spinal disks.

With that wonderful discipline of a dancer and teacher of dance, my spine has always been erect, but unknowingly I had shifted the erect trunk to the left. Only when I formed the WORKGROUP (1971) did I learn from my fellow dancers that I was over to one side. Looking in the mirror, it was suddenly obvious. My left hand was hanging more than two inches away from the thigh, while the right hand hung down partly over the thigh.

Explanation? I was "saving" and "protecting" the muscles on the left side; the muscles that had been so savagely torn up seventeen years earlier. By shifting the torso to the left, most of the lateral support of the back was being performed by the muscles of the right side, *but the muscles of the left side were healed years before and no longer needed protection.* To the cerebellum it made no difference because *it* couldn't forget, and the conscious mind knew nothing of this.

Did the mere learning of this correct the misalignment? No. Even further, I began to notice that when I entered a stressful state, the shift would be even more exaggerated. I realized it was a metaphoric gesture of getting out from under some unattractive burden or situation, i.e., literal pain and emotional stress mixed up.

How many teachers wrestle with hunched postures! First there is the puzzled resistance of the student who "feels funny" when standing corrected and erect. Second, there is the secret history of the student. Was there a physical trauma? Was there a history of abuse, be it physical or emotional? The hunched posture can be a metaphor for self-protection, or a ducking away from pain, assault or insult, or a poor sense of self-worth.

We dance teachers are not psychiatrists or therapists, but I think it is time we all realize that posture is metaphor. Posture is philosophy. Posture is who we think we are. Posture is our emotional history made visible. Poor posture is not merely bad alignment. It is often the bitter memory of bad experiences in life.

Without attempting therapy or going into the student's personal history, I think that it is helpful to indicate generally and specifically that in order to correct alignment profoundly and significantly, a dancer not only needs to know the physical elements of correct placement but also to rethink her/his sense of self. Of course, I don't know how one can become a fully expressive artist, or realize one's potential, without a profound self-examination.

In addition to everything else, the cerebellum is stubborn, and merely bringing a significant memory to light is far from sufficient. To explicate the problem and suggest ways of coping with it, I'm going to pursue the rest of this personal experience.

I tried to correct the imbalance, but without the pressure of any pain or limitation of movement I was neither persistent nor inventive and my unconscious habit continued to have its way.

In 1978 I tore the right knee cartilage. It was removed by one of the most brilliant orthopedic surgeons in New York, who skillfully left a barely perceptible two-inch scar. Wonderful? Not quite. When I was back on my feet and ready to begin my first foray into retraining my body to resume dancing, I asked him, "Shouldn't I be working with a physical therapist?" "No," was his reply. "Do what you can. Stretch, build up with the weights, start dancing gradually, and if it hurts, don't do it." I am certain that as I stood there while this conversation was going on, I was so full of the fear and anxiety that would afflict anyone, let alone a man who earns his bread by dancing, *that I was standing in his full sight twisted laterally to left.* In addition to my old habit of shifting to the left, there was now the reinforcement of avoiding weight on the right leg, which had been sliced open a few weeks before. Did he see this distortion? Not see it? Was he indifferent? That brilliant orthopedic "hotshot" surgeon treated my knee, not me.

Suffice to say, in the ensuing months I developed a tingling in my left leg which in time became an intermittent numbness, until finally onstage at the University of Hawaii, as I did the last few steps of a solo called *PATH*, my left foot blanked out so severely that I did not know where the floor was and staggered badly. I soon learned that lateral pressure had malshaped a disk, causing pressure on the spinal nerve, and seriously blocked sensory information from the left foot critical to correct coordination and muscular response. The payoff? As I continued to dance, create new material and tour, I kept injuring the left foot. It was numb half the time. Finally, by the year's end, it was such a mass of strains and tendinitis that except for dancing, I locomoted about the studio in a wheeled stool to avoid walking.

But I was inventive, finally. First I dealt with the back. At the start of every day I would get in front of the mirror with little or no clothes on and rehearse an endless variety of common tasks. Example: I would pretend to drop something, bend to retrieve it, and, straightening up with my eyes closed, pause, relax and then open my eyes to see whether I was straight or crooked. At first it was dismaying and even frightening when, certain that I was erect and centered, I discovered that the destructive lean to the left persisted. It took much time and simulation of many tasks—getting in and out of a chair, turning to go somewhere, combing my hair, etc.—with my eyes closed while attempting to stand erect, and then opening my eyes to check. In other words, daily and often more than once a day I was forcing into consciousness the muscular behavior necessary to correct alignment. I think it took almost a year for this task of "surfacing" to take effect so that the morning drill was no longer necessary. That was solved.

The foot was a different matter, and I took a lead from an article I had read about the strange problem that had limited the work of the fine concert pianist Gary Graffman. He had pain long after a vicious muscular strain should have healed. Was it possible, I wondered, that the protective mania of the cerebellum was restraining the formerly injured muscles in my left foot so fiercely that their resistance to being used only created more pain?

On the basis of this speculation I adopted a procedure that would have startled and bemused any observer. I would walk, run, leap and skip in the studio while *talking to my left foot*. Please do not put down this book! Hear me out. In time you too may find it necessary, even helpful, to talk to your left foot, or some other part of your body that needs such attention. It went something like this:

Now, Left Foot, I want you to observe Right Foot. Carefully. See how the weight travels through the foot from the heel through the pads into the toes. It is using all the muscles fully. Now you, Left Foot, do funny unequal things. The ball lifts and won't accept full weight, throwing stress on the outside, which is also tight. Left Foot, I want you to study and learn from Right Foot. I know it hurts now but move right through the pain using all muscles fully and generously as though nothing is the matter. There! That was perfect! Yes, I know it hurts, but keep studying Right Foot.

Personally, I hate cutie-pie, and the above discourse is one step removed from baby talk, but the cerebellum is not bright. It is a primitive part of the brain. It can be reached, but with difficulty, and *you must address it positively*. From the very first of these weird sessions there was improvement. Within three months I was free of left-foot pain and on my way to getting back my jump, which had gone by the boards during three and a half years of constant pain and weakness.

In summation: When an injury has had sufficient time to heal but limitation and/or pain still persist, bring the action up out of the depths of the unconscious home of habit into consciousness, persistently and patiently. This may reveal that only a "Remembrance of Things Past" is causing the trouble, and, best of all, that it can be overcome.

I'm glad this chapter is over. It felt like making a quick dash across Death Valley. To tie up: Many years ago on the wildly beautiful northern coast of California, I stood before a gymnasium full of long-limbed, golden-haired beauties twisting, turning, giggling and talking, talking, talking. Somehow, I was to give these stunners a master class in Dance. Looking into the ground before me as if the center of the world lay there, I began to tread the ground as a fierce kitten would tread his mother's belly. Slowly a wave of silence seeped across the room. When every one of those sun-kissed goddesses was quiet, I tread on for a bit more. (I have a tendency to push my luck.) Finally, from the pit of my stomach, the words came out, "If you want to go left, you must first go right." The silence took on an added depth. I looked up sharply and said, "Do as I do," and led them into a class wherein they hung on every gesture and word of mine.

I call these Broadway Gibran utterances "guru-farts." They have their uses if the listeners listen but don't knock their heads on the floor in front of me. They often cause me a reverberation of embarrassment, not because someone might think I'm "wise" but

Danger

because I might get that idea myself, and that would be the beginning of the end. All of which is a singularly devious circumlocution and excuse to say, "Dancing crazy wild is where we all want to get and the road leading there is called Caution." Now how's that for a guru-fart? So true, and what a ring to it!

CHAPTER IV

HEALERS
AND TREATMENTS

Doctors

Recently I heard someone say, "All doctors should be considered guilty until proved innocent." Let one person in a social gathering tell a bad-doctor story and a flood of terrible experiences with the medical profession is released.

> In California, the average award in a malpractice suit has climbed to $650,000 . . . [nationally] the average was $338,000. . . . Between 1977 and 1983, premiums for medical professional liability increased to almost $1.6 billion. . . .*

> U.S.-educated doctors are sued for malpractice twice as frequently as are doctors trained abroad, and U.S.-trained women physicians are sued half as much as their male counterparts . . . the study was conducted by the Committee for Fairness and Equality in Medicine. . . .†

What's going on here?

*From James Kilpatrick, "Malpractice," an article syndicated by Universal Press appearing in *The Arizona Republic,* March 5, 1985.
†From a United Press International report appearing in *The Arizona Republic,* March 12, 1986.

HOW TO DANCE FOREVER

To whom does a sick Eskimo turn? To a shaman. An ailing Plains Indian turned to a medicine man. An African, to a witch doctor. The Yaqui of northern Mexico have the sorcerer. The Chinese, even now, make use of the herbalist and the acupuncturist. For these people and for many other cultures, the choice of healer is simple.

So, you're in trouble. To whom do you go? The options are staggering and yet there is at the center the obvious: the doctor. Who are the doctors? We all know they are men and women who have plowed through a long, arduous, intellectually demanding and very expensive education. Their credentials are impressive. Most of us have looked to them with great respect. We have been willing to pay them large sums of money for their expertise and for what we hope will be certain protection of our health and future well-being.

There is a multiplicity of healers out there but doctors, the members of the American Medical Association, have all the advantages.* They and the doctors of osteopathy are the only ones who can legally prescribe medicines; they are the only ones who can cut us open when we need surgery; they have access to the best schools and the best facilities; they receive almost all the research money; only licensed M.D.'s and D.O.'s may order X rays.

What happened? Why are we inundated with so many other kinds of healers? Why are there people who will try anything rather than go to a doctor? The news is not good.

If you call yourself a dancer, you are expected to be able to fill the stage with exhilarating movement. If you are a doctor, you are expected to heal the people who need your skill and help. You carry the burden of a moral role in society. We have always assumed that you do what you do to help us. Imagine our shock when we hear some of you say, "I don't have time to answer all these questions,"; or when we realize you have not listened to us; or when you glibly tell us, "You simply will have to give up dancing,"; or when you put us in a cast for an interminable length of time in a position that will take us years to correct; or when you cut us open needlessly; or when you tell us to rest when we need to rebuild; or when you prescribe doubtful medicines with-

*From the *Occupational Outlook Handbook*, U.S. Dept. of Labor, April 1984: "The average of all physicians' net income for 1982 was about $100,000; general or family practitioners' and pediatricians' average was around $70,000; anesthesiologists, radiologists and surgeons average slightly more than $130,000."

out any warning about their possible negative effects, or when you outpace all inflation levels and price yourselves beyond the reach of anyone with less than a modest income and no medical insurance.

Does this sound biased? Read these words:

> The dilemma of modern medicine, and the underlying central flaw in medical education and, most of all, in the training of interns, is the irresistible drive to do something, anything. It is expected by patients and all too often agreed to by their doctors, *in the face of ignorance* [emphasis added]. And, truth to tell, ignorance abounds side by side with the neat blocks of precise scientific knowledge brought into medicine in recent years.

This is from a book review, with the title "What Doctors Don't Know," by Dr. Lewis Thomas, president emeritus of the Memorial Sloan-Kettering Cancer Center, writing in the September 24, 1987, issue of *The New York Review of Books*. He was reviewing a book on the training of doctors by Melvin Konner, M.D., called *Becoming a Doctor*. A paragraph earlier, Dr. Thomas quotes a pithy lesson Dr. Konner recalls from one of his teachers:

> "If it's working, keep doing it."
> "If it's not working, stop doing it."
> "If you don't know what to do, don't do anything."

Dr. Thomas continues:

> . . . it is the ambiguity arising from this plain piece of sense that is principally responsible, in my view, for most of the problems that face contemporary medicine, including the unprecedentedly bad press, the mutual mistrust and disillusionment among doctors and their patients, the escalating costs of health care and insurance, including malpractice insurance—in short, the state of crisis in which the profession finds itself today.

Doctors, instead of your self-righteous fury with the outrageously large jury awards in malpractice suits, ask yourselves what has caused this state of affairs. Hazarding a guess, I would say that every one of these jurors is not only passing judgment on the case before them but also on another doctor—the one who mistreated them instead of treating them. Harsh words, but they have to be said. Blaming the insurance mess on lawyers and greedy patients won't wash. The juries are filled with angry people and probably angry judges.

There is a Jewish expression, *Abi gezunt!* Literal translation: "At least healthy!" Actual meaning: "Okay, so you lost your job, or your sweetheart walked out, or the world is ending tomorrow, but at least you have your health."

Abi gezunt! may be a Jewish expression, but it is also a national phenomenon, and on the wave of that passion, the medical profession has us. On the basis of *Abi gezunt!* too many doctors are the most important causes of inflation, unnecessary or even harmful treatments, operations and prescriptions and, to top it all, a contemptuous, manipulative and secretive attitude toward their patients. *In no way is this a blanket indictment. There are not merely good, generous doctors out there but great ones.* Of the others, I am not prepared to say how many there are who in essence betray their role in society. Survival demands that should you unfortunately need the services of a doctor, you cannot safely engage just *any* doctor nor entrust yourself uncritically and unquestioningly to *any* doctor. *En garde!*

About six months after a vicious back injury which had ostensibly healed, I still could not palm the ground with straight legs. My orthopedic surgeon laughed when I complained and said, "You're getting old, Daniel." This was 1954, more than thirty years and a thousand concerts ago. I was thirty-seven at the time. A year later, coming back to him for some other ailment, I tipped forward to touch the floor with straight legs, palms flat, arms bent and from down there said, "Hey, Doc, you're right, I'm a year older." At least he had the graciousness to laugh. How many dancers have the same story—a dire, authoritative prediction disproved by their passion, knowledge and skill?

Late one spring I developed in both knees a terrible pain while in deep flexion. Going to the then "in" surgeon for the dance community, I received from him a pessimistic picture of age—arthritis and a damaged meniscus. Period. He had nothing to add to that summation of the situation. The ensuing summer workshop was a misery. Came the fall I was no better and grimly thinking something serious had to be done, I rang his office again. He was away and his nurse suggested another doctor. With no little trepidation, I went. Stretching and testing my strength, *he* laughed and said, "You may not have the strongest thighs in New York City, but you certainly have the strongest fifty-five-year-old thighs. You just have not been stretching the quadriceps enough. In deep plié they're yanking at their roots." I stretched them and in six weeks the problem disappeared.

Two instances: One is solved by the dancer's persistence; the second by a radically different diagnosis. *En garde.* Take nothing for granted from any doctor, particularly when your well-being is at stake.

At least one positive story: While I was still at City College, I finally arrived at the point where I knew that I had to make a stab at becoming a dancer. Among my gnawing self-doubts were a chronic lower back pain and the fact that I was starting dance study so late in life. I went to the clinic at the Hospital for Special Surgery, and to a quite young orthopedic surgeon put the problem "I want to spend my life as a dancer. From your point of view, what do you think of my equipment?" The question seemed to challenge and excite him. He ordered a mess of X rays. I returned the next week for his opinion. Just before speaking with me, I saw him consulting with an elderly physician. Attending to me, he said, "It all looks good, with two exceptions." He indicated a malformation in one of the spinal processes of the last lumbar vertebra and thought I had much too little freedom moving the thigh backward. Right on both scores. Not for one moment did Plisetskaya have anything to fear from my arabesque. The back? The moment he described it, I understood how I had to work at lengthening my spine to relieve the pressure created by this irregularity, and it worked.

Would I recommend this procedure to other young dancers? Uncertain. That was a massive dose of X rays. There were at least a dozen of my entire bony structure. The physician would have to possess a genuine knowledge of dance. I was in luck. This man even used the word *plié.*

On one score, we are all victims of the healers (medical, holistic, mystic or whatever): Hardly any of them truly recognize or admit the staggering complexity of it all. If they did, their answers could never be so simplistic, or so readily given, or given in such a tone of unequivocal authority. The great majority of healers of every stripe take information from a very narrow base: their own, period. Anyone thinking, reasoning or operating from a different

HOW TO DANCE FOREVER

set of premises is wrong, fraudulent and a quack. Information is not shared. Respect is not given to other schools of healers. Their very existence is ignored.

Could there be a dialogue between a Navaho medicine man and an internist? I most certainly believe it is not only possible but that it would be productive in the healing work of both of them, given a mutually genuine desire to learn from each other and a dedication to using information and tools, regardless of their source. Ultimately, this flow between different ways of thinking and doing would enrich and help heal all of us.

There are a few remarkable cross-cultural leaps. One is the discovery by psychiatry in the fifties that primitive Hindu medicine had used snakeroot (Rauwolfia) not only for snake bites but for hypertension, insomnia and insanity.* A derivative, reserpine, thought to be an ideal tranquilizer, came into use, overuse, misuse and now disuse in the handling of mentally disturbed people in our own country.

Another such bridging is the way the Chinese medical profession welcomed into their hospitals and health-care practices the acupuncturists and herbalists. That these collaborations are so rare is a major cause of our profound ignorance of many human afflictions. If only the hearlers recognized each other and had constant dialogue.

What a mass of them are out there! One of the least noted aspects of the sixties/seventies upheaval was the emergence of many new forms of health care. The key word was *alternative*. Adele Davis was an early high priestess of nutrition. Her books probably played a significant role in the proliferation of health-food stores and food co-ops. The list goes on: Shiatsu, acupuncture, the macrobiotic diet from Japan. Books such as *The Well-Body Book, Diet for a Small Planet, Foxfire Book, The Whole Earth Catalogue,* and *Our Bodies, Our Selves* became new guides to living. Since then, Madison Avenue, the pirates of our culture, label everything "Natural, with No Preservatives Added!" Esalen and the Zen twins, Suzuki and Watts, seduced people away from the psychiatrists' couch to encounter groups and sitting cross-legged in meditation. These were the alternatives to conventional health care. They are all, in one form or another, very much alive today. The

*The Pharmacological Basis of Therapeutics, by Louis A. Goodman and A. Gilman, (New York: Macmillan, 1970).

entire spectrum of health care, from conventional medicine to the most esoteric "holistic" healers, presents a variety of choices which is nothing less than dazzling. It is not improbable that, discounting the deliberate fakes, each of them has elements of value. If only they would talk to each other, how lucky we would all be.

The remainder of this chapter will explore three sources of healing: ourselves, with our own skills and resources; other dancers; and the pros.

Patient, Heal Thyself

The premise of this book is that over the long haul, survival depends on what you do and not on the magical panaceas offered by others. In a profound sense, it is the reason for this book. Give up the idea that anyone is going to "save you," "make you over" or "cure you." Realize that who treats you and what treatment is given you are ultimately your choices, since you do not have to do anything or allow anything unless you accept it. Can any treatment work without the profound effort and life-force assertion of the patient?

Continuing this thought a bit further, it is a false assumption that doctors automatically know more about you than you do. It is possible they do, in some matters, but since you reside in your own body, there are things of which only you are aware. Pursuing this, what are we to think of a physician or healer who is aware of what you can do to heal yourself without his/her aid and who withholds that information? Unspeakable.

Follow your hunches. If a diagnosis or plan of treatment makes you uneasy, doubtful or even resentful, trust your reaction and ask for more detailed explanation and *express your misgivings.* You are not beholden to the doctor. He/she is supposed to be working for you. If you receive no clarity, evasive replies, a brush-off or an answer to which your intuitive reaction is no, say so and/or go to another doctor. You know more about your body than anyone else does. You've been around it longer than anybody. Trust your hunches.

When you're in a quandary, even after going to more than one doctor or healer, there are your fellow dancers to talk to. Over the years, the most sustained wisdom and the most useful experience has come to me from other dancers. Years ago, the Baroness Bethsabee de Rothschild sponsored a modern dance festival on Broadway. I was invited to appear. At the same time, I was dancing in the musical *Plain and Fancy*. Some "brilliant" ideas forced into the turbulent second act ballet by the producer set up a hazard that took its toll on my knee six weeks before the festival. The meniscus cartilage was pinched and shredded enough to force a three-week rest that made me doubt whether I would be strong enough to appear.

I had heard that Martha Graham, who was to be the centerpiece of the festival, recently recovered from a knee injury she had incurred in Paris and that weights had helped her. I rang her up to ask her advice. It was a long call. She explained in the most precise detail the procedure that had helped her. It helped me. To this day I use elements of it when I sense a weakness or strain.

Other dancers are gold. Up to now, we have shared our bits of experience and knowledge about injuries and healing with our narrow circle of friends and colleagues. Hoping to widen that circle of information, as part of the work of this book, I have enlisted the help of the Survey Research Laboratory of Arizona State University to conduct a national survey. It went out to a wide sampling of dancers, asking them about their major injuries, the healers and treatments used and their opinions about the results. More of this later. In fact, you will find the survey and its analysis in Chapter XI. Fair warning: The survey will not be easy reading; statistics rarely are, but it contains the bitter and sometimes hopeful experiences of a large and varied group of professional dancers. I believe you will find it worth the effort it will take to read it.

Self-Healing

Notes from my work journal, April 2, 1985:

> Few things give me greater joy than working it out myself. Scribbling this on a Tuesday evening. Last Friday, during a workout got into some wild torso work. Toward evening, felt a small, tight knot just inside and below the right ilio-sacral crest. The next morning it wasn't so small. It turned Saturday into a nightmare. No workout possible. The few household chores and a bit of shopping were barely managed. Sunday was worse. Again no workout but I rolled around on the floor doing slow stretches trying to get a handle on the spasm and pull out of it. It was all so discouraging that I began to fantasize that I would finally try out the local guru, who practices something called Myopractic, sworn to by a few of the dancers here. But it was Sunday; I was still on my own. More

work on the book and intermittently rising to stretch, hang from the chinning bar, moving the waist as if trying to wriggle out of the muscular vise or just quietly "talking" to the crazed muscles asking them to ease off.

Came Monday, carefully rolled out of bed and, following breakfast, gingerly went to the studio to do a slow, unadventurous workout; hardly doing "anything." Late afternoon, it was easing a bit. Why go to the "guru"? By evening, it was as bad as ever. "Go to the guru tomorrow, Daniel." Rising this morning the same routine, only a little freer. Still pain plus burning and tingling in the feet. No fun. Dressing to go to the studio, a surprise. The knot was softer. A very careful workout, forgot about the spasm. Here it is evening and once again, I can easily reach the floor with straight legs and there is only the slightest echo of that savage pain. Nothing gives me greater joy than working it out myself.

I have yet to visit that guru. The point of all this? Our greatest healing resource is our own bodies. Most dancers have a wonderful backup, their *kishkas*. That juicy word is Yiddish for your internal organs. There's no question that though our musculature is the envy of the rest of the population, it's the part that takes the worst beating. But our insides! The furious activity of our work is precisely what invigorates our hearts, lungs, kidneys and circulatory system. The stomachs would be fine too if it weren't for the crazy life that many professional dancers lead. The tension, the touring, bad diet and the irregular hours probably wreck quite a few digestive systems. Otherwise, we usually have strong support systems to carry us through and over any difficulty, whether it be a twisted ankle or knee surgery. Most of us should be among the best and fastest healers.

The awesome power of your mind also costs so little, if you use it. There is news about that most subtle of mind trips—meditation. On May 13, 1986, there appeared in the "Science Times" section of *The New York Times* the following headline: RELAXATION: SURPRISING BENEFITS DETECTED. The article lists an amazing range of troubles alleviated by *relaxation*, the word they use to cover everything from traditional yogic meditation techniques to Dr. Herbert Benson's suggestion of "sitting quietly with eyes closed for fifteen minutes, twice daily, and mentally repeating a simple word or sound." Dr. Benson is director of the Division of Behavioral Medicine at Beth Israel Hospital, a part of the Harvard Medical School

HOW TO DANCE FOREVER

in Boston. Reports from him and over a half a dozen clinics, hospitals and research centers have indicated that in many patients, any one of a variety of relaxation techniques can:

1. Reduce muscle tension

2. Lower blood pressure

3. Slow the heart and breath rates

4. Strengthen the immune system by increasing the number of cells that attack tumors and viruses

5. Decrease the body's response to stress-provoking hormones

6. Improve blood flow to the heart

7. Lower cholesterol levels

8. Lessen the severity of angina attacks

9. For the most common type of diabetes, improve the body's ability to regulate glucose

10. Relieve chronic asthma

11. Lessen or relieve severe pain of backache, chronic migraine, and cancer, allowing the decrease or even totally discarding of the use of pain-killing drugs

12. Lessen side effects of kidney dialysis and cancer therapy, irritable bowel syndrome, insomnia, emphysema and skin disorders

13. Increase defenses against upper-respiratory infections

This list sounds like the label on an old bottle of snake oil, but it does come from a variety of responsible research scientists. "The experts caution that intensive training (of several weeks) followed by the regular use of the techniques may be required before many medical benefits appear." By relaxation they do not mean ordinary concepts of relaxation such as gardening, reading or watching TV.

Healers and Treatments

"Just sitting quietly or, say, watching television is not enough to produce the physiological changes," said Dr. Benson. "You need to use a relaxation technique that will break the train of everyday thought, and decrease the activity of the sympathetic nervous system."

More on self-healing: hot and cold. The debate never stops. Quite a few of the respondents to the survey spoke of icing as particularly helpful. My principle may be simplistic, but ice early for an injury and heat for healing after swellings and inflammations have subsided. Detailed discussion of hot versus cold specifics is beyond the scope of this book, *but* hot and/or cold treatments are among the most potent therapeutic aids at our disposal. Best of all, they can be self-administered and cost so little.

The mind. We all would do well to train the mind to be on speaking terms with the muscles. In the terrifying decision to become a dancer, I set up a safety net. I shifted my college concentration from psychology/sociology to health education, part of which involved gymnastics. While I was attempting my first forward somersault, the gym instructor, who was supposedly holding the safety ring attached to my belt, turned away to talk to someone precisely at the moment I took off. His hand dragged my motion and I landed clean on the top of my skull. That started a history of stiff necks. Every few months my head would freeze between my shoulders; no movement and much pain. These intermittent attacks went on for years.

I cannot recall what did it or what taught me, but one day I beat it. I was caught in the first stage of one of those neck sieges that would last a minimum of four days. Lightning shot up from my right shoulder into my head and the breath went out of me. I also got angry. I had enough of that. I stopped cold, closed my eyes, and directed my mind to the core of the tension and *spoke to it*. I spoke as if I were addressing an intelligent entity. I said, "Enough of that. Let go. Easy does it. Soft. Soft." I stayed with that, concentrating as if there were no question that it would be driven away, and it was! An hour later, I realized that I had never done anything like that before. It was a new world of power, which to this day I have never let go of. I imagine many of you are familiar with this experience. If you're not, know that tool is there, in you, waiting to be used.

When to use what is partly a matter of experience, but it really

HOW TO DANCE FOREVER

should be supported by knowledge through in-depth study. My getting a bachelor of science degree in health education was both an act of caution and a bore. Courses in education were a blur. One was like the other and all were equally useless. The rules of soccer, badminton, etc., were tedious and totally irrelevant to my concerns. This was my self-imposed bridge to a dance career. Three courses did entrance me and made up for the grind: Anatomy, Kinesiology, and Fundamentals of Physical Examination. The latter was designed to help physical-education teachers detect signs of ill health. I think I really started this book then. I'm certain the knowledge I gained through these courses circumvented many of the disadvantages of starting my career late and contributed to the fact that I'm still dancing.

Look out, here comes the preacher again, but I'm probably right this time: *If you have never studied anatomy, study it. If you have never studied kinesiology, study it. If you have never studied physiology, study it. If you have never studied nutrition, study it.* Does a racing-car driver know automobiles?

Feeling Good, Feeling Bad

Feeling bad? Panic. Grief. Get the doctor? The guru? The chiropractor? Help yourself? There's a physiology to feeling bad. Knowing it would help you know what to do.

In America, we're always greeting each other with the question "How are you?" In fact, it's considered gracious and friendly to be even more specific by asking the people with whom we associate, "How do you feel?" Discussions of this order take up much talk time. I would not be surprised if other cultures and countries regard this focus of ours as peculiar. I know that unconsciously I start each day by checking out how I feel. Feeling good is great and feeling any other way is deplorable. I've come to regard this focus as deplorable. It's all part of the *"tsutsik"* syndrome.* As a mental discipline, I try to put my mind on what there is to do rather than on how I am feeling as I do it. I succeed at times! There's no escaping awareness of how one feels, most of the time. It's simply a question of what you put in the forefront of your consciousness.

Objectively, feeling good, really good, is JACKPOT. There are many odds against it. If you pause for a moment to consider the

---

*A *tsutsik* person, upon entering a room, immediately heads for the thermostat to raise it half a degree or lower it half a degree.

staggering complexity of the human organism, the complexity of human relations and the general mess of human society, it's a great day in the morning or any time when things line up just right. JACKPOT!

Take the body: There's the muscular system, the neural system, the skeletal system, the circulatory system, the digestive system and the respiratory system, plus eight major glands, each one depending on all the others to work perfectly in order to work perfectly. When they do, it's JACKPOT and you feel great! Feeling "Okay" or "Just so-so" or "Not very good" should really be one of the givens of being alive.

What I'm getting at is that most of the time it's not that bad if you don't feel good. Several reasons. First, feeling fine demands the perfect confluence of a myriad of factors. Second, the moment you cut yourself, you begin to heal. All of you is filled with an energy to set things right. Enter a room with a crooked picture on the wall and you have an impulse to level it. The body responds to all negatives with an attempt to right them. There's no guarantee of success, *but that energy is there in all of us*. If we nourish, nurture and support that talent, we have a chance to *survive for a very long time*.

One of the great healers is the blues, particularly the inexplicable blues. They're saying, "Stop. Lay off. Back off. Enough—for a while, at least. Postpone everything. Go slow. Go easy." Accept that slow wave, curl up inside the circle of your misery, float in it and you are healing. You are pointed straight toward getting better.

Or deny it, be brave, keep a-going, don't let it slow you down, paste a smile on your mouth, be cheerful and never let anyone know. I suppose that regimen will get you through the day or even through a miserable and unexamined life. I have no proof but I suspect that's the wrong way. I think the blues, depression and, yes, even breakdowns are profound efforts of the body-heart-mind to return to health and happiness. They are not unlike what Camus said was at the very heart of freedom—the power to say, "No." There are ten thousand things and more that we cannot do, but there is always at our command one power: the power to say, "No." He, of course, was talking about politics, rebellion. "What is a rebel? A man who says no, but whose refusal does not imply a renunciation. . . . He means that 'this has been going on too long,' 'up to this point yes, beyond it, no.' . . . Rebellion

HOW TO DANCE FOREVER

cannot exist without the feeling that . . . somehow one is right."*
The blues, depression and breakdown are forms of rebellion.

We are talking about the body, the mind, the heart. "No" can
be the beginning of healing and health, if you know when to float
with it. True, there are times when this is a luxury that cannot
or should not be indulged, not unlike those rough moments when
we must work and perform with injuries. In five years I created
three new works, concertized and toured with multiple tendinitis
in the left foot. I'd rather have rested, but I wanted to dance the
new dances more. Also, I would never have been able to pay the
rent if I hadn't kept on. It'll all get perfectly simple one day, but
I won't be here to know about it.

Then, of course, there are those blues that won't go away, even
after a rest in the cool dark of your cave. The awful word is
depression. Sometimes there's a wall that won't let you move,
won't permit a single constructive act. Sometimes, your head is
in trouble. Out there are a multitude of psychotherapists to help
you. How many good ones are there? Here we go again. And
again I'll say, "Patient, heal thyself, if you can." On rare and brief
occasions I've consulted with them; had luck with one and the
other was a horror. I much prefer to cope on my own.

My usual practice when the blockage, a bad feeling, drags me
to a halt is to sit down and write it all out. Just thinking at these
times is counterproductive, because the mind tends to go in circles, literally going nowhere. By its very nature, writing out the
problem demands going forward. Usually, I gain some clarity,
finding a toehold to start the climb back up to functioning again.
I have hidden a few of these misery notebooks which I hope no
one ever reads. Aside from the intensely personal material, which
is no one's business but mine, the picture would be of a man who
would make Dostoevski's most depressed character appear a blithe
spirit. Why not? I only write in them when I am in the pits.

A few years ago, I came across a book that actually opened a
way to gain personal insight and the clarity to move ahead and
yes, to make changes. I have since then given out at least ten
copies to friends and students. It offers a process that should
make particular sense to dancers. Dr. Eugene T. Gendlin, in *Focusing*, asks people who are having problems not to *think* about
them but to present them to the body, asking it what it senses.

*From Albert Camus, *The Rebel* (New York: Knopf, 1954), p. 13.

He says the body answers by the way it feels. This is how I make dances and probably how you deal creatively with dance. Using his technique, I have learned things about myself that had puzzled me for years. Is this a plug for the book? By all means, yes.*

Healing

You've had trouble. What can you do? Getting well is a tightrope act. Keeping balance is a matter of leaning this way and that. Restoring the power of an injured body is balancing between rest and action. Resting heals, *but* resting also weakens. Muscles atrophy at a frighteningly faster rate than muscles can be strengthened in *any conditioning program.* Here is a specific challenge to researchers in the fields of kinesiology and orthopedics, and to trainers of dancers and athletes: Compare the length of time of immobilization of a muscle group with the amount of time it takes to restore it to its former strength.

The whole business, like balancing on that tightrope, is a game of juggling opposites. On the one hand, when rebuilding, if there's any hesitation about going past a certain point of effort, I would say when in doubt, don't. Respect the uncertainty. On the other hand, I am reminded of the material I read on how the Chinese handle serious leg injuries, including bone breaks; compared with procedures in our country, they rarely use a cast. More often they use a firm splint, *which allows a minimal amount of movement.* The literature I read indicated faster recovery rates than with our procedures.

I had the misfortune to incur an inguinal hernia. I had heard remarkable things about a procedure practiced in Toronto at Shouldice Hospital. The operation is performed with a local anesthetic and the patient is expected to get moving quickly. I went for it. Not only did they only use a local anesthetic but when they finished stitching up the four-inch incision, they told me lunch was already being served and I had better get downstairs or I might miss it. True, they did help me off the table, but from then on I was on my own, walking unaided. I made it down three flights of stairs—in time for lunch. It hurt like hell, but in three and a half days I walked out to the airline limousine carrying my luggage, and I *never* travel light.

Focusing, by Eugene T. Gendlin, Ph.D. (New York: Bantam Book, 1981).

HOW TO DANCE FOREVER

I am in complete sympathy with this way of healing. Not only is the body a perennial healing factory, but action, making demands on the injured part, speeds recovery. A good part of the medical profession leans toward inactivity for healing. This is particularly true of general practitioners and orthopedists, who have little or no experience with dancers and/or athletes. This advice ranges all the way from "Stay off it for . . ." to "You have no alternative. You must give up dancing." Big question: How many doctors' decisions are made to cover their tracks, to limit their responsibility, and how many decisions are made for us, their patients?

More on healing through action: We lost a light in the shabby elevator of our WORKGROUP studio building. To change the bulb, I had to hoist up one of the dancers to reach the socket. Searching for it in the dark, her hand suddenly slashed downward, striking me with karate force exactly where the shoulder joins the neck. I gasped with the pain, realizing she had been jolted by a live current. She seemed okay and so did I. We solved the problem with a flashlight. The next day, I started to do my workout in front of the mirror. My first gesture at that time was a contraction of the upper back which drew the arms up to a release above the head. Something peculiar was going on with my right arm. In the repetition of the phrase, glancing out of the corner of my eye, I noticed that the right arm was only shoulder height while the left was above my head! I tried to make them move together. No way. The right arm lagged far behind. I guessed what had happened. A nerve was damaged and one arm was partially paralyzed. I never learned which were the specific muscles affected, but this presented a particularly nasty problem because at the time I was still touring *The Peloponnesian War* and in it was a rifle dance, and I do mean a rifle. An old Springfield, ten pounds of hardwood and steel, never easy to move around, and now at least half a dozen moves would be muffed or diminished.

Once before I had had a bit of nerve injury with consequent numbness and movement limitation. I remembered the doctor's vague prognosis. "Recovery? Six weeks, more or less, but there's no telling how much will return." No medicine. No treatment proposed. No physical-therapy program. Just that vagueness, and, literally, *a stepping away from that problem.* Again I'll ask: What's going on here? The tendency is to leave nerve injury to fate.

Healers and Treatments

Anyone out there who has been close to stroke victims knows exactly what I'm talking about and what I'm getting at.

More on that paralyzed arm: I did not even try to get to a doctor. Instead, I immediately picked up a pair of five-pound dumbbells and went through my torso stretches, which involve much arm movement, and then added some special arm moves with heavier weights. The tour date was only two weeks away. In spite of the daily use of weights, there was little change and the rifle dance was a mess. Came the day to go, I loaded up, literally. *The Peloponnesian War* was performed with two tape recorders, too precious and delicate to entrust to strangers and which I always carried on my person when traveling. One on each shoulder, they totaled more than fifty pounds, always heavy but usually not that much of a problem. Now, with one dumb arm, the anxiety, and the exhausting two weeks rehearsing *The Peloponnesian War* and my company, the WORKGROUP, walking under that load was too much. Halfway across the waiting room of Pennsylvania Station I was visited by a spear of pain between the right shoulder blade and the neck so severe that I sank to the ground and spread out on the station floor, lying there until the pain subsided. Finally, rising and readjusting my burden of tape recorders, I realized the right arm was different, *lighter* and yes, *stronger*, strong enough to bluff my way through the rifle dance the next evening.

The arm recovered completely in the course of two more events; again, *both involved enormous effort*. One was a near disaster when a heavy old upright piano was being moved up the four steps leading into my Bleecker Street studio. The person on my side lost his footing and I had half the piano's weight. Somehow I held on and somehow we got the piano into the studio. As I walked away with relief, again I felt a surge of lightness in the right shoulder. When all the muscles work beautifully, we are weightless. Let one set of muscles lose power and we learn how heavy that limb is. The piano episode gave it more strength. The last episode involved *PATH*, a dance in which for eight minutes or more I carry before me a twelve-foot-long two-by-four. I always specify that the beam be softwood, otherwise the weight would be too much for that length of time. A month later, just before a concert somewhere on the West Coast, the beam was missing. No one had ordered it. Dashing out, the assistant stage manager could only locate a wet length of spruce, a hardwood. Wet hardwood made it at least twice as heavy as a dry softwood beam. As *PATH* progressed, I became certain that the biceps tendons would be torn out of my forearms. The dance was somewhat shorter than usual, but as I disposed of the beam at the end of the dance and crossed over to stage right removing my work gloves, I knew from the air in the right shoulder that the muscle paralysis was completely gone.

I cite this incident in detail only because I suspect there is a line of inquiry for which it might yield useful results. It has been substantiated by the families and loved ones of some stroke victims who had been given up as hopelessly paralyzed. In the face of the most pessimistic predictions by the medicals, these people would come to the hospital day after day, helping, encouraging and schooling every possible motion that surfaced until some of these "hopeless cases" were able not only to return to work but to their favorite game of tennis. With nerve impairment, constant attempts to reach and activate immobilized muscles may be successful. The additional suggestion I would like to offer is that intermittently an enormous effort should be made with whatever resources are available, i.e., a push to the limit. I think the push fires up dormant nerve tissue. Speculation, but borne out by my experience. I hope one or more researchers in the field will test that hypothesis.

Conditioning

After telling me that I would have to work assiduously with knee weights, the orthopedic surgeon to whom I went with my first knee injury went on to say that dancers make an error by never using knee weights until they get into trouble. He said, "What you people demand of your knees in your profession is not sufficiently met by your technique, whether ballet or modern. Dancers should not wait until they suffer a knee injury. While they are strong, in good shape with happy knees, they should be on a weight program, specifically for the strengthening and protection of the knees."*

Between this man's advice and Martha Graham's specifics, I kept a slightly shot-up knee going and performing quite a few

*This deserves research and verification. See Chapter V, Questions Asking to Be Researched.

outrageous knee shticks for twenty-four years, before I made one error too many and finished off the injury with a torn cartilage.

I believe that specifically focused work with free weights, machines, tension springs or surgical rubber tubing, intelligently done, can work. *All are dangerous.* Five principles can make them safe and useful:

1. A negative: Ignore that slogan on the wall of most weight-conditioning rooms, NO PAIN, NO GAIN. *Do nothing that hurts.*

2. Start with light (*within* your limits) repetitions and go for endurance, *not for strength*, particularly after an injury. Healing is no different than sewing up a garment or darning a sock. There's an early stage in the mending of damaged tissue where it resembles a basted seam. For those of you who are unfamiliar with the craft of sewing, basting means stitching together material with a large single thread stitch to line up what will need to be strongly sewn together. Move actively in a pair of pants that have only been basted and every seam will pop loose. Just try to move vigorously with a recently torn ligament or muscle. Somewhere along the way you have to develop the antennae to sense what's actually happening in your body.

3. When endurance begins to create strength is the time to start adding weight.

4. *No giant steps.* Never, ever, go for the big one. All advances should be no more than small increments. The distance between step two and step three should be weeks. How many? How should I know? You'll know when the floor of strength has been built enough to start adding weight.

(You are thinking, "But that's a complete contradiction to what you just proposed. Didn't you suggest occasional massive efforts for nerve damage?" Yes, but that problem is special. The seat of trouble is nerve tissue, not muscle tendon, or ligament, and besides, the procedure is suggested for research. I haven't the faintest idea as to whether there's any validity to it. It *seemed* to be the operative factor in my case, which proves nothing at all. It is an indication that deserves investigation. When it comes to conditioning, whether rebuilding injured and/or weakened muscles or adding strength to healthy tissue, I'm quite certain all the experts in the field would advise against attempting any sudden big increase during conditioning work.)

5. After every intense working of a specific set of muscles, stretch them in a nonweight-bearing position.

It's no news that dancers are a strange lot. I first encountered Phoebe Neville when she was a student in a Pennsylvania college, and upon conversing with her instructor I learned that she was working very hard on the bagpipes—to increase her wind. Hilarious, I thought. Today she uses tai chi chuan. Some dancers run. Again, it's a matter of going left in order to go right. Conditioning, whether you're a tennis player or a dancer, is a matter of doing something other than your specialization in order to be super at your specialization. It often works, if you enjoy that particular activity and if your choice is canny and well directed. This touches on a strong personal predilection: I love dance more than anything else and willingly accept all the hazards it demands, but I would feel like a complete fool were I to injure myself doing anything else. Rock climbing? Horseback riding? A little touch tackle? Surfing? Even if I loved doing one or another of them—no.

Swimming is an invaluable reconditioner for the injured body, particularly when there is a serious weight-bearing problem. But extensive vacation swimming when not dancing can throw off our timing. We impact on a hard surface, a floor, and our need is for a miraculously fast response to cushion our descending weight. Traveling through water asks for a radically different timing. A long daily swim for a week or more could slow down timing, either weakening a jump or opening the door to calf tears, which are notoriously slow healers. As a side note, this lack of speed, in both landing and taking off, is the reason some dancers, particularly women, have poor elevation.

Running: There are odd moments in a dancer's life when it seems to make sense. Healing time. Rebuilding time. Vacation time. However, I can't imagine extensive running while intensive dancing is going on. Why? Running has a built-in danger, particularly for dancers. The beauty of our work is its continually shifting demands on the body. This way and that we move: bending, stooping, flying, reaching, turning. Extended running is potentially the most devastating kind of repetition. If you just plain run, the same muscles, the same bone surfaces, the same tendons and the same ligaments are being worked *constantly* in the same fashion with only one step to recover before the same impact is repeated, over and over again. If run you must, keep changing: Forward, backward, sideways, skipping, hopping and in circles. Figure eights are what I do in the studio, mostly to give all the lateral calf muscles and all the structural members of my ankles a working. Time spent is brief at best. Street running I hate; the unfriendly concrete. Grass, earth and sand are okay, on occasion. Real running—twenty minutes or more at a shot, a mile or more—I've never attempted, never having had the impulse or the rationale for it. Still, some dancers do it and thrive.

Therapeutically, a mild, restrained running program can help rebuilding. It truly resembles meditation. It is a repetition. It makes little demand on the intellect. It has a clear focus. One could think of it as a meditation on strength and endurance. Many athletes use it as an integral part of their training, particularly boxers. Louis XIV did, poetically. Every morning under the tutelage and supervision of his ballet master, Beauchamps, he practiced the courante, and for the rest of the day ran the show in France for more than half a century. *Courante* means a running dance. Helen Tamiris had a five-minute sequence of running steps, small leaps, skips and hops which she used to build or maintain endurance, but it was danced.

The best thing about the running craze is the shoes that have been created for it. I hope they someday soon replace dress shoes of all kinds. More and more people are exhibiting poor style and good sense, wearing them with inappropriate clothing. A friend, who sings in smart supper clubs, appears wearing floor-length gowns concealing her bright-red running shoes.

Augmentation

When people have hand and lower-arm injuries, doctors and physiotherapists recommend carrying about a firm rubber ball to squeeze and work the muscles that need rebuilding. I call these "en passant" exercises—exercises that can be done on the way, any time of the day, often and almost anywhere. I invented one which I call Augmentation. Example: The transverse metatarsal arch on my left foot could be stronger and higher. Sitting, waiting

HOW TO DANCE FOREVER

or standing in any idle moment, I can run through Augmentation in less than a minute and a half for a miniature workout. The steps are as follows:

1. Contract and release the muscle group involved ten times. This quickly warms the muscles a bit and also sets the rhythm for all the subsequent work.

2. Contract and release for one count.

3. Contract and HOLD for 2 counts and release.

4. Contract and HOLD for 3 counts and release.

5. Contract and HOLD for 4 counts and release.

6. Contract and HOLD for 5 counts and release.

7. Contract and HOLD for 6 counts and release.

8. Contract and HOLD for 7 counts and release.

9. Contract and HOLD for 8 counts and release.

10. Contract and HOLD for 9 counts and release.

11. Contract and HOLD for 10 counts and release.

12. Repeat step 1, contracting and releasing ten times.

13. Stretch the muscle group you've just been working. This step is a must follow-up for any intense working of muscles.

This exercise can be combined with the use of weights or tubing and note that there is nothing sacred about the number 10— neither the repetitions nor the final holding for 10 counts. For some muscle groups it could be too much or too little. Listen to your body.

It's a strange, funny little exercise that combines the virtues of repetitions and isometrics, and, best of all, it works. There are no limits to your ingenuity in restructuring Augmentation according to your own needs. My first thought upon receiving a strain or injury is that something isn't strong enough. As soon as I think the area can take it, I begin to build its endurance and strength up to "normal" and then beyond.

One word of warning about any unfamiliar activity, whether in dance, conditioning, sports or just plain fun: Never plunge into it fully, no matter what kind of shape you are in. We are quite specialized, each of us. Have fun on the beach throwing a ball half the afternoon. "It's been years!" you say, and then your arm might be useless for a few days.

Touch Therapies

In the lexicon of healing gestures that we ourselves can perform, three stand out as the most thorough and immediately satisfying: a warm bath, a good sleep and touching. One of the commonest and most ancient of human gestures is rubbing a sore or injured body part. Massage. Self-administered massage. Most obviously and eminently useful is stroking and kneading with varying degrees of pressure. Less well known and good for our work are Shiatsu and pressure point therapy. If you are unfamiliar with these, it would be worth your while to get a book on Shiatsu and/or a book on pressure point therapy by Bonnie Prudden. As with too many healers, Prudden presents her stuff as the second coming, making it out to be a cure-all for almost everything. Overlooking that, there is useful stuff for self-treatment in her manuals.

Shiatsu and pressure point therapy: Say there's an unhappiness in the hamstrings. Find it with your fingers. Locate the center of the tenderness. Press into it with your finger hard enough to touch the pain but not so hard as to create worse pain or damage tissue. The Shiatsu people concentrate on specific acupressure points with varying degrees of pressure. Prudden has a magic number—seven seconds—and advocates a steady, firm pressure, one point at a time. I just lean in for the length of a long, slow inhale and exhale repeated four times and then move on to the neighboring spot of the same muscle, tracing its course to the end of its length. Prudden has a good follow-up suggestion: Slow-stretch the muscle you've just pressured.

Another method, called friction massage, is ideal for muscles and tendons. Again, with the fingers find the suffering tendon or muscle. Tracing its entire length with probing and pressure, locate the most tender spot. Now, starting here as if you were a

HOW TO DANCE FOREVER

bass player plucking a string, pass a pressuring finger across, at right angles to the direction of the muscle or tendon fibers. You won't get a sound but you will get some pain and probably relief.

I'm assuming that behind each of these therapies—massage, Shiatsu, pressure points and friction massage—is the body's response to being touched. Touching a specific area calls attention to it, not only from your conscious mind but from a whole battery of internal organs. The gentlest caress can relax a tense muscle. Why? Some of your inner workings respond to that touch with more blood, more juices, more nourishment and helpful relaxing signals from the cerebellum (that part of the brain that talks to muscles).

The pain is a provocation calling on the body's healing resources, *but* too much pain can cause either tissue damage or local tension, which is exactly what you're trying to avoid. When I use friction massage, if the pain is moderate I'll keep up a steady rhythm for about five minutes. If it's very sore I'll do, say, six to eight strokes and rest for two, giving it a moment of recovery time, and continue that for at least five minutes. This is just as effective and not as brutal. Do not be heroic or rough. You can easily hurt yourself. After the concentration on the most tender spot, carry the action up and down the length of the muscle or tendon for a while. You can do this in the middle of a workout or a rehearsal if the pain begins to limit the work. You may discover the pain recedes almost immediately. In addition, it seems to facilitate healing.

Friction massage may do more than help painful muscles and tendons. Physical therapists believe it can break up adhesions. Some claim it can reduce scar tissue. Sounds good, but unproved so far.* I suspect that in the course of our work adhesions may be more common than we think and one of the causes of subtle nagging chronic pains that seem to persist long after an injury has ostensibly healed.

Everything in the body is snug up against something else. Except for our breathing apparatus, there are no open spaces in the body. Even the heart is full of blood all the time. A bad charley horse is really a muscle tear, with minor local hemorrhaging. It

---

*Is there any reliable information about this? More than once I've heard about friction massage breaking up scar tissue. Is it possible that friction massage, while healing is still going on, may minimize the amount of scar tissue that will develop? I suspect that once scar tissue is formed nothing can be done about it.

hurts because fluid has accumulated where there is no room for anything extra. The pressure of that fluid creates the pain. The well-intentioned body begins the healing process immediately. As the fluid pockets drain off, the torn tissue begins to mend. Because everything is so crowded, it is not at all improbable that the torn part will in the healing process attach itself to a closely pressed neighboring bit of tissue. If there is motion during the healing time, this will not happen, but some hurts are so bad we rest, stop dancing or get put into a cast. When we are healed and ready to go again, there is only that residue of pain we are sure will go away, only it doesn't. The subtle demands of motion ask various parts of that particular muscle group to respond differently. Trouble is that two parts that should be sliding past each other at different timings are tied to each other by *living tissue which should not be there*—adhesions. It is believed that friction massage, properly focused at the seat of tenderness and pain, can help tear loose connections that should not be. Tricky business and, I think, best self-administered. We know when to stop working on our own bodies. I'm sure there are pros out there who are sensitive enough. You need the luck to find one who is and the assertiveness to beg off if you sense you're being manhandled by one who is not.

Since this section is about ministering to yourself, we can touch on over-the-counter remedies. I think mild painkillers, such as aspirin and any of its variants, make much sense. Pain is double-edged. Without it we would kill ourselves. It certainly keeps us in line, warning us to go easy or even to stop for a while. On the other hand, it causes tension and overreaction from the neighboring body parts. Most spasms are the cerebellum's instructions to the muscles surrounding an injury to protect, meaning to immobilize that area. They freeze up and you can't move. If you try, it hurts. If you force, you tear more. The pain is provocative and freezes an even larger area, until one little tear snowballs into an entire back spasm if you keep moving against the pain. A mild pain suppressor doesn't dismiss the pain completely but decreases the chance of a riot of spasms in the unhappy area.

Liniments? Ben Gay? Tiger Balm? I really don't know. Hotshot doctors dismiss all of them, saying that the warmth evoked is skin deep and does nothing for the deeper muscle tissue. Athletes and dancers the world over have stunk up locker rooms as far back as the Greek Olympiads and the Roman Circus games. I don't use liniments and that proves nothing, either way. Can anyone out there bring forth some clean, clear evidence, one way or the other? It's a draggy smell, but if it's useful—okay; but if not . . . ?

DMSO, claimed to be a miracle healer of muscle injuries, has yet to be cleared in the United States by the Food and Drug Administration, which means that the stuff you might buy in hobby shops or hardware stores could be anything. It is potent stuff, having built-in hazards. The unregulated product could easily be harmful. A gamble at best.

Almost all dancers and athletes develop an almost professional skill with adhesive tapes and elastic bandages. Only one note: If and when you tape, you should be very clear as to your specific intention. Is it immobilization? Support with a little motion? With moderate freedom of motion? To protect a blister or skin break from infection? It's necessary to have a clear intention to know which to choose.

DIP: Dancers' Information Pool

Finally, there is an aspect of self-help wherein we dancers have consistently failed over the years. In close quarters we can and do help each other as friends and colleagues, but as a group I can think of half a dozen attempts that survived but a few years. In the thirties, there were the Dance Repertory Theatre, left-wing dance organizations, the National Dance Congress, and the short-lived Federal Dance Theatre of the Works Progress Administration. The Writers' Project, the Artists' Project, and the Federal Theatre Project lasted longer than the Dance Project because the writers, the artists and the theatre people stuck together. Though the dancers put up a strong resistance to the dissolution of the Dance Project, they had a long history of divisiveness.

For a few years there was the Association of American Dance Companies. Two teachers' organizations persist—the American Dance Guild and the dance section of the American Association of Physical Education, Recreation and Dance—plus CORD (the Congress on Research in Dance), a group of scholars. At present, the unions that hold us together are the actors' and the musicians'. They have much to teach us about self-help, support groups and mutual help.

Here is a beginning, a proposal, a get-together-and-help-each-other fantasy. Many, many odds against it, but give it a listen.

Healers and Treatments

To help you listen, here's a background note which may sharpen your interest in the dream proposal. There are now in existence throughout the nation newly formed organizations called, in some cities, Physicians Alert. Alert to what? Threats to our health? No, threats to their burgeoning medical prosperity. The name of anyone who sues for malpractice is entered on a list made available to other doctors. This is an alert to the "wrong" kind of patient. Does this mean they will blackball such a person? Deny him/her medical treatment?

We too could use an information pool. We could call it DIP: Dancers' Information Pool. Every dancer who joined would furnish to a central computer a personal history of his/her dance-related injuries under a secret code name. Any dancer belonging to DIP who is injured and in sore need of advice would have a way of getting information from dancers who have had the same problem. Say X has developed chronic shin splints. X calls DIP, describing the specific condition. The computer is fed that problem and comes up with, say, half a dozen phone numbers and *code names*. X phones, in turn, Ahab, Min, Mary, Wary and HoHum—all dancers in his/her city who have had chronic shin splints. X describes the problem and gets advice on self-treatment and/or their experience with treatments and therapists that helped and didn't. *No one giving or receiving the information has to or is expected to identify herself/himself.* Does anyone out there have a few thousand to get DIP off the ground? Or is there an ex-dancer with computer skills, a computer and a little capital to set up a business that would help him/her and us?

The Healers

Enough with self-help. Times are when we need help. Let's try to take a look at the help, that multitude of healers and treatments that are supposed to do just that—help us. What follows is one man's experience, given not as cut in stone but as the beginning of a discourse that may help all of us find an overview of a confusing and at times a dangerous mess.

THE MEDICAL PROFESSION

GENERAL PRACTITIONERS

By and large, they are inappropriate for any dance-related injuries, no matter how minor. Even a sprained ankle, diagnosed inaccurately and treated improperly, can snowball into a chronic horror.

ORTHOPEDIC SURGEONS

If your hunch is that you need to see one, hunt one up who has had extensive experience treating dancers, and check the physician out with the dance community. Lacking doctors experienced in treating dancers, check with professional or university athletic teams regarding which doctors have helped their players. There is a proliferation of physicians who call themselves sports doctors. Just what it takes to justify this self-naming is probably vague enough that none of us should take it for granted that Dr. X, self-titled as a sports physician, knows all about the vigorous body in action. As noted before, *En garde.* Orthopedic surgeons whose experience is primarily with the general population rarely understand what we do and what recovery means for us. To them, recovery is healing the trauma. For us, recovery means quickly recovering what we lost—our incredible speed and strength—and the return to dancing.

Early, I only went to orthopedic surgeons. As the years went by, I avoided them as much as possible, preferring physiotherapists unless the problem looked too intricate and/or serious. When the grim indication was a torn knee cartilage and the probable necessity of surgery, there was no question about seeking a second opinion. When the knife is suggested, a second and even a third opinion should be sought.

NEUROSURGEONS

My few brief encounters have been unnerving, if I can be forgiven an all-too-accurate pun. I think that most of them know little about dancers, their powers and their needs, and that this field has more than its share of uncertainties. Witness their fatalistic attitude to nerve damage and what to do about restoration of neural response. I'm not at all surprised that an intuitive person like Irmgard Bartenieff* achieved results with children suffering from infantile paralysis that surprised the medicals, the neurosurgeons in particular.

---

*Irmgard Bartenieff was a woman of many talents. She developed a therapeutic technique of movement, was an expositor of Rudolf von Laban's theories and practiced connective-tissue massage therapy.

Healers and Treatments

OSTEOPATHS AND CHIROPRACTORS

Call it a quirk, but I have a fear of manipulation as a therapeutic technique, even though I was helped by it once. (I was also disconcerted by her therapeutic technique. When I returned later with a radically different problem, the treatment was exactly the same.)

Behind the fear lies this thinking: From time immemorial, humans, and I suspect all animals with spines and bones, heave a sigh of relief when some painful joint gives a click or a thunk, sometimes audible, and the pain is suddenly eased away. In many of the farm areas of the country I have seen large osteopathic clinics and hospitals. I have little doubt that manipulation can not only relieve but profoundly help people with back spasms and other joint problems, particularly manual workers. However, I do have trouble with the idea of manipulation as the basis of almost all healing.

As *Consumer Reports* noted in its skeptical article on chiropractic in September 1975 (there was no discussion of osteopathy that I recall), the founder and creator of this technique, Daniel David Palmer, claimed to have manipulated the neck of a deaf handyman, restoring his hearing. Very impressive, but, as the article pointed out, the nerves of hearing are not in the spine; they exist entirely within the skull.

Still, there probably is genuine substance to osteopathy and chiropractic, but the practitioners have been fenced off by the orthodox medical profession as interlopers, and there never has been a genuine objective study of what they do and what they claim. Vested interests feel threatened by a technique they neither understand nor command, while those committed to it declare it to be *the* answer. Could it be that such a study would meet resistance from both sides?

To return to that magical thunk or click induced by our own motion or by a skilled manipulator: My sense of what takes place is based on an image of the body as a collection of bones held together by the fierce strength and tension of ligaments and the tone of muscles tugging on tendons attached to those bones. Injury or strain of any of these—ligaments, muscles or tendons—sets up that well-known protective device of the body, a spasm or deep muscle tension. The spasm immobilizes the injured part to protect it, sometimes overreacting to the extent of creating problems elsewhere in the body. The increased tension makes for

HOW TO DANCE FOREVER

an uneven pressure in the joints, throwing that part of the body out of symmetry. The tolerances of the body are fine. Everything is in its precise place in the well body. However, the taut ligaments and tendons of an unhappy body part stretch across bones in the wrong places. The bones have uneven surfaces, lumps and bumps, some of which are calcifications from earlier injuries. A sudden movement or a manipulation by the osteopath or chiropractor will cause the strung body wire to slide back to its proper place, making it twang like a plucked string and producing an audible thunk or click. Two things are happening. The symmetry is restored, giving relief of pain and tension. The other is that the movement releases some fluid, which is the axle grease of the body. The surface of the protuberance has been oiled and the next movement is too smooth to be noisy. This explains why people who crack their fingers get no sound the second time around, unless the protuberance is very prominent.

Now, though the symmetry is restored and the painful pressure of unequal tension lifted, nothing is healed, but the protecting muscles may "think" the problem is over and a general relaxation ensues. Since the injury is still present, the muscle may tense up again and return the related joint to its imbalance. That is why one usually must have a series of treatments over several weeks with the osteopath or chiropractor. Of course, the injury is healing itself regardless during those same weeks. Obvious question: Say the treatment took six weeks. Would you have recovered in that time without treatment?

Now to my basic point: I think dancers risk specific hazard from repeated manipulation. Most people, other than dancers, move their bodies and their limbs through a very restricted range. Dancers, on the contrary, are constantly pressing against their outermost limits. What happens in the course of an "adjustment"? We stretch out in a quiet booth, usually being left there for a while with heat of one kind or another. We relax as best we can and assume a kind of passivity. We are in someone else's hands—the hands of a healer-helper. Finally, the osteopath or chiropractor enters, and from then on there is a gentle, firm grasping of opposing body parts, a pause of uncertain length and then, when we don't quite expect it, a very swift and forceful pressure. Please take special note of the swiftness and the unexpected timing. They circumvent what is known as the stretch reflex—an automatic contraction of a muscle when it senses that it is being stretched too far.

The fact is that the stability of our entire physical machine depends on this very stretch reflex and the power of all those "wires" to hold us together through all the demands of our dancing, no matter how extreme or wild. Too loose and we begin to bobble, or, as we say, "slip out." This is the question I would like to place before the body manipulators: Is it possible that these powerful twisting motions applied so suddenly to dancers' bodies will gradually, over an extended series of treatments, *permanently stretch what should never be stretched*? We all know that a stretched ligament is permanently stretched. Another question: Which is smarter, the manipulator or the stretch reflex? One interesting sidelight: More and more I hear of chiropractors who perform all kinds of physiotherapy with a multiplicity of devices but *with little or no manipulation*, and when they do use manipulation, it is of the most gentle kind. What's happening?

LICENSED HEALERS

Chiropractors should have been included in this group, which is distinguished from medical practitioners, but it is convenient to group them with osteopaths since the methods of both involve manipulation even though their training differs vastly. Osteopaths undertake four years' training in a medical college and a one-year hospital internship. They have to pass the same exam as medical doctors. The training of chiropractors is considerably shorter.

PHYSIOTHERAPISTS

This is a growing field which I think may prove to be in the long run our best source of healing. Combined in the same person are the skills of someone trained with a fairly comprehensive knowledge of anatomy and kinesiology, skills in the use of a variety of devices, from heat lamps to Cybex to laser machines plus, when necessary, a thorough competence in massage techniques. In the few that I have encountered, I sensed an openness not characteristic of most monomaniacs in the field. Since most of them work in conjunction with a medical doctor, it is easy to get their treatment covered by insurance and/or workers' compensation. This is less likely than with the more exotic forms of treatment.

HOW TO DANCE FOREVER

Every dance company and college department should have on call a physiotherapist and/or a massage expert.

MASSAGE EXPERTS

In this business of writing, there is the constant temptation to deliver an odd, shocking and unexpected thought. What follows is anything but that, though it may sound like it. Massage is wonderful, even when we feel good. When we're in trouble, a competent masseur/masseuse will help. A less than competent one is, of course, a waste of time or a hazard. A great one is a blessing.

There is one person in your life who needs to know little or nothing about massage and yet can help as much as any super massage expert—*someone who loves you.* Anyone who really cares for you and your well-being has magic in their hands, an innocent skill that will ease away even more troubles than all the work of an indifferent skilled masseur. One of the miracles of this kind of "healer" is that simple, gentle caressing, or even a gentle pressure of the troubled area, can ease many physical difficulties. Try it. At the very least it will be comforting and its efficacy may surprise you.

A young dancer here at the university came to my house to do some yard work. On entry he complained about waking with a terrible painful tension in the right side of his neck that was shooting into his back. I said, "Sit down," and for about two to three minutes I softly touched his neck and upper back in about six different places where I assumed there was tension and then said, "Well, let's get going." He swiveled his head around left and right like an owl, and then back around to me, and said, "What did you do? Were those chakras?" "No," I said, "I just asked you where it hurt." I didn't really. I only sensed where the knots were.

What is going on here? It's very complex, but I suspect it goes back to that time when he, you and I toppled over and banged a bone or two, howling "Mama!" and bawling vociferously. If he, you and I were lucky, Mama's warm arms gathered us up, touched the boo-boo, we cried a little more, then we felt a little better and then we forgot about it. Kindness, love and warmth are healing agents and should be at the *head* of the list of all treatment. A good massage is, before any other quality, kind, warm and loving.

Healers and Treatments

ATHLETIC TRAINERS

Never having been on a school team, my experience with this type of healer is severely limited. In my tours I have had occasion to use their services. Some of them are afflicted with a macho ethos that I have learned to fear. I remember needing some ice for that aggravated ankle tendinitis mentioned earlier. A trainer shamed me into putting my foot into a pail of nothing but small ice cubes. Why I suffered that for an excruciating twenty minutes I don't know, except that I literally quailed before that tough-guy challenge. Leaving the training room somewhat stunned, I muttered under my breath, addressing myself, "Schmuck!"

PODIATRISTS

They do certain things better than anyone else—things other people don't even want to do. In a very real sense, our feet are our front line, constantly receiving the brunt of whatever's going on. It's a good idea to have the telephone number of a reliable podiatrist. Some of them invest in heavy hype advertising campaigns in newspapers and the Yellow Pages. Better to seek out references from fellow dancers than from friends who are not dancers. Our needs and pressures are different.

Podiatrists and some orthopedic surgeons design orthotic devices. In case this is an unfamiliar term, these include anything from arch supports to wedges to lifts, which are put under the foot to change weight-bearing alignment. This particular field of research has received a boost from the widespread and fevered interest in recreational and competitive running. The best results of this study are some of the remarkable running shoes which I and many dancers have learned to prefer to conventional footwear. Specialized solutions are reputed to be helpful and, should the occasion arise, deserve to be investigated. The problem with dancers is that most of the devices are either too hard, too big, or too clumsy to fit inside a dance shoe and are almost never of help to our barefoot brothers and sisters of the modern dance.

SPECIALIZED FORMS OF TREATMENT

These usually require a certificate from a training center and some are licensed by state government agencies. I will rely on the alphabet to preserve an air of impartiality.

HOW TO DANCE FOREVER

ACUPUNCTURE

Who's going to argue with a four-thousand-year-old method? Again, my own experience is limited. From all that I've heard and read, and from the film showing the smile and wave of the little old Chinese lady walking away from the hospital table upon which she had just lost a gall bladder without losing consciousness though stuck with pins, I am convinced there is something substantially useful in this art or science, whichever it is. But, with the probable exception of a few of its members, the majority of the American Medical Association, and particularly its anesthesiologists, have allowed acupuncture to exist in America unnoticed, unexamined and unresearched in the odd corners of our urban centers.* Is it valid, good, wonderful, dangerous or fraudulent? It certainly awaits serious research here in America. I gather there are a few people here who have a command of acupuncture based on long and profound study. Any number of people, including a surprising number of chiropractors, have received some training and some pins. I'm in no position to judge them, but that doesn't stop me from being leery of them. As is the case with every one of these healers, it would be foolhardy to trust a serious condition to any-one who is not highly recommended, preferably by other dancers.

FELDENKRAIS

For those of you who are unaware of the work of Moishe Fel-denkrais, there's neither the space nor do I have enough knowl-edge to say anything more than to describe it as a therapy that uses a multiplicity of exercises as a means of breaking up old responses and making new and more efficient ones possible. There's comparatively little touching. The aim is to allow the body to find the easiest and most efficient ways of moving. I personally found a few of its exercises useful and liberating. Beyond that I've heard nothing but good reports.

CONNECTIVE TISSUE MASSAGE

I had a brief personal contact with this treatment from Irmgard Bartenieff. It is weird and gentle. During the six weeks or so of treatment, I reached a stage of limberness beyond anything I had ever achieved. I really would like to learn more about it. There

*There is strict licensing in some states and loose licensing in others.

seem to be very few people in America or even the world who are trained in this technique.

IDEOKINESIS

This is a staggeringly brilliant concept developed out of the theories of Mabel Elsworth Todd, who wrote a book called *The Thinking Body*. Her theories were developed further by Dr. Lulu Sweigard and Barbara Clark, R.N. Today their theories are being carried forward by Irene Dowd and André Bernard in New York and Pamela Matt here in Arizona. The briefest compression of this complexity is one that should be familiar to most dancers. It states that the concepts that exist in the mind about the body, its structure and its motions, are fundamentally what determine our alignment and motion. By mentally clarifying the actual structure and functioning of a well body and learning to image these, a repatterning is supposed to take place.

Underlying so many of the alternative methods of healing and living that are current today is a common bond with the Ideokinetic way of understanding the mind as a source of health or a source of pain. Take a book like Norman Cousins's *Anatomy of an Illness*, a description of his personally designed struggle against what his doctors had handed to him—the prognosis of a fatal disease. At the core of his healing was *laughter*.

As I write this, I realize that a subsequent chapter of this book, Chapter VI, The Heart-Mind of the Dancer, is based exactly upon this reverberation between concept and action. I believe Ideokinesis is worthy of the most extravagant research efforts. It says if you have the right concept, idea and/or poem of the motion, the motion will be right. Isn't this the way most of us work in the classroom, in the rehearsal hall and onstage?

ALEXANDER TECHNIQUE

This is a subtle set of concepts devised by a British teacher of actors and public speakers. F. Mathias Alexander's work deals with one of the most difficult tasks of all: correcting body alignment. The goal is an efficient, effortless way of moving and the techniques are directed toward changing muscular patterns that are hidden deep beneath consciousness. All that I have heard about their thinking and the experience of those who have worked with them is positive.

I myself had a brief contact and some help from a practitioner of Alexander technique. Due to my own fierce predilection for working things out myself, I discovered a personal resistance to how the teachers impart their information. It is generally one to one, one session a week, sometimes extending over a period of more than a year. The heart of their method is that one is led by the practitioner into the correct way of standing and moving by gentle pressure of his/her hands and a continuous stream of quietly murmured suggestions. It is very relaxing and leaves one open to its influence. My problem is, sooner or later I turn a corner and back off from the loving-parent/dependent-child relationship. My ideal human is that two-foot child I once saw poised on a New York City curb between two very large women. They each took a hand preparatory to crossing the street. Ms. Two Foot yanked her hands free, howling "No! No! No!" and strode forth, crossing the street, swinging her arms fore and aft.

Still, I do know several people whose truly grievous and threatening back conditions did not respond to any treatment until they spent a significant amount of time with an Alexander therapist. It seems to serve some very well.

What I regard as a very healthy development is the increasing number of muscular therapists who list among their credits extensive training in Feldenkrais, Alexander *and* Ideokinesis. It is exactly this kind of wide-ranging knowledge, techniques and approaches that makes for flexible, resourceful healers. Welcome.

MENSENDICK

At the time I started to dance, way back in the mid-thirties, much was made of this therapy. Some early modern dance techniques were influenced by it. To my knowledge, there is only one such practitioner left in New York City. She is recommended for postoperative therapy by some orthopedic surgeons performing back surgery. The reports are quite positive; people have been helped after many other treatments failed. An important part of the therapy is exercises using very intensive muscular contractions, particularly in the gluteal region. Most modern muscular therapists teach relaxation as opposed to such tension. Citing this apparently contradictory technique to Irene Dowd, she replied, "Daniel, the back is a funny thing. Sometimes almost any change or anything

1. Warming up for a photography session at State University of New York, College at Brockport, where *The Peloponnesian War* was created and first performed 1967–68
Photographer: Mel Simon

2. *Indeterminate Figure* (1957)
Music: Robert Starer. Photographer: Marcus Blechman

3. *In the Dusk from Spring '65*
Music: Charles Ives. Photographer: Oleaga

4. *The Peloponnesian War* (1968)
A Dance Theatre Collage
An evening-long work. Photographer: Carol Stein

5. *The Peloponnesian War* (1968)
An evening-long work. Photographer: Arthur Alexander

6. *Ruminations* (1976)
An evening-long work of dance, music and talk
Photographer: Beverly Owen

7. *Strange Hero* (1948)
Music by Stan Kenton. Photographer: Marcus Blechman

8. From the Broadway production of *Annie Get Your Gun*,
DN as Wild Horse in "The Wild Horse Ceremonial"
Photo credit: Vandam(m)

you do for it will work." I suspect there is an uncanny piece of wisdom here.

PILATES

This is a well-organized system of personal exercises and supervised exercises on spring-loaded machines. I use a few of the floor exercises, having learned them years ago in the army air force from Barton Mumaw. This is basically a conditioning program of which I have never heard anything but good reports. In the hands of a skilled practitioner, the exercises are modified for each person's need and lead to a repatterning of motion.

ROLFING

I have absolutely no personal experience with this technique and little information from those who have dealt with it. The extent of my knowledge is the awareness of the myth that surrounds it. It hurts. The fact that it hurts seems to be part of its mystique. There are a number of therapies that seem to demand the administration of pain. Rolfing is the most notorious. I am always struck by the awe with which people speak to one who has been through it. They ask in a hushed voice, "Did it hurt very much?" The answer is almost always given with an air of diffidence, whether the pain was little or great. We do know this person knowingly dared to accept the pain. This romance of pain has an edge to it that should not go unquestioned. Friction massage, Shiatsu, and pressure points, which I feel are remarkably efficient ways of ridding the body of many chronic weaknesses, can only proceed by creating pain. The spot chosen to massage *is* the most tender, i.e., the most painful.

All of this about pain brings to mind a conversation with a physiotherapist about friction massage. I can still see/hear her solemnly nodding her head and intoning, "Yes, it hurts and you have to do it for a real long time."

Therapists, a question: How long *does* it take to be effective? Will some of you please get together to investigate and research this matter? *It should be as short a time as possible.* There is that old and classic cartoon image of the masseur pounding the helpless victim, for his own good of course. The question is, For whose good? There is no judgment here, either about Rolfing (since I'm ignorant about it) or about this matter of treatments involving pain, only the question.

Types of Treatment

So what is out there to help us? Alphabetically, there are connective tissue massage; cryotherapy (ice); diathermy; diet modification; conditioning exercises; friction massage; heat; hydrotherapy (whirlpools, saunas, hot and cold contrast baths); laser; manipulation; massage; prayer; pressure points; rest; surgery; traction; ultrasound; weights (free weights, Nautilus, Cybex) and, as the car salesmen rant in the commercials, much, much more. Every one of these is potentially dangerous and potentially useful. As we say, it all depends. I seriously doubt that any one of these is either miraculous or the only answer for healing. The correct choice of one or more of them depends upon a combination of the wisdom of your therapist, your sensitivity to what is working, and luck.

Medicine and the Medicine Men

This next section will explain why I left medicine out of the above list of treatments. "Twentieth century medicine, which has worked so many miracles, has been chemically, not structurally, oriented."* The most serious flaw of the medical profession lies in its very name: *Medical*. The doctor sits in his office as each year and every day thousands of people come to him with trouble, much of it of obscure complexity and not easily treated. Into that same office comes mail—tons of it—from the great pharmaceutical companies: brochures and printed matter designed by the best graphic artists of our time, written by the best copywriters, since the pharmaceutical corporations can afford the very best. I knew a leading American poet who made his living writing advertising copy. Vividly and confidently the slick literature announces that *the* cure is here, with all the reservations in blindingly small print.

When a doctor sits facing a person with a complex complaint, there are *two* troubled people. One is sick and the other is often not certain what will help, but gets paid to be certain, and so fills

*From Dr. Ida P. Rolf, *Rolfing* (Santa Monica, CA: Dennis-Landman Pubs., 1978), p. 17. It is a structually biased book, but interesting nonetheless.

Healers and Treatments

out a prescription. It's an easy way out. There is mutual collusion here. It is a definitive act that satisfies most patients, physicians and the pharmaceutical companies.

I am certain there are many doctors who are not merely "medicine men" but physicians who make the enormous effort to be sensitive to the complexity of this person who has come for help. The best physicians are aware of and open to the wide range of ways to deal with the problem, other than medicine. Not for one minute is this meant to be a diatribe against medicine, as such. That would be as simplistic as those who rely primarily on pills. Bitterly, I must state from my own experience the existence of too many "pill pushers." That nasty, disrespectful slang term is unfortunately accurate for too many physicians.

Question: How many medical doctors are pushers—drug pushers? Story: Several years ago I had a breakup which broke me up badly. At the time, I went to a doctor for a long-delayed checkup. This doctor had been recommended by the estate of my wonderful physician who had died a few months before. In other words, I didn't know the man. As he was lashing my arm with the gadget they use to read blood pressure, I remarked, "I'm crazy now with upset about a separation. I wonder what you're going to read." Said he, "Don't worry. We'll give you a prescription for Librium." In old Chinese novels, when a man gets very angry, the convention of the storytellers was to write, "He made round eyes." Well, I made very round eyes and asked, "Are you saying that if something is upsetting I shouldn't be upset? Are you going to save me from being disturbed? I have every right to be unhappy. A sad and terrible thing has happened to me and no one is going to make me feel good or indifferent about it. I'll get over it, in time, and in fact I'll work at that, probably with a different lady, but certainly not with a pill." Let us call things and people by their proper names. This man was pushing for a pharmaceutical company, pushing me into a dependence on an unnecessary drug and pushing me to mindless indifference through a tranquilizer

Another medicine story: Recently, I had a nasty boil in the center of my back. I found a local doctor who upon digging out a deep sebaceous cyst found it necessary to pack it with surgical gauze to let all the gunk drain before letting the opening heal and close. Fine, but just as I was leaving, he said, "Oh, we'll have to put you on an antibiotic." I couldn't believe my ears. I said, "Doctor, doesn't my body have a pretty comprehensive defense system of its own? Why do I need antibiotics when my body can do the job of demolishing the enemy?"

I'll say this for him. He backed off, saying, "Well, we'll see how it looks when we remove the drain on Friday." No antibiotics were necessary.

In self-defense, you absolutely have to become knowledgeable about your body, and in this interaction and dialogue with the medical profession and all of the healers, you cannot afford to be awed, cowed or elbowed into an unnecessary dependence. So much for treatment.

CHAPTER V

QUESTIONS ASKING TO BE RESEARCHED

Back in 1967, I taught at a summer arts camp in Idyllwild, California, high up in the San Jacinto Mountains. I had made a radical teaching experiment, which I occasionally still do: not teaching. For a few classes, I tell the dancers they will be responsible for teaching and learning from themselves. It does wonders for some and terrifies others, particularly the younger ones. It also caused a furor among some of the faculty, and in the aftermath I was asked to give a lecture to explain what I had done.

In the course of the question-and-answer period, a gentleman rose to ask whether I had subjected this procedure of mine to a controlled experiment. I have no idea what ticked me off, perhaps his manner? Was he addressing me from a smug and arrogant height? I launched not into an answer to his question but into an attack on the medical profession and particularly on orthopedic surgeons, charging that they knew little of the problems of the dance profession and cared less, because most of us were too poor to afford their exorbitant fees. After the meeting, I learned that this man was the head and leading teacher of an orthopedic surgery clinic at a major university and that he was certain I had attacked him personally. I had never seen or heard of the man.

HOW TO DANCE FOREVER

A weird leap on my part, but in one respect, seen from today's perspective, that was a bad time for us. We have come a long way since then. There are sports medicine clinics all about, even a few centers and surgeons focusing on dancers and, most important of all, *pursuing research specifically about dancers*. The fact is, there is money to be made from dancers—now. There are significantly more professional dancers all over the country. Possibly half of all middle-class families send their daughters and even some sons to study dance for a few years at least, and then there are all those teachers for all those daughters and sons. Now that's a lot of leotards—and also a lot of sprained ankles, twisted knees and back spasms, all needing attention. It's finally here— some attention from the medical profession, kinesiologists and university researchers. For whatever reason, our beat-up bodies and tired tendons are at last being studied.

This chapter throws a few questions and challenges to the growing group of scientists and scholars who are studying us.

1. Nothing would please me more than if some skilled researcher were to take the survey from Chapter XI of this book, examine it critically, revise it where necessary and *repeat the entire study*. First of all, such a procedure is a distinct part of the scientific method. I welcome that. Second, should this happen, I do hope the new team will be larger and generously funded. This one was not. To do such a survey properly consumes much time from skilled people, and they are, as they should be, expensive. Our study was performed with barely any grant support and enormous amounts of kindness and generosity.

To do it properly, a truly representative sample of the *entire* dance profession would be necessary to give a broadly valid picture, but before this is possible we must learn once and for all who the dancers are. How many are there? How many are performers, choreographers, teachers and students? How many are ballet, modern, folk, etc.? How many are male and how many are female? The study we did may be furnishing us with the correct answers to these questions, but without a more extensive and better funded study we will never know. We should know who we are. The results of our study may be right on the mark, much of it appearing reasonable, but still it needs the verification or contradiction of another study.

Questions Asking to Be Researched

2. The research literature on aging is proliferating, and yet I am of the belief that to draw any conclusions from it about dancers is dead wrong. I will guess, and I am probably right, that the general population, i.e., those who are being studied, are the victims of a culture, a mythology, a way of life, a diet and, worst of all, their own expectations. All of which conspire to slow them down, enfeeble them and, plainly put, cause them to grow old at a time when they could have been zestfully digging into each day with a wisdom that matched their vitality. They and our culture have made them old in the worst sense of the word.

The dance profession, as well as athletes and all intensely active people, needs studies on the aging process, but the studies should compare young actives with "old" actives, young dancers with "old" dancers, young athletes with "old" athletes. Don Sutton of the California Angels pitched his three hundredth victory at forty-three, Raymond Floyd won the U.S. Open golf tournament at forty-three and Jack Nicklaus won the Masters golf tournament at forty-six. All this in the month of June 1986.

Undoubtedly our bodies change as we go on, *but how? How many changes are there for the better?* I myself am in some ways faster than I ever was, physically and mentally. Unless there are tests comparing young, older and "old" professionally active dancers, nothing can be assumed about the matter of aging dancers. Quoting from *Research on Aging*, June 1983, Vol. 51, No. 2, "A Review of Aging and Cognitive Process" by Diana S. Woodruff: "More than at any time in the life-span, there is diversity in old age in different individuals' cognition, ranging from senility to wisdom, and in a given individual some abilities fade while others are *maximized* [emphasis added]." This material focused upon the quickness/slowness of response. A complete study for us would include neuromuscular behavior, metabolic rate, healing powers, sleeping patterns, etc.

In recent phone conversations with Dr. James L. Fozzard, director of the Baltimore Longitudinal Study of Aging, and a colleague, Dr. Edward Lakata, I learned that new studies point in the direction of what I am claiming, i.e., that physical activity, not time, determines much of aging. "Self-proclaimed physically active men," as they described them, who, for example, have been running many miles per week for years, have twice the aerobic capacity not only of their sedentary contemporaries but of sedentaries in their twenties! I suggested a specific study of dancers maturing rather than athletes because our lifetime of activity is not so full of the impacts and traumas that characterize most sports. Dr. Fozzard thought this worth considering. Let's hope someone studies us in depth someday.

3. To give a true perspective to this study of dancers of varying degrees of maturity, the next essential investigation would be to compare us with the rest of the population. How would we compare in terms of our health profile, our longevity, etc.?

4. The matter of sex and injuries: As noted in the survey in Chapter XI, the women suffered significantly more injuries than the men. This must be examined. First: *Is this actually true of the profession as a whole?* Second: If it is true, why? Third: If we discover why, can we do something about it, even if it means giving up some treasured shibboleths about what a female dancer must look like?

5. The next proposal is on dangerous grounds. I'll state it cleanly and then point out the difficulty and hazards that would inhibit such an investigation. We have before us a dazzling multiplicity of technical disciplines, from Polynesian to point work. The research question: *What is the injury profile of those people who intensively study and practice a particular style and technique of dance?* Do the men who practice and perform those Slavic dances that amaze all of us with their virtuosity in Cossack kicks and leaps from deep plié have more, the same or even *less* knee trouble than most male dancers? How does the injury profile of a flamenco dancer differ from that of a ballet dancer or one trained in and performing the Limón technique?

The danger of this research? First, if the researcher is a dancer or someone who has danced or even a nondancer who is mad for dance, the odds are that she/he loves this and can't stand that in dance, i.e., it will be difficult to find a cool researcher.

Another difficulty: Researchers must expect no cooperation from some schools of dance if they became aware of the specific nature of the investigation.

Good news! Work has begun precisely on this question and, not surprisingly, was initiated by a dancer, choreographer and teacher. Professor Ruth Solomon, director of the dance-theatre program at the University of California, Santa Cruz, and Lyle J. Micheli, M.D., director of the sports-medicine division of Boston Children's Hospital, gathered material in 1983, analyzed it and published their findings in *The Physician and SportsMedicine*, August 1986. Despite the depth and complexity of their findings, Professor Solomon wrote me that the article ". . . only scratches the surface of what needs to be researched. . . . The data . . . asks more questions than it answers."* In the conclusion of the article, she makes a most astute observation: "Athletic trainers are usually in daily contact with the athletes they train: many sports medicine physicians have participated in the sports of the athletes they treat; sports scientists know the techniques involved in the sports they analyze. In contrast, most physicians have relatively little access to the daily interplay between dancers and their art form. . . . We contend that the more physicians learn about the training and activity of dancers prior to and at the time of injury, the better able they will be to manage all aspects of dance injuries."†

A related research question was raised earlier in this book in a section called The Balance Beam of Teaching, in Chapter III. Danger. In essence, it asked, What is the comparative injury profile experienced by students, performers, choreographers and teachers?

6. Examine the belief that professionally oriented dancers should engage in a weight-training program specifically designed to strengthen the muscles of the thigh even though there is no evidence of knee trouble. Suggestion: Get the interest of several conservatories of dance and base the research on dance students who volunteer to do the program and those who choose not to. Follow their careers as students and professionals for several years.

7. Compare the length of time of immobilization of a muscle group with the amount of time it takes to restore it to its former strength and limberness. I understand that ligaments usually heal in six weeks, even if immobilized, while muscle tissue atrophies when unused. The rate and degree of muscle atrophy and then the subsequent recovery time, though subject to many variables, should be known, even if only approximately.

*From a letter from Professor Solomon, February 4, 1987.
†From *The Physician and SportsMedicine*, August 1986, p. 89.

HOW TO DANCE FOREVER

8. There is a schism running through the entire dance field and it revolves around the buttocks. No, not what you are thinking. There is a school whose battle cry is "Firm those buns." "Tighten your rump." Others regard this as a false and unnecessary tension that produces back spasms, pressure on the sciatic nerve in the area of the piriformis and a multitude of woes. This battle extends to physical therapists and people who develop conditioning programs. One very expensive therapist, who is the only one recommended by some hotshot New York orthopedic surgeons, is fierce about strong repetitive contractions of the anal sphincter while you're standing on the curb waiting for the green light.

Can this matter of firming or relaxing be researched? There was a time when I taught a body-alignment sequence that followed an energy flow of pulling up from the feet through the thighs, the waist and the neck only to be answered by a downward flow through the shoulders, down the back to a firming and pulling down of the buttocks and through the legs into the feet, whose downward thrust produced a relevé. It felt great and fit everything I had been taught, until as an aftermath of my knee operation I developed what was apparently a severe sciatic irritation that produced numbness and tingling in the feet. At this turning, grabbing those gluteal muscles began to feel wrong, and when a therapist in Seattle suggested that the piriformis, which is part of the gluteal complex, may have been strangulating the sciatic nerve, which passes through it in some bodies, I gave up on that buttock tightening maneuver completely, *but I don't know how right that was or is.*

I am certain that whomever I would ask in the field of dance or physical therapy would give me an answer untinged by any doubt one way or the other: "Grab it," or "Let it be." I suspect there has not been any significant study of this rather crucial matter by any qualified movement scientist. It is long overdue. There is a profound difference in how the human body moves and feels depending how one uses this powerful set of muscles at the center of our motion.

9. The next proposed area of research is possibly the most subtle and the most difficult to pursue. It concerns two sets of interrelated dichotomies: slow/fast dancers and soft-touch/hard-touch dancers. The slow/fast relationship came up in Chapter II, Diet. I proposed the possibility that dancers who tended to move slowly

would generally be heavier than dancers who moved quickly. In Chapter VI, The Heart-Mind of the Dancer, I speculate whether dancers who have the "soft touch," i.e., who tend to use a light dynamic through most of their dancing, would have a characteristic injury pattern, and, conversely, whether dancers whose movement is pervaded by the "hard touch," i.e., a continually forceful style, would have a different injury pattern.

Setting up quantitative measurements for who is slow and who is fast, who is soft and who is hard, would be tricky indeed. Still, it could and should be done. One of the most difficult therapeutic problems is helping overweight people, including dancers. If learning to move faster, and when necessary, to be ahead of the beat, will alter a dancer's metabolic rate and thus reduce weight, that would be a bit of a victory. If learning to give one's dynamics a broader range would result in fewer injuries, that would be more than a bit of a victory. This is the logic behind the UP-TEMPO weight-loss regime outlined in Chapter II, Diet. Researching that would be an intrinsic part of this area of investigation.

10. Compare the meat eaters with the vegetarians among high-output people like dancers and athletes. Are there significant differences in health? Achievement? Virtuosity? Injury profile? Longevity?

11. Will skilled and responsible researchers ever examine, with all the impartiality at their disposal, the strange and exotic treatments and diets that exist on the periphery of our culture? Acupuncture? The macrobiotic diet? Homeopathic medicine? Yes, even reflexology, which makes no sense to me and yet some very smart people swear by it. I don't mind discovering I'm wrong. That would only mean I learned something.

12. Speaking of the unusual, the unexpected and treatments that exist on the periphery, take a look at the statistics from the Survey on page 293. There are six different forms of body retraining that were given a perfect score of satisfaction by the dancers who experienced them: weights, Alexander, Feldenkrais, Pilates, exercise and conditioning, and Rolfing. There were a total of 69 such treatments of 12.2 percent of the dancers having had one form or another of body retraining.

I would like to direct the hope for research that will study the

HOW TO DANCE FOREVER

effectiveness and validity of these new forms of healing, all under the umbrella of body retraining, to Martha Myers, who is on the faculty of dance at Connecticut College, is the dean of the American Dance Festival at Duke University and has organized many conferences at which exponents of these therapies have spoken. She is a great listener and has been in touch with almost everyone in the field of body retraining. I can't think of anyone better qualified to direct a comparative study of these therapies.

13. In Chapter IV, Healers and Treatments, I describe an incident of partial paralysis in my arm and the strange course of nerve recovery which I experienced. Summing it up quickly, in the course of my daily light exercises following the injury, there were three unexpected super-demands upon that arm. Each of the first two was followed by a spurt of recovery, and the third one appeared to bring on a complete dispelling of the neural incapacity. The research, probably best performed by physiotherapists in association with a neurological surgeon, would train patients suffering a negative neuromuscular response to make persistent, light demands on the incapacity. Intermittently, that is, after there has been even a minor buildup of strength, an unexpected heavy load would be imposed. This procedure of persistent light work and spaced sudden demands for much more strength would continue with tests and observations. Admittedly, there is an element of danger here, but carefully calibrating the sudden heavy demand with some caution might ultimately tell the researchers how far they could go. My nerve recovery was so complete and so directly connected with the sudden heavy exertions, I sense something of value here.

14. What is the ideal work week for people who have to deliver top performance physically, i.e., dancers and athletes? Five days? Six days? Seven days? Or is it different for each individual?

15. Research the strange surge of energy that will rise after a sustained physical effort and considerable fatigue. Is there an efficient way of getting to that place *earlier*?

16. There are, in our language, in our consciousness and probably in our deep unfocused feelings, strong associations with limberness and its opposite, a very limited range of movement. We

advise others to "hang loose." The implication is that if one does so, one will be better able to cope. Referring to another as "uptight" is a flat-out pejorative. With limberness, we associate emotional health, ease of mind and a ready and joyous access to one's sexuality. A narrow range of movement seems to speak of undue tension, inhibition, fear, unresolved inner conflicts and/or an unrealized sexuality. These associations are probably not all that conscious, but they are there in our language and in subtle hints from dance teachers, physiotherapists, psychotherapists and our best friends.

By this token, would the happiest and/or most relaxed people in society be contortionists? Are those dancers whose leg can bounce off their ear privy to deeper sexual gratification than those whose major achievement is barely grazing the ground with fingertips and straight legs?

The research problem: Do limber people have more in common with each other emotionally and mentally than unlimber people? Is there an identifiable personality portrait for these two different body types? Does a person who overcomes limited motion by stretching experience a change of emotional and mental patterns? Ideally the investigation would compare dancers, for whom limberness is professionally desirable, with nondancers, for whom it is not a central issue.

17. All animals, including dancers, upon being injured touch the hurt area if they can. They lick it, press it, rub it, etc. This common action has been developed by healers through the centuries into many different forms of therapy: from Gypsies' bears walking up and down the sprained backs of Romanian peasants to massage, acupressure, Shiatsu, friction massage, connective tissue massage, Rolfing, etc. To a greater or lesser degree, they all work, including the bears. Touching a specific area calls attention to it, not only from our conscious mind but from a whole battery of inner organs which operate in the dark beyond our cognizance. The gentlest caress can relax a tense muscle. Even harsh and painful touching helps. Why? The body responds to being touched with more blood, more juices, more nourishment and helpful relaxing signals from the cerebellum—that part of the brain that talks to muscles. These come surging into the touched area and we not only feel better but it appears that healing is facilitated. As children, when injured we got the fondest attention:

HOW TO DANCE FOREVER

"Does it hurt? Mummy will kiss it." It helped and we stopped crying!

Around many of the touch therapies there is a heroic mystique that assumes pain as a concomitant of the treatment. Of those listed above, only classic Swedish massage and connective tissue massage are painless. The others vary from awful to nigh unbearable. I'm against pain—giving it or receiving it. Still, it works. I have materially helped myself with friction massage, and that hurts.

Recently, I have for myself and for some of the students here used a subtle form of pressure with the most amazing results. Wherever there has been a pain, instead of the usual theatrical, deep, harsh force associated with so many touch therapies, I've simply placed a firm but gentle pressure upon the affected area, either with the palm of the hand or with a finger or fingers, for a small area. To draw Stanislavski into this therapy, the "inner action" of the pressure is "to comfort" and "to reassure." I do not use any movement, only direct strong/soft pressure into the painful region. For how long? I pretend it's a crying child and keep comforting contact until it stops. Give this method the name Pressure Therapy.

An experiment: You dancers are an ideal group to try this. Rare is the day when you haven't a single ache. Keep a dated record of your musculoskeletal injuries, rating them as MINOR, MEAN or MAJOR. MINOR = present, but interferes not at all with movement. MEAN = you can dance but the pain is affecting your movement. MAJOR = you have been forced by the pain to stop dancing. Treat one side of the body with Pressure Therapy, the other side with any other form of therapy. Note when each injury started and the rate of recovery. Keep the record for five weeks. Try to get at least ten other dancers to do the same. Compare your experiences and draw your conclusions. Of course, there's nothing to stop professional physiotherapists from researching this. My guess is that this is a very useful adjunct for almost all MINOR injuries, many MEAN injuries and even some MAJOR injuries. Very early, I was grounded by a violent back spasm and treated by a chiropractor. She started every session with cupping and stroking my feet gently with her warm hands. That felt so good *all over*, I used to wonder whether that alone could serve for the entire treatment. Can this be researched?

One can go a step further: An ex-lover, whether from inspiration or experience I'll never know, introduced me to what very easily becomes an erotically provocative "massage." I use quotes because all it is is weightlessly gliding fingertips over the skin. The surprise came when it proved to be amazingly efficacious for muscular tension and pain. Research this. Whatever happens, you can't miss.

18. More than once I've heard about friction massage breaking up scar tissue. Is it possible that friction massage, while healing is still going on, may minimize the amount of scar tissue that will develop? I suspect that once scar tissue is formed not much can be done about it. The other belief is that friction massage breaks up adhesions. How much research and how much assumption are we dealing with here?

19. Next is possibly the subtlest and most complex question of all. In Chapter VI, The Heart-Mind of the Dancer, I go into a matter that has many names: "getting high," "going with it," "letting go" and their opposites—"not losing your head," "acting civilized," "keeping in control." Each of these means something slightly different, and yet they are all a cluster of meanings that surround the dialectic of human experience: control and release. Some cultures regard one aspect as reprehensible, to be avoided at all costs, and the other as an ideal and even a holy state. The glorious ancient Greeks regarded both as sacred and essential to a full life. One has been dubbed Apollonian and the other Dionysian. Innumerable rituals are used by every society either to stimulate what they value or inhibit what they fear. Some of these rituals are social ceremonies, some are personal practices and *some employ agents:* a cold shower or a tranquilizer for one side of the seesaw, alcohol and drugs for the other side.

Characteristically, here in our society in America, we have a great mishmash: the "uptight" ones polarized against the "wild" ones, with the modern "Greeks" and the confused ones in the middle. Great concern is being expressed about the astronomical amount of alcohol and drugs used by an amazing number of people from all walks of life. The question: *Is it possible that the heavy users of flyaway agents such as coke and booze are people who have neither the talent nor the knowledge nor the personality to release without the help of some kind of stuff?*

The research stated is in two parts. The first is the subtle and

HOW TO DANCE FOREVER

complex aspect, which may defy clarification. If we, for simplicity's sake, describe one aspect as the capacity for control and the other as the capacity for release, is it possible to devise a test of a person's capacity for each? I have a great suspicion of all such attempts to quantify human states of being and yet I fantasize that it might be feasible to make a roughly accurate profile of a person's ability in respect to these two diametrically opposed human functions.

Assuming this were possible, the next step would be to examine two groups, each representative of the United States—one having a heavy dependence on alcohol and/or drugs and the other using little or none of these agents. My hypothesis: The alcohol and drug users do not have the talent or the freedom to release. They are caught in the net of self-consciousness and can't lose themselves without stuff of some kind.

I raise this suggestion because I suspect that the entire campaign against drug abuse is misdirected. If a mate beds down with a third party, where is the problem? With the third party? No, it's the mate that has to be understood and dealt with. If the coca leaf is harvested in the mountains of Peru, Colombia and Bolivia, burning it solves nothing. The real question is, Why does the bright young stockbroker need to sniff cocaine? The drug pusher isn't the problem. Without a user, the whole distribution apparatus would disappear in a flick.

There is, of course, that group of people who have a rigid necessity *to control their release, and to control its frequency, its timing and its intensity*. Some of these are professional performers in the arts and in sports. Terrified of performing and not being "with it," when that ecstasy is the identity they present to the public and the public expects of them, locks some into the contradiction of *controlling the opposite of control*. Among all the professions appearing before the public, I suspect that dancers resort to this less than any of the others, and that too would be worth an investigation.

20. I have a reluctance born of possessiveness to explicate the next and last research proposal. Why? I would like to initiate it myself, find a qualified associate, receive a barrel of money to fund the work and participate in the research from beginning to

Questions Asking to Be Researched

end. I would also like to study and understand physics, modern electronics, algebra, differential and integral, and learn to read Greek and Chinese. George Bernard Shaw was right. Our life-span, at best, is too short. By the time we get the faintest hint as to how to deal with existence, it's time to turn in. He suggested a minimum of three hundred years as a decent life-span. One of the great Japanese watercolorists, Hokusai, was painting away while his daughter was preparing lunch. This was two weeks before his death. He was eighty-nine and one of the giants of art. (His illustrations, found on newspapers used to wrap imported pottery, shook and inspired the artists of Paris, who in turn created modern art.) His daughter called him to come to lunch when the food was ready. "In a moment, daughter, just one more moment. I think I am getting the hang of it."

I am digressing to avoid opening up this idea. Here goes: One of the most fundamental aspects of a basic human motion, walking, is rarely discussed or studied in depth: pelvic action.* I see three broadly different ways that the human pelvis can deal with walking:

1. The Seesaw: The pelvic girdle tips laterally up and down. Put weight on the right foot and the pelvis tips down on the left side. Put weight on the left foot and the tip is to the right. Mae West gave an all-out, mocking version of it. In a subtler and less aggressive version, many people from all walks of life seesaw their way through every day.

2. The Forward-back: In this version, the hip moves forward with the leg that is stepping forward, and by that token, the opposite side of the hip moves behind what would be a centerline from one side of the pelvis to the other.

---

*There is a massive study on all aspects of walking, including the pelvis: *Human Walking*, by Inman, Ralston and Todd (Baltimore, MD: Williams & Wilkins Co., 1980). But most of the studies were of fewer than ten adult male athletes and the orientation was to discover what characterizes walking, as if there is a norm. There may be. What I am always aware of are the differences.

HOW TO DANCE FOREVER

3. No Motion: These people walk slowly or quickly, maintaining an immobile and stabile pelvis, almost as if they have a gyroscope within.

There is no question that most people have a blend of at least two of these or do one or the other in different circumstances. Still, one can easily observe the major differences just described. The subtle variations from person to person are staggering. The three main types can be useful variations to study as long as we understand that they are simplifications of a complexity.

My hypothesis: I think that each style of motion is the expression of an attitude toward self and society. I am by trade a people watcher. Much of my dance is gleaned from looking, guessing and living with people. My favorite sport is watching or falling into the walk of someone I see on the street and speculating a mental portrait of that person.

Seesaw people call up to me an unhurried ease and a sensuality. They tend to accept themselves and the world as it is. If anything, they lean toward the negative pole of energy. The Forward-back people are all too familiar to me. I'm one of them. Whenever I pick up their walk, I have the sense of someone who is concerned that they might be late. There is a sense of drive, ambition and a need to control things. Sensuality may be there, but it often takes a backseat to "more important matters."

The No-motion people amaze me because of the astounding coordination required to move the massive weight of the limbs back and forth *without moving the hips*. If I slip into the skin of a no-motion walker, my pelvis turns into a tightly clenched fist attempting to keep that entire perilous area from moving, as if moving were dangerous, and yet it always carries an aura of "cool." It feels puritanical, forgoing all sensuality, not only sex.

Not one bit of this thought stream has a basis in fact, as yet, *but I think there may be substance to it.* How to determine it? Again, here is a fascinating but extraordinarily subtle set of variables we would have to find some way of quantifying, a dangerous procedure at best.

There is potentially more to be learned in such an investigation: What effect does each mode of walking have on health? *Which of the three has the least amount of back trouble, or is a blend of motions best?* Does each type of walk have a characteristic skeletal structure? (If that were the case, then my entire psychological specu-

Questions Asking to Be Researched

lation would fall down in a heap, since the determining factor of walking would not be a mind-set but rather a given physical structure.)

The complexity of the research would be compounded if one were to add the motion of the shoulder girdle. In fact, the shoulder girdle should be studied, but probably after the initial pelvic-motion study, which in itself is complicated enough.

CHAPTER VI

THE HEART-MIND OF
THE DANCER

 is the Chinese ideogram for "mind." It also means "heart." The spoken word *hsin* is exactly the same for both. The linguistic history of this unexpected melding is unknown to me. However, if you think of "heart" as a metaphor containing both the passions and the body, for it to become one with the "mind," you have a poem living in the single word *hsin*, a word that should be quite understandable to dancers. This is our ideal—a oneness of body and mind, passion and reason, the darkness and the light. Not that this oneness is easy to encompass.

Most of you reading this book are the children of Western European history and culture. Within the psyche of each of us there is an unresolved war that we have inherited. Mind and body are presumed to exist in a state of irreconcilable conflict. From infancy, with the first gestures and the first words given us, we learn through an infinite variety of hints, restraints, urgings, slaps and pats of encouragement that part of us is bad. Whole areas are off limits. Parts of us must be hidden. Inner longings of unbelievable strength must be suppressed and denied, and if ever released, only under carefully prescribed rituals and conditions. Crudely put, in order to be GOOD, you must not be as BAD as you would like to be. This is our heritage and it lives to a greater or lesser extent in every one of us. It becomes a central theme in our art,

HOW TO DANCE FOREVER

our dreams, our fears and our victories, and keeps our psychiatrists very busy and very wealthy.

Speculating on why people come to see us dance is just that—speculation. Nonetheless, I will postulate that as we plunge through space, reaching, stretching, twisting, embracing and strutting our bodies about for all to see, we are sending signals and signs to our growing audience that it is not only all right to have a body, no, it's even beautiful. Taking a long view, this is a new and radical thought in our culture. The phenomenal growth of our audience may very well be a response to the good news we bring.

Whether you know your dance history or not, the bitter fact is that for a thousand years before the discovery of America there was no such thing as a professional dancer in any respectable arena, stage or space in all of Europe. A thousand-year hiatus. Music, architecture, painting, sculpture and literature flowed on. We were prohibited. Put aside for a moment what that meant in the loss of traditional skills and the continual development of our art, technically and artistically. Our work was considered outside the pale of acceptable human and social behavior. To this day, there is hardly a major university in all of Europe that teaches dance, though they teach the other arts. Few of the Ivy League universities of America teach dance, and if they do, it's as a minor diversion. Many people in our culture, both here and in Europe, believe even now that our art is neither a serious nor a respectable human activity. Some of these people are our parents, even our mates! Unwittingly, some of these people are *ourselves*!

It is not inconceivable that trace elements of this self-doubt and guilt exist in all of us. I have witnessed more than a few dancers who are either hamstrung by contradictory inhibitions or fly to the opposite pole—dancers who make this moral disapproval a justification for defiant vulgarity. Dancers who shun sensuality, as well as those who direct every stage moment toward an erotic connotation, are all not merely in trouble as artists but as people. In the middle are the uncertain ones, pushed this way and that.

It's a safe guess that almost all professional dancers reading these thoughts will not consider them a digression from the question of survival. It matters not how sharp and well our bodies are; when the head's not right, the body is in danger. When the sense of self is an unresolved battlefield, there's work that has to be done.

The Heart-Mind of the Dancer

Who Are the Dancers?

On the face of it, this is a ridiculous question. Obviously all kinds of people become dancers. Perhaps, and yet what kind of person is it who in order to help people must cut them up? Certainly not "all kinds of people." I'll wager we have more in common with professional dancers from Argentina or China than with the surgeons in our own town.

Here is an attempt to outline the profile of those who are drawn to dance as a life work:

Before anything, we are people who repeatedly have an almost mystical experience. It comes unbidden. It can never be called up on demand. We are dancing, in class, rehearsal, performance. It usually happens when the body is hot and flowing, and not infrequently, deep in the heart of fatigue. We are dancing and there is a shift. We never notice when it happens. We no longer have any skin. The floor becomes pliable, the music is coming from everywhere at once. It is being made in our body. The walls dissolve. There are no walls. We have no limits. We can do anything. We are a universe where everything in us and outside us is us and all of us are whirling about in the dance. We are in the middle of a multicolored soup and our dancing, our body, is stirring it all up. We never notice when it begins, and only when it ends can we look back and know that it has happened, for while it is happening we are as happy as we can ever be, and the beauty of it all is that while it is happening we are too busy to know we are happy. Briefly, it's called a high.

Sometimes weeks go by, even months, without this exquisite high. We go on because we know that having happened, it can happen again. If ever it stops happening for a very long time, our survival as a dancer is at stake. Without it, why dance? Without it, dancing is just a job and dancing is too hard, too risky and often too unrewarding to be just a job. So dancers are people who get high on movement. It may very well be the most profound reason we dance.

Second, for dancers, the body not only occupies a major portion of the horizon but becomes the most significant metaphor for who we think we are and what it's all about. When I took my first university engagement as a teacher at the State University of New York, College at Brockport, I asked my students on the first day of technique class what they hoped to achieve. More frequent

HOW TO DANCE FOREVER

than any reply was, "I hope to gain control of my body." On the surface, what could be more obvious? Yet, if you back off and consider the tribe of dancers and what it is they do year after year, another meaning attaches itself to "gaining control of my body."

Dancers work deep into fatigue and not too rarely through pain. They are constantly disciplining not only their bodies but their appetites, their time, their pleasures and the joys of their personal life. Is a deep part of this matter of "control" a matter of keeping the beast body in line? Is the constant regimen of ordering its motion—lining up the spine, the feet, the arms—all a poem of not letting the body run free, or it might do something—bad? Is this not that classic conflict of body and mind? I'm reasonably certain that this is not the case for all dancers, but it's a great profession for people who hunger for an ascetic, controlled existence and, yes, an existence carrying the shadow of self-flagellation. Think. Don't all of you know dancers who answer to this description? Do you? Is this bad? Unhealthy? Who has the right to judge you? I will, however, say that if this is where you are, if this is what you are doing with dance, you should at the very least know you are doing it. It's one thing to make sacrifices for the work you love and a different scene to enjoy the sacrificing more than the work.

How many joinings have been torn asunder by the zealous discipline of one of the partners, the dancer? More than one marriage or union has started with an admirer inflamed by the gorgeous, liberated body and the sensual motions of a dancer. Then, as the heat of the early encounters cools, our admirer of voluptuousness is faced with the all too frequent "Darling, I had a brute of a rehearsal," or "Honey, I open tomorrow night!" or "I'm sorry, but my back is just about gone." When is the plea for restraint discipline, and when is it fear of flesh dressed up as discipline? It is hard to know anything for sure.

The third defining element of being a dancer is not all that obvious. It is something we carry with us onstage. Being a dancer, all we do points to that time when the eyes of many people are filled with our presence. Some people study-study until they finally arrive onstage only to discover they hate performing and/ or appearing in public. I think it is critical that anyone aspiring to be a dancer find occasion to perform intermittently throughout the entire time of their training. You never know when you will

The Heart-Mind of the Dancer

change and what once seemed the pinnacle of existence will not only lose its charm for you but, even worse, will fill you with fear and a sense of inadequacy. Ironically, and sadly, this can happen to highly talented dancers. To get on that stage you have to bring more than your body. One of the most glorious dancers of the early days of the modern dance would retch violently or throw up backstage before each entrance. The other dancers would have to push her on. Yes, she quit and became a teacher. She suffered the absence of a quality critical to dance performance.

Every craft and art has a unique spine, without which it is not possible for a person to qualify. Lacking a sure sense of pitch, the most gorgeous-sounding voice wouldn't be enough to call that person a singer. A pianist with perfect pitch and a flabby sense of rhythm would be in an unredeemable position. An actor with a wonderful voice, a magnificent and magnetic presence, but an inability to pretend that what wasn't so was, would leave every audience as unconvinced as he/she was. A tone-deaf percussionist only needs a magical sense of rhythm.

A dancer can have everything—appearance, virtuosity, even the passion to dance—and still fail to convince and draw an audience into her/his expression and performance. What a dancer needs in performance, above all, is peculiarly subtle, compared to the other arts. To my way of thinking, a sense of pride in one's physical presence is the spine of the dancer's craft and art. Onstage we have no secrets from an audience. A dancer with a profoundly negative attitude toward her/his physicality inevitably diminishes her/his stature and credibility. Without this sense of pride in one's physical presence, performing can only be a torturous experience for the artist and a negative for the viewers.

I have seen in my time some of the strangest and most unfashionable shapes appear and take center stage with zest, conviction and pride in that they were about to offer a theatre full of people a gift of inestimable value—themselves seen dancing. Without question there is not a dancer, including the most "beautiful," who does not have a secret fury that he/she is not taller, shorter, blonder, darker, larger-breasted or smaller-breasted, more muscled or less bulky. In fact, the more conventionally beautiful often suffer even more than the plain ones with this problem of self-denigration. They have been so conditioned to hinge success on appearance that the slightest mess, deviation or change with maturity can destroy them, while the funny ones, the odd-shaped

HOW TO DANCE FOREVER

ones and the plain ones enter the stage trembling and triumphant with the ineffable poem of their motion.

A vital dancer-performer is invigorated not only by pride in her/his physical presence but by *the presence of the audience. Being looked at* makes such a dancer stronger, more alert, more creative and, yes, happier. All those eyes are like water, sun and earth for the roses; the true dancer-performer blossoms before the intent gaze of all those eyes.

Beyond pride, there is the ultimate challenge to the performance art expressed in the Spanish word *duende.* Federico García Lorca, the Spanish poet and dramatist, wrote an exquisite, albeit complex, essay on this word.* Plowing through it, every performer would come away with a piece of gold. Briefly, to have *duende* in the act of performing, one gives over being careful and risks opening the dark gates of one's inner being. It is that supreme level where all the years of craft and training give one the right to forget craft and create with all that is within. I think every performing artist should read this essay at least once a year.

To return to this business of pride in one's physical presence, there is a distortion of it that can diminish or even wreck our performances. For a period of time, I gave lecture demonstrations for elementary school children; so little, their legs could swing freely as they sat. In fact, the swinging was my barometer as to how well I was doing. Fast and furious, I was in deep trouble. I was boring them. Unpardonable. The ultimate accolade was when their legs stopped swinging altogether.

In that lecture I was trying to give them an idea of what had led me to dance. As part of the session I asked them whether any of them danced, followed by the question "Why?" One day an eager little gentleman shot his hand up, answering, "To show my mother." That hit home.

Among our tribe, people come to the stage for a variety of reasons and showing or showing off are as important as any but also potentially treacherous to our artistry and equilibrium as humans. Some dance primarily to show their beauty; others, to show their virtuosity or their sexuality or their strength, etc. Too bad.

Among the Jews there is an expression used only sparingly: *"Er ist ein richtige mensch"* (or *"Sie ist . . ."* if a woman is being

---

*Federico García Lorca, *Poet in New York*, trans. Ben Belitt (New York: Grove Press, 1955), pp. 154–166.

The Heart-Mind of the Dancer

discussed). Translated literally: "He [She] is a right person." The meaning is much more complex than the words and is indicated by a subtle emphasis and retard in the voice on the word *richtige*. The speaker is conferring the highest praise possible, saying that this person (*dieser mensch*) is endowed with many wide-ranging qualities. He/She is thought to be intelligent, strong, creative, capable, sensitive to others, generous, considerate, delightful, self-resourceful, socially responsible and in all probability a lively and lovely lover. Looks, good or unattractive, are never the issue. No one quality is indicated, only the complexity of a rare human being who contains fine qualities in many directions.

"Coming on" to show off but one facet onstage is not merely to denigrate oneself but to limit one's artistic range. Trusting only to virtuosity or looks or whatever will drive a dancer into a corner of limited possibilities. A limited dimensionality will even affect musicality. A dancer who *always* tends to drag the beat may be giving signs of laid-back energy, uncertainty and/or a tendency to follow. A dancer *always* ahead of the beat may be unduly aggressive theatrically or putting out high energy all the time, regardless of the need of the moment. A dancer who is *always* square on the beat could be a goody gumdrop, i.e., cautious, safe and, yes, dull.

Real musicality invites being before, after and square on the beat, as the case may be. Each is an exquisite metaphor with many shades of meaning possible. *Ahead of the beat*, the dancer could be challenging the musician to go faster or by her/his motion is creating the music. *After the beat*, the music creates the motion and the dancer is swept and carried by it. Finally, *on the beat*, the music and the dancer are one and the dancer is alive at the world's center. There are thousands of other images for these musical choices and the rich dancer has many of them at her/his command. The poor dancer is stuck with one rigid response to all music.

Again, the heart-mind configuration shapes the style and defines the artist. It colors every motion and even determines the structure of the spine. As indicated in Chapter III, Danger, posture reveals secrets. It is a revelation performed without plan or consciousness. Posture is politics, philosophy, the barometer of the moment and, to anyone who can read bodies, a clear message from deep inside. Your insides will out. It matters not how well you have mastered correct alignment; an unresolved tension makes "correct" look like a straitjacket, an inner pain makes a beautiful back look fragile, and self-hatred makes an elegant line invisible. No avoiding it: To study dance, one must also study to become a *mensch*.

Surviving Criticism

A dancer who survives and does well is one who has a clear and quite objective awareness of the scope, magnitude and quality of his/her talent. Yes, but what about the opinions of other people? If we are lucky, we are nourished by their love and faith in our talent. Sometimes, despite that talent, we experience teachers who discourage us, choreographers who ignore us, dancers whose competitiveness leaves us frozen and isolated, and finally, there are the critics who can on occasion draw and quarter us. For some of us, negative feedback is the hardest load of all. It was for me, for many years. Any unfavorable opinion from others, real or imagined, would fill up my mind, wall to wall.

My very first job was both wonderful and traumatic. It was at Unity House, that summer resort of the International Ladies' Garment Workers' Union which I mentioned earlier. I was raw, barely trained, uncertain, terrified musically and I didn't think I "looked good." I was surrounded by an extraordinarily skilled and talented group of dancers, singers and actors. All were first-rate professionals. I knew that the paucity of trained male dancers (this was 1940) was the sole reason I was hired. I felt like a lumbering hairy goat. My failures were many. Criticism was harsh and probably justified. The best part of the summer was that my fellow dancers were kind, supportive and helpful. They schooled me when they could. Somehow I survived the three months, learning, learning and suffering.

The very last night before leaving, I had half packed and then gone down to the lakeside casino, the combination ballroom and theatre, to collect my work clothes and makeup. It was deserted. I was quickened, as always, by the empty dressing rooms, the sweet-and-sour smells and the ghost presence and vitality of the actors, dancers and singers. Walking out on the darkened stage, down onto the ballroom floor streaked by long moonmade shadows, I held my breath as I always have whenever in the emptiness of a theatre space waiting to be used. I thrum with the awareness of what could occur there. Leaving the hall and coming down the steps, I was rocked back by the sight of a high moon haloed by racing clouds, silvered and black. Standing there, my eyes filled with that light, all of a moment I knew with more power and more strength than I had ever known that I was going to be a dancer, a good dancer, and that I was going to make beautiful dances. Never had I been so sure of anything in my life.

Less than a month later I was thrust into a despair that threatened my sanity. The Shuberts had seen our summer revues and decided to produce our strongest material for a Broadway show. Not even half a year out of college, hardly any training, and I was going to get my Equity card and appear on Broadway! Good luck? Yes and no. Not only was I back again with all those beautiful artists who I was certain had witnessed all of my weaknesses but a new dancer had joined us. Bitterly, I must grant he was fabulous. He could do a descending back attitude turn and flow, without the slightest interruption, into a spiral fall, spin into an outrageously arched back on the floor, pause for just an instant and swing himself back up the way he came down, finishing in a hovering attitude of perfect balance and stillness. I would have admired and carefully studied all he did but he was the personification of arrogance and the living proof of my hopeless ineptitude.

Parenthetically, from the vantage point of this distance in time, I will hazard a guess that this man whom I envied so and saw as an aloof snob was probably living at that moment in close quarters with his own fears and self-doubt. The show was rehearsed for three weeks, and for those three weeks from the moment the alarm opened my eyes, I could hear a broken record in my head repeating, "You are not a dancer. You will never be a dancer. You are not a dancer. . . ." In the middle of a plié, while eating, while talking to others, while sitting down or standing up, "You are not a dancer. You will never become a dancer. . . ." continued without interruption, accompanying me to bed, into my sleep, my first thought upon waking and all day long, every day. If I ever came close to a breakdown or madness that was it.

The show opened—and closed in one night. For me that was luck, leaving me free of my brilliant nemesis and all those people who I was certain saw me as an incompetent. It matters not what they actually thought. I believed I was incompetent and it followed that they would too.

In the ensuing years, the agony never quite ceased. As dance captain for my first Broadway show, *Up in Central Park*, I couldn't give anyone notes or corrections if I thought I had danced badly that night. In *Annie Get Your Gun*, there were men dancing behind me in the chorus who could spin out six, seven, eight pirouettes and warm up to the overture doing double turns in a perfect second while doing a grand pirouette. It was clear to me that everybody was better than I and everybody thought I wasn't very good. All this, even though there were marvelous reviews of my performance and audiences were unfailingly enthusiastic.

An "important" critic dismissed my first half-concert, in which I presented all the solos I had at the time, as mere "Broadway slick." Shaken, I did not create another solo dance for five years; this in spite of the fact that that first program included *Strange Hero, Spanish Dance, Dance in the Sun* and *Man of Action.* Years later, this same critic dismissed my new work saying it did not hold up against my earlier "urban classics," which she had previously put down. It took me a long time to transfer my resentment and anger against her to where it really belonged: *me.* Nothing I have done in my life fills me with more shame than the fact that I allowed myself to be so thrown by the public comments of this woman that I stopped working creatively as a dancer for five years. For five years I denied the essence of my being.

Finally, one evening I filled in for a sick dancer in a mixed bag of a concert. It was in the little Roerich Museum Theatre on Riverside Drive. I was performing *Strange Hero.* The entrance finished downstage left with a pause to drag the right foot into a soft kick and a held balance that had to be maintained while a sidelight came up from black to blinding in my face. The balance problem always made me a little nervous, but this time there were at least four heads belonging to some very young dancers peering out from behind that downstage wing. Young, inexperienced, unknown, it mattered not. They were dancers and that was sufficient to fuel my fear. My slight bobble developed into a sway suitable for a tidal wave. I was instantly furious with myself. I not only danced like a madman but that instant became a turning point for me. A slow turning point, but as time spun out, it finally took. I gradually tore myself loose from the focus on the opinion of other dancers and/or the pronouncements of the critics. From then on, neither blame nor praise—from anyone—would ever be the deciding factor in my opinion of my work or in my artistic choices and decisions. I could and would listen to anybody and everybody, but when the click time of conclusion came up, I finally learned to consult one authority, myself. Significantly, over the

The Heart-Mind of the Dancer

years I have been harsher and more demanding in my self-criticism than anyone else.

I suspect my experience is not all that unusual. Ours is a performance art, and as such we live and work in a climate that always contains some element of judgment. If we can't learn how to deal with constant judgment, we either suffer throughout the entire time of our professional existence or fall away, giving up. Is there an answer? I think there is. I think secretly each of us knows the extent of our talent. I think that along with the skills and artistry we acquire, the taste we develop is critical. The power to pass whatever we do through the sieve of our own values is the major source of our self-confidence. It is easy to think that those who have "made it" are often vain. On the contrary. None are more ruthless in self-judgment than those who have made it.

There are some very odd performances when we feel great and look awful or when we feel a fumbling mess and deliver a touching and strong performance. These are rare and complex events. Generally we *know*. To survive in our field, we must develop the ability to pay attention to all responses to our work, favorable or negative. Learn what we can and where we can, but ultimately have the strength and clarity to do the final toting up *pas de seul*, alone.

The great golfer Bobby Jones was playing a game with a friend. On the fourth hole Jones slammed a drive off the tee that seemed to go forever and landed in the exact middle of the fairway. His friend exploded, "That was fabulous. Wonderful, Bobby." Jones said nothing. Later, walking up to the eighteenth tee, Jones said, "You shouldn't have said that back there. Only I know where that ball was supposed to go." Ungracious perhaps, but spoken like an artist.

Learning can be so damn slow. It took the presence of some very young dancers who had practically no history compared with my professional stature and past successes to make me realize how stupid and self-destructive I had been. I finally learned the obvious. Our profession and purpose in life is to dance for people, among whom are a few who happen to be dancers, and that ultimately we resort to one authority, one critic, ourselves. Laying claim to that prerogative and that responsibility gives us the right to consider ourselves as artists. By allowing anyone else final authority in our choices and actions, we disallow that right. An artist is a person who is ultimately responsible for her/his creation.

When it says "choreographed by" or "performed by," that's precisely what it means—or what it should mean.

Competition

Getting ahead. Ours is a competitive field. (Does it really have to be that way?) Here is another aspect of our lives where, in a profound sense, we write our own program. For some, getting to the top is what it's all about. For others, status level is less important than living the life of a performer, choreographer and/or teacher.

Anyone who has to be number one, the one out in front of the pack, is laying their happiness on the line. Even if you are the best, you still may not come out on top. So many factors come into play. You have to "be born at the right time." You have to be in the right place. All this, in addition to having the talent and all that it takes to realize it. If you do get to be king of the hill, there's always the next wave hungering to be where you are. Not for one second am I attempting to dampen ambition in these warnings. As I said earlier, I never tell anyone what to do. I'm only pointing out that needing to be first in your work is no light risk.

Speaking for myself, I never wanted to be better than anybody. I only wanted to dance superbly, to be a rock-solid technician and to make beautiful dances that would engage the heart-minds of audiences. By my own lights, I succeeded only partly. If I had truly mastered technique, if it had come up to the level of my performance style, I think many of my artistic statements would have been more compelling and more widely influential. It's not difficult for me to be objective about my "achievement." At best, I am a minor but interesting artist who distinguished himself by making a personal expression that repelled many and attracted the fierce loyalty of a few. The irony is that by operating within my technical limits I evolved a personal vocabulary and, yes, a personal virtuosity that inspired and freed quite a few young artists who didn't fit the conventional mold. They could see that if one was crazy enough and persistent enough, they too could come bearing gifts, and somewhere out there was enough of an audience that needed those gifts.

All this is by way of honoring the minor artist. One could mutter, "Daniel, isn't this little discourse a bit self-serving?" My reply: "If that's the way you take it, there's nothing I want to do or say about that." Getting on with it, I have a long-standing private war with the critics. (Which of us doesn't?) One of their favorite ploys is that only time would tell whether so-and-so was a *great* artist. The implication of this gratuitous pronouncement is that what you now think is great, lovely and beautiful may in reality be dross, junk and bad art. Even more pernicious is the corollary that what isn't great ain't much at all. I deny this with heat. This ploy is of course self-serving for the critics, since in their scholarly "objectivity" they are possessed of an overview denied to the rest of us. We, artists and audience, are blinded with the sweat of the moment and so our ecstasy is suspect and awaits the harsh judgment of time—and the critics.

I am going to such lengths in this matter of "minor artists" because I suspect and have sensed the existence of not a few dance performers and choreographers who have enveloped themselves in a painful mantle of failure. This in spite of the audiences they have charmed, changed and inspired. This in spite of the lovely personal permutations they have spun out of the work of the dance giants. This in spite of the concert they lovingly danced way off in the small high school in the middle of the Great Plains of America, or in the lofts of San Francisco, or in Seattle, Minneapolis or New York City. *They are what makes dance in America.* Yes, the leaders and the greats are the source, and the others are the river and every bit as precious and necessary to our flow into the future.

Mediocrity

Minor is one thing, and mediocre is another. I first became aware of a troubling accommodation to the challenges of dance when I began to tour as a concert dancer. Until then I had worked primarily on Broadway and had only experienced the blazing passion of some of the best dancers in the country to make it. On the road, in the university dance departments and in the various summer workshops, I was occasionally disconcerted by a not-so-small number of dance students and, yes, teachers who were operating on some low-grade level of energy that, to me at least, had absolutely nothing to do with dance. It took me some time to fathom what was going on.

There are people who are drawn to dance, but somewhere along the way they realize or come to believe that they are either not

HOW TO DANCE FOREVER

very good, or, at best, ordinary. For one reason or another they don't quit to do something else. Everyone knows they have opted to become dancers and backing out seems impossible, or they're locked into dance as their only means of livelihood. Notwithstanding, something inside has snapped and *they have resigned themselves to mediocrity.* They *look* as if they are dancing, they *act* as if they are dancing, but, as the acting teachers say with total contempt, they're only indicating.

When this leaden energy surfaces in a master class or a workshop, whether in an individual in whom I sense a talent or, even more upsetting, in a group that has adopted a laid-back style, I go a little crazy. I would guess that most teachers and choreographers will sympathize, having experienced and been frustrated by this baffling phenomenon—dancers who look as if they are dancing but aren't.

So many reasons for this. Those who have decided, consciously or not, that they have, at best, a limited aptitude for the art of the dance and *choose not to leave off* not only live a gray tragedy but do no honor to the image of dance, either in the studio or before the public. But what of the inexplicable ones with talent whose low-key energy flattens their expression? I think this is where teachers and choreographers can heal something that may have taken place many years ago. Early grueling experiences with demanding, perfectionist parents and/or teachers implant the conviction in some young ones that whatever they do will never be right and will never be enough. I don't believe these are lost people.

Being human, we possess emotional and physical resources beyond imagination. Being human, we too easily accept limits imposed by others and/or our own complicity. And yet, subject us to a crisis, an accident, a turn in the road, a challenge and surprise—we discover resources we never knew we possessed. Rich powers may appear in that desert of mediocrity.

A loving and encouraging atmosphere can and has brought many a young dancer in touch with hidden powers, creating another dancer artist. Somewhere I read that most of the extraordinary achievers had mothers who *expected* them to be wonderful. Mothering—fathering—befriending—choose your style, but letting your students know that you expect them to be wonderful may open the door to flowering for many of them.

The Heart-Mind of the Dancer

The Net of Style

There is a question that has haunted this century. On innumerable couches in innumerable psychiatrists' offices, on an infinite number of porch steps, over drinks in multitudinous bars, the same question is moaned by men, women and adolescents: "Who am I?" Throughout the reigns of Freud to Erikson to Esalen, the moaning rises in a constant crescendo: "Who am I?" Is there anything more earnest and admirable than this search for identity? It's been with us for at least the last half century and it hasn't gone out of style.

All of which brings up the question of style. "Style" and "the real me" are concepts bound together like the strands of a rope. A rope that weaves an invisible but powerful net. Caught in a net one can move, but just so far. I have come to view style as the most subtly pernicious of limitations upon human freedom and creativeness. The moment you know for sure who you are, you have entered a prison of which you are the architect.

I first became aware of this when I began to work intensively and creatively with improvisation both as a discipline to open up expressiveness and as a basic performance skill. Having always had a relish for the game of "becoming someone else," I was disconcerted by the difficulty so many people in my workshops had with the wonderful exercises involving imitation. It took some time to realize they were *protecting* what they felt was their "essence."

Several of the first exercises or games that I give involve one person finding on impulse a sound and motion phrase and, after allowing it to flower, giving it to someone else. To "receive" what is given literally means to imitate, duplicate, "become" the giver—to take over the sound/motion of the other and even more profoundly re-create that persona. It's an exercise that becomes a delightful, challenging game when it is done fully, innocently and with daring. Too often a reserved dancer, upon being offered an outrageously raucous "gift" from another dancer, would tone it down—"civilize it" or freeze up entirely. The reverse could just as easily take place. A high-energy person would receive some delicate set of gestures and replicate them up to the tenth power. In either case, the given task of imitation was shunned in favor of preserving one's style. Blow it up or refine it, but never accept what is given, which is precisely what the exercise is about.

HOW TO DANCE FOREVER

Provoked, I have launched into the following tirade:

The power of all artists runs on two legs, craft and creativeness. Craft rests on the talent to imitate. By imitation, we learn from our teachers. By imitation, we learn from the life about us. By imitation, we verify the accuracy and truth of our observations. By imitation, we discover resources we never realized are ours.

When we are confronted by a pattern completely alien to us, the uncritical, uninhibited immediate mirroring opens up new doors for us, not only as artists but as human beings. Some of you have a secret terror that you will stop being you, whatever that means. You're always you, and as an artist, to "become someone else" with your craft, your taste and your creativeness, you reassemble bits and pieces of who you are like a mosaic to re-create the other person out of the raw material of your own persona.

It's the equivalent of an artist having the craft to sketch accurately what is seen. This skill is possessed and used by most of the great abstract artists.

The word *style* suggests a stance. *The American Heritage Dictionary*'s definition: "The combination of distinctive features of literary or artistic expression, execution or performance characterizing a particular person, people, school or era." Very early in my career, in Anna Sokolow's company, at a time when I had the barest outline of a dance technique, an older man in the company informed me, "You're coming along, but as yet you don't have style." "Style? What's that?" "Can't be explained," he said down his nose. "You'll know when you have it." A few years later, sitting on a park bench in Madison Square Park in New York City, exhausted after a brutal rehearsal with I don't remember whom, it came to me and I spoke into the cold night air with conviction: "Style is personal authority."

That neatly served for a number of years, until it slowly began to dawn on me that always having a firm grip on the reins was a surefire way of finding only what I was looking for and learning what I already knew. "Personal authority" is precisely what all those young dancers at Brockport told me they wanted. Their way of putting it was "to gain control over my body," and, by implication, over themselves, their totality. From the word go, control, authority, discipline and, yes, *style* are assumed to be as much a part of what it takes to become a dancer as pliés.

Well, yes and no. We do need control and we don't. Nothing

The Heart-Mind of the Dancer

of any importance to what it takes to be a human being exists without paradox. Style, as I claimed a moment ago, suggests a stance. A stance suggests a possible rigidity. The deliberate and conscious embracing of a stance brings to mind a tennis player who with correct form misses the ball. Closer to home are dancers who cannot cope with an unfamiliar choreographer giving unfamiliar movement. Even worse is not expecting the unexpected. Locking into a style, consciously or inadvertently, means that tomorrow or even the next five minutes contains a threat if your style is not up to it.

The last thing any person who has worked long and hard at a craft has to worry about is having a style. There's no way that a distinctive style will not flourish. Freedom exists when that style is a garment easily thrown off *if it gets in the way*. Prison is when it gets glued to your skin and even seeps down into your bones.

It must be obvious by now that I'm getting at something. Yes, a suggestion for an ideal way to be. Being ideal is probably impossible, but reaching for it may be the richest and most exciting way to do it all. The goal is to *be*, without giving yourself a name, without saying who you are, without defining your limits, without spelling out your weaknesses or even your strengths. You will never be anything but what you are, but, once again, being human you are an awesome creature with powers, complexities and possibilities beyond your imagination. Not naming yourself, not defining yourself, opens gates, knocks down walls and makes it impossible for anyone, including you, to anticipate your scenario.

Is this dangerous? Of course! Is living in a prison safe? Living out in the open, you expose yourself to the surprises created by you yourself. Bad impulses could rear up. Bad for you or cruel to others. So, don't do them. Having an impulse and pursuing it are two radically different things. Act out every desire and you will go to prison—not to a metaphor, to a real one. Not armored or frozen in your style, your hidden insides will surface more easily. The question being raised here is, Can a person live well without self-knowledge? Can an artist?

Free of the net of a rigid style, one can approach the scary ideal of the Greek demigod Proteus, who had the power to assume many shapes and forms. I think, being human, we are all protean, if we allow ourselves responsiveness to the moment. The Taoist ideal is water. It takes on the shape of whatever container holds it and yet is never anything less than itself. Certainly we of the

HOW TO DANCE FOREVER

theatre should have that talent as a matter of course. In our work, we play roles exactly like Proteus. One of these might be our own self, but even that requires an imaginative leap outside in order to step back inside to make a creative statement. My premise is that all people have that Protean capacity, yet few exploit it, except under the pressure of extreme adversity or extraordinary good luck, say, winning a million-dollar jackpot.

Speaking of good luck, for us a great performance is a jackpot. I was into the first minute or so of a solo concert at the University of Arizona in Tucson when I became aware of a frame of mind that was giving me a power of dance that I had never before experienced. It was good, so good and so right that I wondered why I had never used it before. I roared through that evening with an inner triumph and joy. I do not really know what the audience experienced, but for me I had never felt so on. A few days later, I had another concert scheduled; where, I do not recall. The forgetting will explain itself in a moment.

I couldn't wait to get to that town, to set up the show, to get on the makeup and dance and do that again. Came curtain time, I dived into the evening with a zest. It did not take long to realize that something was seriously wrong. It was not working. I was in that worst of all performing states, that cold place a few feet off, back and to the right, *watching myself*. There was not one moment when I could slip into the folds of what I was dancing. I was locked into that dispassionate, judgmental distance. Does any other profession have a comparable state of mind? For me, it is the bottom of the pit. I have always known that if it were to recur too often, that would be a sign to get off the stage—permanently. That night was only half a nightmare because I was smart enough to realize that whatever it was that ignited me in Tucson was not available. I think it was someplace in the early part of *Indeterminate Figure* that I thought to myself, "This misery has to stop. Forget Tucson and do what you can with what you have here." That may have been the smartest thought I've ever had in my whole life. Chuang-tze would have been proud of me. If I read those venerable Taoists correctly, they are saying, "No history." Each moment, each day, each turn in the road, gives birth to its own conditions, rules and creative demands. The rest of the evening was tolerable, not great, but, as the expression goes, I could live with it.

Every performance since then, I come onstage curious as to

what I will find there and gird up to turn *that* into magic. If ever I think of the Tucson performance I'm happy it happened to me, but I will never try to make it happen again.

There's nothing startling in the statement that an early success can haunt and even hurt a career. Going further, one could say *all* success becomes a hurdle when one clings to it. Having success should give you joy. Period. The next task is the next task. Using the rules, formulas and "secrets" of past successes will blind one to the realities and the specifics of the present. All of this applies equally to past failure. Engaging the present loaded down with the guilt and self-doubt of past failure guarantees less than your full power. To sum it up: Do not let your history determine your style.

To this point, we have discussed style that is self-generated, coming from within. There is another source of style, equally powerful, coming from without. In its most insidious form, it shapes us while we are not looking. A few years ago I was looking, unsuccessfully, for the address of a potential sponsor when I recalled that she had attended a concert given in my Broadway studio theatre the previous season. Whenever I did these concerts, my manager would leave a loose-leaf notebook of blank, unlined pages open on the desk directly in front of the elevator entrance. Coming or going the audience had to notice it and, beside it, a little sign asking, WOULD YOU LIKE TO BE ON OUR MAILING LIST? Following each concert the pages would be filled.

I found the guest book and leafed through it to find her name—with no luck. Certain that I had missed it, I started over again, but this time, after turning three pages, I was distracted by an irrelevant but startling observation. The first page was headed by a neat someone who had entered his name off to the left in a tight small script and then his address, on the same level as the signature, an inch to the right. *There were sixteen more names on that page, all in a row, directly below the first one, all but one neatly written and all but one with small characters.* The addresses, similarly, were all spaced off a bit to the right and on a parallel line with the signature.

The next page had only three names and addresses filling it completely. The first signer had begun in the upper center of the page with block letters half an inch high, his street address directly below, and city, state and zip on a separate line below, all of which went two and a half inches down the page. The next two took the same format of large printing and a line for each name, street address, city and state. The next page had the same format, with one exception: The first person had a small and somewhat florid lettering, with the three lines taking up about an inch. There were a total of seven such blocks on this page, all an inch or so in height, the last one being one of the current young hotshots of the avant garde. In fact, these people are some of the most sophisticated New Yorkers around. Who else would come to Daniel's concerts?

Page after page the pattern was consistent. If the first person took up a discreet, small, three-line block in the upper left-hand corner with a line drawn underneath, there would be two columns of such blocks. The most astonishing page was headed by a large block formation of three lines, written in a chaotic high-energy script, with an unruly capital letter *J* that slashed down through the other lines. All the other names and addresses were high energy, large and messy. Two were squooshed in on the diagonal, along the right side. Actually, there was one neat, controlled script, but in a block the same size as all the others.

These are not docile people, but they are subject—as you and I are—to a phenomenon labeled by the psychologists as imprinting. *The American Heritage Dictionary* defines *imprinting* as "a learning process occurring early in the life of a social animal, whereby a behavior pattern is established through association with a parent or other role model."

I hope it frightens you. It frightens me. In a way it's the story of culture and tradition. *The first person seen sets the style.* How many critical choices in your life and mine have been decided by someone who got there first and, conversely, how many were determined out of our own necessity and insight? How many were determined by imprinting? The shocker in those mailing-list pages is that not only did people adopt the format established by the first person but most picked up on the energy and the *size* of the letters. One would think these are too personal to be affected, but they were.

Observation is a great thing, important for all people as well as artists, and having the talent to "become what you see" is part of the performer's craft. However, becoming what you see *without realizing it or, even worse, believing that is what you chose* is sacrificing your individuality unknowingly.

I promised you paradoxes and this one is a lulu. Being able to

The Heart-Mind of the Dancer

imitate expands your capacities when it's a deliberate, conscious act within the practice of your craft as an artist. Imitating unwittingly and believing you are making choices spontaneously when you aren't are actually steps toward becoming the clone of what you see and of your peers. The latter hardly qualifies as a description of an artist and the former is part of the tradition of all art.

To draw all of this together, the net of style is made of a subtle and barely visible weave. In the warp, we define ourselves and so limit our possibles. In the weft, our society, parents, peers and critics define who we are and can be. Warp and weft, subtle yet so strong one can live a life and never know one was trapped from the start.

A third factor can enter into style. It relates to the weft of society. It is fluid, flexible and anything but rigid. It's called charm. It's the style of many politicians, salespeople, conmen, conwomen and some very sweet people. They are all observant and sensitive to you and me, quickly determining what it is we want and would like to hear. Some use these acute observations to package and ribbon whatever they want to hustle in a fashion we will find irresistible. The sweet ones want more than anything to please us and to be loved. Their other hungers, demands, beliefs and needs, which might conceivably dismay or ruffle us, are repressed, hidden from sight. One group charms to manipulate, the other, to be loved.

It is so easy to view this way of relating to people and to audiences as the ploy of *other* people. I'd be lying if I claimed that I never resorted to this manipulation of others in life and onstage. I hate it when I do it. Sometimes I rationalize that it's necessary and so do you. The horror is when it becomes *a way of life* and the essential style of one's art. If at the center is aiming to please, to charm and to direct all of one's creative talent in such a direction, where is the charmer? Who is the charmer? What is left when you take away the smile?

This is the curse of our business—the need to be loved. The brilliant actor Frank Langella, while playing on Broadway in Arthur Miller's *After the Fall*, said in an interview:

> It could be the single worst trap for an actor to want to be liked. It's a stultifying insecurity. It's in me, it's in all of us, and we must fight it. To want to be liked is to ultimately compromise. You begin

to live for other people. It shouldn't rule your life and it shouldn't rule the roles you play. I have failed as Quentin whenever I overplayed the sympathetic side. Whenever I tried to entertain, I lost the audience.*

In a class called Acting Technique for Dance Performance I asked the students to write down the earliest stage instructions they could recall. What they related were horror stories about never looking at the audience, "giving it your all," "feeling beautiful," smearing Vaseline on their teeth and smiling, smiling, smiling. What was being danced was the least of it. Being loved and successful was all.

I remember coming offstage while working in Broadway musicals and finding my upper lip stuck because the gums had dried out from the constant exposure of the constant smile. We are again caught on the cross of a paradox. Which of us doesn't enter the stage, after the trembling in the wings and the many years of preparation, without the passion to be loved by that anonymous mass out there in the dark before us? And yet, if we are to be artists, true to our convictions, dare we bend the vision we have so lovingly shaped, so that it will be liked, loved and applauded? If we bend our work to guarantee success with the many, have we bent our vision out of shape? Do we sometimes end up saying what we didn't mean and, worse, not saying what we mean, all for love—of audience and, worse, of the critics? And what kind of love for an audience, or for anyone for that matter, is it that lies and conceals an inner truth to guarantee acceptance and/or success?

If we back off and look at this "charm" style, be it by conmen, conwomen or artists, then the only value is success. Who you are, what you are and what you have to give get dumped in the process. Well, that's one way to survive. Something gets lost along the way, or perhaps one should say "someone" gets lost. What is left? A style.

Control and Release

In all of this hammering about the net of style, having a style might appear to be exactly like having a disease. Not at all. To repeat an earlier thought, you can't spend years learning and

---

*The New York Times, November 5, 1984.

practicing a craft and an art without acquiring a style that defines you and makes much of what you do recognizable. The great English silver craftsmen set their personal seal on the bottom of all their work. Most of us have only to be seen to be recognized, even without the aid of a program. The net I was discussing above is mostly what comes to us from the outside, obscuring or blocking what is inside.

There is another interaction or seesaw of energies that springs from our inner depths. Every act, choice and motion that we perform is colored by two opposites: control and release. The balance, the *proportion* between these, is the profile and the very texture of how each of us dances—and lives. One can even precisely call up epochs, cultures and nations by describing them in these terms. In the court of Louis XIV, even the removal of a handkerchief from the pocket was performed as if in a prescribed and controlled ritual. Seventy-five years later, during the French Revolution, France, particularly Paris, took off in a storm of released passion, jubilation, triumph, individual freedom and rage. In the next century, again in Paris, a new "war" raged between two beautiful dancers, Marie Taglioni and Fanny Elssler. To quote the erudite Lincoln Kirstein writing of Taglioni: "Under the vague outline of skirt and bodice, there is pure strength; geometry the base of every arabesque."* Théophile Gautier on Elssler: "Fanny is quite a pagan dancer . . . exposing her thigh . . . she bends freely from her hips, throwing back her voluptuous arms. . . ."†

I think many promising careers in dance are either cut short or never quite realized because in spite of the talent and the craft ability, there is a destructive imbalance between control and release. To ensure clarity, I'll define the terms. Control is the ideal of knowing clearly and specifically what it is you wish to do and *doing exactly that, no more and no less.* Release is "going with it," "letting go" and/or permitting an impulse to flow *without needing to know or control what will happen next.*

Controlling all, either as a performer or a choreographer, creates icy, dispassionate and alienated work. Correction: The only emotion visible is the passion to be "correct." Yet lacking control and always "going with it" are literally definitions of self-indulgence,

---

*From Lincoln Kirstein, *Dance: A Short History of Classic Theatrical Dancing* (Brooklyn, N.Y.: Dance Horizons, 1969), p. 244.
†Ibid. p. 247.

sloppiness and the loss of craft. In spite of having a secure technique and all the skill needed, those who lack control disregard their power of control in favor of at every moment needing to "feel deeply" what they are doing. Messy at best.

If the balance between these two essentials is so vital and delicate a matter, how much conscious choice needs to be exercised? I think none, *unless you sense something is not right with a phrase of movement or a particular role or, most serious of all, what is happening to your career.*

This interplay between control and release operates within a single measure of music. The waltz can present a stumbling block for young dancers if they try too hard to be correct by precisely and deliberately spelling out each beat. It becomes a waltz when they learn that the downbeat must be *done* and the "2, 3" just happens. A musical and dynamically right downbeat, or "1," creates, gives birth to, the "2, 3." To dance the waltz, you don't *do* the "2, 3," you let them happen.

Every movement we do, every performance and our entire lives are sculptured by where we choose to direct our actions and when we allow ourselves to flow with the moment.

On the Cutting Edge

Dr. Cary L. Cooper, a psychologist from the University of Manchester Institute of Science and Technology in England, did a study rating the stress of various occupations in the workplace. The ratings range from 2.0 for librarians to 8.3 for miners. Upon my query, he wrote admitting to not having rated dancers, but he did do actors, giving them a 7.5 rating, *the same as pilots and prison officials!*

You dance? You live on the cutting edge of existence. Your body, your mind, your heart, all go out periodically to touch your limits. Few professions demand that. Not many people venture out there. It's a thrilling game and we come away exhilarated and extended—if we get away with it.

From your very first dance class to the one you took this morning, there is suspended out there, in front of you and your imagination, an exquisite motion, but so damn elusive. In the plié preparation, you are a tiger crouching to spring and finally capture that dazzling tour de force you just know you can do, yet to date have never achieved. In technique classes, when I find a group of students infected by an unwelcome timidity, I drop one of my favorite guru-farts: "This room and this time are dedicated to reaching the impossible."

In this reaching, we constantly risk failure. Can it be that the wrong choices, the missteps and the boners are the glue of success? Of course, too much glue and . . . ! Clarity, beauty and the rare moments of perfection are partially the profits of learning what not to do. Listen to Dennis the Menace advising his friend Joey as they watch a sculptor chisel a statue of a horse: "It's easy, Joey. Just get a big rock an' chip off all the pieces that don't look like a horse." In spite of Dennis, ours is not an easy way to live. Exciting, yes, but it takes its toll, and we need strength to pay the fare. Perhaps the core talent at the heart of success is how good you are at picking yourself up.

Consider the hub of our work: rehearsals. They are laced with wires of tension which sometimes make it almost impossible to get anything done. There are the leaders and the led. Leadership and followership. Toughies. "If I only knew then what I know now": a sad and pathetic remark. In years past, at several intervals, I directed and choreographed for dance companies. Some of these experiences were the best times of my life, but some were the opposite. I had a profound misunderstanding of what it means to be a leader. I now know that there is no way to be in a position of telling people what to do without at some time discovering that you are not loved by one or more company members; nay, they may even *dislike you*. Whenever I would encounter this rejection, I'd be crushed. Ironically, during some of the worst times, I managed to do some of my best work, but at a cost I did not care to face.

It's not impossible that this vulnerability on my part played a role in the extensive amount of work I have done as a soloist. Of course there have been times when I disliked *myself*, but that was always coupled with enough empathy to get me past that worst of all hurdles.

I think successful leaders, aside from being talented at what they do, are never derailed by hostility from their followers. On the contrary, they will even take this negative attitude and turn it to their advantage, either by taking time out to make a convert, isolate the adversary, make concessions, or by letting them go.

A rather young film director was asked how he handled the awesome task of leading so many people who were all his seniors.

HOW TO DANCE FOREVER

Behind his smart-aleck reply is something every director needs to know in order to survive. He said, "The first day on the set, I fire someone." My other weakness was that I could never fire anyone, always rationalizing that I needed the malcontent. In one case, finding an equal talent for a troublesome dancer in the middle of summer and in the middle of rehearsals seemed impossible. The anchor of his negative competitiveness was dragging every rehearsal down into a misery for me and for the rest of the company. Without him, I would have made do, *and any other like him would have thought twice about playing the same ploy.* I didn't fire him and I suffered.

Following is equally complex: Most performers are proud, skilled, intelligent creatures. It is not rare that they are given uninspired and unbeautiful direction. How many have the good fortune to work with first-rate choreographers? A dancer has but two choices. Whatever movement is laid upon them, their sole responsibility is to make the choreography look beautiful. Those who do this are called dancers, truly professional dancers. If the material is unspeakable and an offense to the taste of the dancer, leaving is an alternative. It's a big world and there are a few more opportunities today than yesterday.

Yes, but what if you are fortunate enough to work with that great artist whose work does inspire you but from whom you are receiving a hard time? There is no justice and few things are neat. There are angels whose choreography creates pure yawn time and there are cruel devils who have made dance history.

What to do when you are being cut at, insulted and manipulated by one whose work you love? You find a quiet spot, clean your head out and set a scale before you. In one dish you put the value of the association and what you can gain from continuing it in spite of the negatives, and in the other, what you are losing as a human being and ultimately as an artist by staying. You have all the elements of a painful decision.

I myself never could handle or accept disrespect and/or insult from any teacher or choreographer. I either fought back or quit. For years I carried a card with seven unused classes remaining on it. The teacher had backhandedly made an uncalled-for disparaging remark and that was it. I never returned. Yes, he was a very good teacher. But knowing myself, it was clear that I was no longer capable of learning from the man.

The Heart-Mind of the Dancer

Early on, I was a terrible follower. My gods and masters were few and far away, up on the stage. With one exception, I drenched every one of my teachers in critical disapproval. Later, as I became stronger, I was more pliable and appreciative. Now I'm a pussycat when directed.

Reaching for the impossible, risking failure, leading and/or following, there's no walking away from the fact that dancing is layered with stress. From student to company member to company director, and from the classroom to the rehearsal hall to the stage, we are forever yearning for the impossible, being asked to do the impossible, and as we accept this task, we are constantly being watched and *judged*. To boot, our pay for all of this heroism is more often than not meager or, at best, uncertain. Talk of testing a love. All the while our capital investment is an expensively trained, nonrenewable, vulnerable, mysterious mass of bone, sinew, muscle, guts and mind, all of indeterminate staying power. How do we do it? Why do we do it? Love is the easiest answer, but it's not enough. Love needs help. We all have our own ways to cushion and drain off that ever-present stress.

For me, for years, there was no question in my mind that I had to have cigarettes to concentrate, to do my work and to relax. I finally was convinced that this was dumb, but when all of my attempts to quit smoking failed, I gave up and sought help. In my case, it was the Smokenders program that worked. Quitting after forty years remains my proudest achievement to date. Without belaboring the issue, if you realize you have become what the social therapists call chemically dependent and wish to be free but cannot do it yourself, waste no time, get help.

The entire process is about expanding our limits. Alcohol, drugs and tobacco can do just that. There's no question that for some people they produce fantastic results and it is equally certain that a consistent and/or extensive use of "feeling better" boosters to get through the rough times or arrive at the "high times" will in time produce the exact opposite.

Occasionally, a self-portrait has value. Below is an alphabetical list of some methods people use to feel better when burdened by stress. Check off your methods, then back off and ask yourself, "What am I doing for myself?" Or should it be "What the hell am I doing to myself?"

___ alcohol

___ cocaine

___ eating

___ grass

___ meditation

___ napping

___ partying

___ reading a book

___ resting

___ seeing something: a movie, a play, *a dance concert*?

___ sex

___ sleeping

___ smoking a cigarette—or two—or twenty

___ the hard stuff

___ TV

"Stop the World, I Want to Get Off"

This was the catchy title of a Broadway musical revue and it probably sounds as if in the last few sections of this chapter I've been talking about just that. They are all about dealing with the difficulties and "too muches" of our particular kind of existence. Thus, they all carry a negative charge: the stress of living on the cutting edge, cooling it by meditating, turning off with ten-minute naps, etc. Actually, I believe there is a hunger implicit in all of them. This hunger is intrinsically a positive energy and, not simplistically, "getting away from it all."

I think "getting away from it all" may very well be a deeply

The Heart-Mind of the Dancer

hidden metaphor for the opposite: getting *to* something, a state of being going back to our earliest form of awareness. At some point in our moist nascence, as Mama went about her business, we became sentient. When we finally tumbled out, the world of sensation enlarged fantastically, but in one sense it didn't change at all. Both inside the warm, salty sea and outside in the stinging air, for quite some time, there is no self apart from what is not self; everything is us and we are everything. We cannot distinguish between what we feel, see, smell and taste and what we are. We do not know that we are separate. We do not know that we are alone in our skin. It takes months for an infant to begin to recognize dimly that there is an outside, another other than self. Self is a discovery that probably takes place in bits and pieces. It just happens without our ever taking note of the transition. In all probability, this explains why we don't remember anything from that time.*

On the other hand, I am speculating that it is a mode of existence to which all human beings intermittently long to return or do return. I believe we hunger for it, we need it, and it is probably necessary to our mental and emotional health. Back in the beginning of this chapter, I describe a form of it—the dancer's high, those moments when we merge with the music, the floor, the air, without any awareness of self. Coming offstage we might mutter under our breath, "I was really into that."

I believe all people need this experience, this total involvement. The fortunate ones are those who can find this intermittently in the course of their daily work. I've been getting it writing this book. Still, when the work is done, I get that hunger. Imagine the craving of one whose work never gives them this merging of self and other. I'll use the image of swimming. Some people fear the water and at most might dangle their feet in it. Others will only paddle about in the shallow water. Some will swim out but always keep their head up out of the water. Finally, there are those who plunge completely and for a little while disappear from view; in our case, from *self-view*. There are an infinite number of ways that humans choose to plunge, plunge completely. Take my handy checklist of stress blotters: alcohol/cocaine/eating/grass/meditation/napping/partying/reading a book/resting/seeing some-

*One school of therapy violently disagrees with this assertion. In fact, they imply that full health and self-knowledge is not possible without recalling or, unbelievably, reliving prenatal existence. Of course, they might be right.

HOW TO DANCE FOREVER

thing: a movie, a play, a dance concert/sex/sleeping/smoking a cigarette—or two—or twenty/the hard stuff/TV. You can add religious experiences, rock climbing, building a bench, talking long distance to a dear friend and taking a shower. Probably most important is the capacity to become so completely involved in our life's work that we lose from time to time all self-awareness.

Some of these can kill you, some will make you fat, one will gain you a bench and many will make life worth living. If you are aware of what it is you are doing as you plunge completely, then there are three questions worth exploring: Is your choice a lovely, enriching submersion or is it stupid beyond belief, i.e., one third of a day slogged out in front of the tube or damp with alcohol all through the day? Is it an action that is pervading your life and mucking up your productiveness? Of the innocent diversions, do you grudgingly spare yourself only a few brief moments of what could be a lovely part of your life and probably as necessary as vitamin C? Worst of all, if work, the job, never gives this release to a person at the end of eight hours, he/she is in trouble and will desperately need three beers, or a double Scotch, a joint, a snort or devastating multiples of one or more of these. Or, still another path "away from it all" are those pretty pills that school one in indifference, distancing, complacency and not feeling: the tranquilizers with their elegant Latin names.

In a very real sense, this section is a repeat of an earlier one in this chapter: Control and Release. I'm coming at it from a different angle, hoping that it will help focus attention on an ideal of which the Greeks spoke and wrote much. They had a word for it: *sophrosyne*, which literally meant "moderation." Poetically and as a way of life, *sophrosyne* represented for them a balance between the Apollonian and the Dionysian, the rational and the ecstatic. Without this balance, survival is either difficult or a drag. With it, it's a rich life, every minute.

Wealth and Beauty

These are two states of being most of us envy. Ironically, each is an obstacle to survival as a dancer. By wealth I mean having, from the beginning, sufficient means and income to live very well without having to work for the indefinite future. Beauty? The Russians have a word that does it better: *krassieveye*. Upon entering any space, a man or woman possessing *krassieveye* will stop conversation and turn heads.

The Heart-Mind of the Dancer

The wealthy have the privilege of turning away from difficulty and unpleasantness. The beautiful know they can disintegrate hurdles with one luminous glance. These difficulties, unpleasantnesses and hurdles demand from most of us all our efforts. We poor, plain ones get strong in the struggle. The early, easy victories of beauty do not create that core of steel. Silver Spoon, triumphing over the easy obstacles of survival, is left too weak for the tough ones of artistic survival. No one makes it in our business without a profound put-out. The beauties and the wealthies are poorly schooled for necessity.

However, becoming wealthy after having been poor rarely weakens or slackens the energy, and becoming successful endows the funny-looking ones with an ineffable attractiveness. I salute all those dancers with *krassieveye* and wealth who survive, persist and go on to make fine dance art in spite of their "advantage." Theirs can be considered a moral victory.

The Mind Can Use a Journal

In the early seventies, I brought the WORKGROUP, the improvisational dance company I was directing at the time, to Johnson State College in Vermont for a summer residency. Early on, I gave a solo concert and a young Vermonter became a fan. A recently graduated architect, he didn't seem to have any work. He spent much time hanging around the dancers, always sat in on my choreography class, and usually joined us at lunch.

Wherever he went, he had one of those black notebooks favored by artists for sketching, only I discovered he wasn't sketching. He was taking down what I was saying! Never having bowed to a master, whenever I realize someone is shoving a pedestal under my feet I kick it away. I snorted at him, "Man, you want a guru? You got a guru. You. You're the only real guru you ever gonna get." (Part of my deromanticizing process is to talk slightly gross English.) I have such a resistance to anyone listening with a noncritical mind, I found myself constantly mocking him. Gently of course, for he wasn't a fool by any means and I was flattered, in spite of myself. Returning the next summer, I learned he had found a genuine guru, one who made a living being wise. Still, my Vermont architect attended to my words and just as carefully noted them down in the black sketchbook that was always with him.

A few years later, needing a vacation badly, having little money for it and loving that area, I rang John the architect to ask whether he knew of an inexpensive place for rent. Unbelievably, he offered his home, an apartment over a four-car garage on a rather elegant estate with a little pond for swimming. He said he could spend that week happily with friends. I accepted gratefully. The place was wonderful—spacious, comfortably furnished, and stuffed with art books and records. But to this day what I remember most are the two towers of black sketchbooks. Each stood three feet high on either side of his desk. They were all identical with the ones he had lugged about those two summers.

I found myself shifting from my memory of mocking his note-taking to a secret envy. I thought of those thousands of thoughts, mine and others, which I had jotted down on thousands of scraps of paper. Where were they? Terrible to relate, I have them somewhere, since I throw nothing away. They're never available, except by accident or during an episodic housecleaning. Too bad. There have been times when some creative turmoil I was going through was clarified by the good luck of finding and rereading notes of the previous year. Here this man had his entire intellectual history—questions, quotes and musings—within reach. I admired what I saw and wished I had done likewise. A journal is a good thing for an artist. A day doesn't pass that doesn't contain something worth noting—an event, a passing thought, a teacher's trenchant remark or an astonishing newspaper clipping. These things are gold and should not be lost.

Footnote to the the above: John has now become some kind of guru to a circle of builders and artists. With a small group he started to remodel old houses. Then, not only designing but contracting to build some private homes with his small army of young colleagues, he snowballed the operation into an enormous success. Now he's retired, barely forty, with enough money to do what he really wants to do: paint and teach. He acquired the beautiful old mill beside the bridge over the Johnson River and has started an art school. He is now probably surrounded by attentive young people carrying black sketchbooks.

Read a Book

Though in another passage in this book I put down the experience of working on Broadway, there were actually wonderful moments still vivid in my mind. Almost all of them occurred during rehearsals. Most of the work was done with a great woman who happened to be my wife, Helen Tamiris. To participate in the creative process with that golden fountain of energy was a privilege and a constant roil of excitement.

But I did learn to dislike one aspect of Broadway. Almost invariably, when I think back to a particular show, one part of the experience vanishes or shrinks to a paper-thin moment in time: the auditions. The entire process was always a horror, no matter how considerate and thoughtful Helen tried to be. There was no escaping the brutal logistics of selecting eight dancers out of four hundred who had migrated from every part of the country to "make it." I wonder how Saint Peter feels? I hated participating in that part of show business. Usually, I demonstrated, taught the audition material, called up the dancers, each in their turn, and then joined in the worst part of it all—the final judgment. It was hard watching those restless, aching bodies pretending poise and assurance in a thin, exposed line of eight at a time shifting from one leg to the other, hanging on to the casual smile like a lifeline in a storm. All the while, just ten or twelve feet in front of them, behind a long table, sat the gods of their fate: the choreographer, the director, the author, the music director who had heard them nervously attempt a scale or a tune, one or more of the producers and Daniel.

Some of these brilliant people, poets of the theatre, writers of heartbreaking love songs, played a game of pure cruelty: *They made jokes.* They would use these trembling vulnerable dancers to make sotto voce sardonic and "witty" remarks, literally trying to get the rest of us to break up. The antennae of the judged were supersensitive, and the ripples of discomfort would jostle their bodies. I think they missed none of those "humorous" sallies, even though they acted oblivious to the shards of laughter.

Once while auditioning in a theatre, a rather short young woman came charging onstage like a confident gladiator entering the arena, thrust her sheet music at the pianist and began to belt out a song with a force and volume that was awesome. It was painfully loud and loudness had nothing to do with the song she chose. She then whipped into a dance routine that was violent, virtuosic and tasteless. As she finished, was thanked, and turned to go, one of the benumbed authors muttered, loudly enough for us to hear, "All she needs is to read a book." The shock of her power and equally poor taste plus the unexpected witty thrust of his remark kicked all of us into laughter. I was immediately ashamed of myself, but I never forgot her or the sharpness of his criticism.

Dance is, as noted in the first chapter, a profession that yields best to an early start plus consistent, continuous and intensive training and work. This doesn't leave much time for reading a book. (Although these days, as I glance through the program notes of the major dance companies, mostly modern ones to be sure, the biographies of many of these brilliant dancers do mention a college degree and in some cases even a master's degree.)

Still, the reality is that the generation of young dancers entering the field now was nurtured by the boob tube. Books are in danger of becoming exotic antiques. Teaching as I am now in a major university, I encounter an alarming amount of cultural illiteracy. At the same time, I recall all through my tours, both in the commercial theatre and in the concert field, observing dancers digging out the precious books from deep in their practice bags to be read in the first quiet moment after takeoff.

It goes back to that matter of being a *mensch*, a person with depth and range. A dancer is an artist or should be one. A dance artist in our world will be little more than an attractive physical machine unless she/he knows who Voltaire was, has decided whether or not to read any more of Rainer Maria Rilke, and is aware of what it is that we owe to the ancient Greeks, *because they shaped us, they helped create the world we live in and they point to the life we have failed to live.* To survive as an artist, you have to "read a book."

Sex

Undeniably, ours is a sexy profession. There is our crazy, revealing dress; our constant motion of arms, legs and torsos lifting, turning and leaning on each other; costumes that accurately mold every dimple, swell and declivity; choreography that sings of love; and then the constant dressing and undressing all day long. If you include all of us, students and professionals, we're preponderantly young and the young are bursting with sex, running from it or to it. All of this lives in the envelope of an audience that endows us with a mystique lined with fantasies about our sexuality. Onstage, all of us are potential sex objects. Not a few costume designers distinguish themselves by the provocativeness of how they dress us. How many times is the costume emphasis on our sexuality irrelevant to the theme of the dance we are performing? Even without emphasis, just standing there in the full glare of the lights and the attention, we're sexy. If there's a warp and a woof to dance, is sex the woof?

Ironically, dance rehearsals are usually all business, while places of business are notorious for sexual games and pursuits. Almost every woman I know who has done considerable office work confirms this. My own years of rehearsal on Broadway, in films, on TV and in concert work confirm that rehearsal time is usually anything but an erotic time.

This book is supposed to be about survival. Well, in all probability sex, in all its ramifications and problems, affects not only how long we last but the very choice of dance as a profession. At the very outset, when the question looms not as a fantasy but as a hard question—"Do I really want to spend my life as a dancer?" —those who cannot imagine a complete life without a family realize they are facing a decision that will shape their sexual role in life. The men confront an uncertain and often poor-paying profession. "How do I support a family?" The women, in spite of the new freedom of choice, must deal not only with the contradiction and intricacy of working and child rearing, but they too face an uncertain and often poor-paying profession. Both deal with the devastating effects of touring. At this sway moment, how many talented dancers turn away from dance to some other line of work, to what they believe and hope will be a more stable and profitable existence within the traditional configuration of a family? Many careers, particularly women's, are either interrupted or cut short by shifting to a family life, i.e., forgoing dance to have children.

At this moment, I can see an exquisitely fashioned, brilliant dancer improvising at the last party of an intensive summer workshop that Tamiris and I directed years ago in Maine. At the beginning of the summer, she said she was trying to make up her mind between dance and going on to becoming a psychiatric nurse. Breathless, this beautiful black woman dropped down beside me after the music spun out. "Well," I asked, "which is it going to be?" "Nursing," she said, smiling. I nodded and that was the end of it. Hers was a definitive answer and I never tell anyone what to do. Never learned whether having a family was part of that decision. A good guess is that it was.

To her and all such who turn away from dance, I have but one

HOW TO DANCE FOREVER

question: Is this a choice between two loves, or is it a choice between a love and what is "practical," "sensible" or "safe"? To choose a probably successful line of work for which you have neither a hunger nor a passion but only the press of rationalized necessity is to fail as you begin. To succeed at what you do not love is to fail from the go. One should note that there are dancers who have managed to have a full dance career and a family. I cannot imagine it was easy, but, then, what is?"*

For some young people, particularly the men, there is another fork in the road—the matter of sexual preference. There is the myth that most male dancers are homosexuals. Although it has been almost fifty years since I took my first dance class, I wouldn't dare make a guess as to the truth of this assumption, or even try to compare our profession with bankers, religious leaders or baseball players. I don't know. But answer this: In the entire spectrum of occupational opportunities in America, which offers less harassment and the need for concealment than the profession of dance? True of many of the arts, but none as much as in dance. A homosexual dancer does not have to hide. A judge would. It is possible that there are more homosexual men in dance than in most professions. Also, it's possible that there are proportionately just as many homosexual dentists, football players and judges, but have they found a way of living and hiding at the same time? Difficult questions for which easy answers are no answers.

In any event, few young men enter the profession without having to deal with this hurdle. We don't live merely in the dance community. There are parents, relatives, sweethearts and friends —your gang. "A dancer? What are you? A faggot?" Now there's a hurdle. Deny it and you may be believed with a dollop of doubt. Affirm it and you're an exile in your own community. Our society is rarely kind or tolerant of variations on this theme of sex.

In my own case, when I began to realize the fierce hold dance had on me, I began to doubt myself. "Am I a fairy?" Note: This was the late thirties and at that time, homosexuality was unequivocally, in most minds, including the gays', a sickness. I knew I liked girls—hell, I hungered for them—but there had been one or two moments when I had a brief erotic flurry of sensation in relation to men. Then I thought nothing of it, but when dance

---

*Michael Engel, a talented dancer and choreographer from Minneapolis, read an early manuscript version of this chapter and was moved to enlighten me on what it means to be a father and a dancer. His letter is reproduced on page 331.

began to cover my whole horizon, I thought back and went, "Uh, uh," and hastened to the mental-health clinic at the City College of New York, where I was a student. By this time I had a soupçon of Freud and "knew all about repression." You could think and appear to be one thing but in reality you really were something else. The psychiatrist turned out to be a cold creep and I dropped the business after two chilly sessions. I went on dancing and dancing and dancing and never encountered any man for whom I wanted to shift gears; equally interesting, in all that time, except for one brief halfhearted attempt, no man reached out to me. I wonder. Should I feel a little hurt?

As a questioning sidenote, in dance, is sexual ambivalence never a hurdle for women? I doubt it. Dance is widely thought of as a glamorous and appropriate activity for females. Though it's not improbable that some dancers are lesbians, that is not raised as a bugaboo to young women wanting to dance, as is the equivalent to young men.

In some conservative circles, the opposite may loom up. They believe dancers are loose women. As a matter of history, there has been some substance to this assumption, though little is ever said about it by dance historians. One of the glories of the reign of Louis XIV was the establishment of the Royal Academy of Music and Dance, which included the first professional dance company. It was at the same time a pool of lovers and mistresses for the aristocracy and the wealthy bourgeoisie. This was the case in Italy and most certainly in Russia under the czar. To what extent this atmosphere prevailed in this century I am not prepared to say.

I can relate what Tamiris told me. In the early twenties, while she was still a youngster in the Metropolitan Opera Ballet in New York City, she was engaged for one summer with the Bracale Opera Company on a South American tour. At the intermission of their very first performance, the young American women dancing in the company, along with their startled mamas, were inundated backstage by a small mob of elegantly dressed gentlemen who had left their wives to gossip among each other while they, armed with flowers and smiles, besieged the pretties of their choice with generous invitations. It was plain that this was a custom. They came backstage with the air of men who expected to be greeted with delight and assent to a lovely, "enchanted" evening. Almost all the dancers, but not quite all, greeted the lusting gentlemen with slammed dressing-room doors.

HOW TO DANCE FOREVER

My impression is that this world of frivolity, champagne and you know what is not at all characteristic of dance in America. Of Europe I know little and say less. Here there are bound to be some high livers among the ladies of dance, as in any profession, but from all I've seen, the prevailing focus is a fanatic love and devotion to a demanding profession, usually leading to choices that can only be described as ascetic.

To return to that hurdle, the idea that men who dance must be homosexual. For many men, this is no hurdle. They know who they are, hetero- or homo-, and the assumptions and judgments of other people, one way or the other, are irrelevant and of no concern. For them there is no question, no hesitation and no doubt as to which road they'll take. Good. For them at least, one thing in this confusing life is clear. Some, though, are ambivalent and this can be painful. It would be tragic if a man with homosexual longings were to choose a heterosexual way because of conformity, fear and/or shame. It would be equally self-defeating if a straight man bent before pressures, seduction and/or opportunism. There are those in the gay community who spin myths about their way of life as the only real road to becoming an artist and a fine dancer. Women become the enemy for them. They point to a long list of great artists who were homosexual. Others take the opposite tack, saying that homosexuals cannot possibly become artists of any depth because their experience is "barren" and alienated from most of the human race. Both arguments are shallow and self-serving. Great art is no one's private preserve. Both myths are contradicted by fine artists of both persuasions.

Older, successful people are very powerful, be they men or women of whatever inclination, and when they set their hearts on some lovely young thing, any argument or ploy will serve.

Dear Young Person, Man or Woman:

WHAT DO *YOU* WANT? If you're uncertain, go slow. Your body, in more ways than dance, is your only center. Mucking it up for flattery and someone else's need before you know yours will blow your head out so badly, every part of you will read "MALFUNCTION"; this means dancing, thinking and just plain being.

Happy choices,

Daniel

The Heart-Mind of the Dancer

So the choice is made—to dance and to be defined as a man who dances or a woman who is a dancer. By that very action, a complex cluster of other choices can click into place, unnoticed. The choosers enter the treacherous land of GIVENS. Many women and men know, assume, believe, wouldn't dream of questioning what it means to be a female dancing or a male dancing. For them, it is a given that women are delicate, soft, gentle, tastefully sexy, lovely to look at and never do double air turns. Men, of course, are heroic, strong, forceful and dance "big." They are never delicate, soft, gentle, etc.

Early in my study of ballet, I was taking a beginners' evening class with Mme. Anderson-Ivantzova. I was the only male in a class of girls, teenagers and less. She gave a movement I had not done until then, a forward and back diagonal balancé in waltz time. Being in the second group, I watched the giddy zest of the girlettes bouncing lightly forward and back with their wrists flipping ecstatically. Barely breathing in terror, I took my place, center floor, when it was our turn, took a forward 1, 2, 3, and a back 1, 2, and never got any further. I cut it dead, turned and retreated to the safety of the barre in the rear. Mme. Anderson-Ivantzova hissed, "What iss? What iss?" I pointed to a raised foot, made a painful face. "My ankle. My ankle." The next combination was full of big jumps and wide glissades. She never said a word as I plunged wholeheartedly into it.

That same evening I hurried to the studio of the little company with which I was working at the time, dug out a record of Jewish waltzes (great for steady tempos) and spent two hours doing balancés, trying to discover how to bounce forward and back with relaxed, loose flowing arms and *wrists* and not feel like one of those little girls. So, I taught myself to do it like a "man." I was heroic, grand, big and stiffly proud in the carriage of the head. In time, when I had less fear about who I was, I learned to float as well as to stamp and pound.

It all comes down to image. Some women are locked within the narrow parameters of their particular female image. Whatever movement is given them by teachers, choreographers or even their own choreography is tightly walled in by SOFT on one side and SMALL on the other. Force is a quality best left to men. A large, grand gesture is not ladylike. A percussive attack is bad taste.

This unspoken, unthought given is a "gift" from their earliest days, when their mamas and papas, each with their special input, lay the groundwork for the creation of a "lady"—a woman who will never be so vital as to threaten men, but rather be sweetly attractive to a sufficient number of men to give her the choice of the very best mate. Is this what is called "survival of the fittest"? The right motion earns a "That's my little lady!" The wrong one: "Girls do not sit like that!"

Men were once boys, and boys learn quickly and with a vengeance what is "manly." Dancers caught up in this image are butch, macho, harsh, etc. Some things they can do very well and perform with great excitement, but too much is cut out. An artist of dimension not only has a wide range of choices but also has the subtle and compelling vibration of contradiction. The great female dancers carry with the most fragile gesture the implication of a clap of thunder. The great male dancers allow themselves passive, floating, gentle moments.

In our culture, little boys are encouraged to be competitive and daring. Little girls learn that all little girls should be good and neat and careful. Their traditional games are neither aggressive nor competitive. I believe almost all dancers, as they reach for a richly textured manner of dancing with depth and range, have to confront the limitations of those early traditional roles assigned to the sexes and *refuse to be bound to them*. More than once, while giving master classes on tours, I have encountered students submerged in these traditional identities. Working on a strong phrase cutting across the floor, I will challenge the women, "Pretend that you are a group of heroic male dancers." The display of energy and force is usually a blowout. I tell half to watch the other half, asking, "Do they look like men, or do they look like beautiful women?" The eyes go wide. To a klutz-footed man or one with wooden arms I might say, "Find some woman whose feet [or arms] you admire as impossibly beautiful. Then work behind her all through the class and copy, imitate, blot up all that you observe."

The good news is that in some circles, these gender rigidities are softening. In the WORKGROUP, the improvisational dance company that I directed from 1970 to 1974, it was a common thing for a woman to lift a man. Other companies are opening up the entire range of motion, gesture, texture and virtuosity to both sexes. Long overdue and still a great distance to go, except for a few advanced choreographers.

Aside from the stylistic and artistic limitations of the superfeminine and/or the supermale, I think it is probable that by applying a rigid dynamic to *all* movement, these dancers expose themselves to injuries endemic to each type. Here is another interesting line of research. The hypothesis: The delicate lady in any professional situation will tend to suffer from troubles rooted in weakness, lack of speed and endurance. Mr. Tough Guy will tend to suffer from injuries spiked by unnecessary tension and inappropriate force. Not an easy line of research to pursue, but I'll wager the problems are similar among athletes. An investigation that includes both dancers and athletes might uncover results useful to both fields.

Getting Old

The time for memoirs has come. I am fifty-two years old. I already feel the incessant movement of time. I can measure it in increasingly smaller segments. At the beginning of my life, eternity lay before me. Then I got the taste of decades passing by: later on I could feel the passage of a single year. Now I have developed a feeling for months, weeks, days before eternity will engulf everything once more.*

This is the opening passage of a book by Aleksandr Nekrich, a Russian historian who came to the West in 1976. What caused him to pen this bleak summation I know not. I quote it in full only because it is the picture of that state of mind guaranteed to make a person as old as he/she expects to be. Worse, most of us have that remorseless calendar upon the wall of our minds. It is one of those givens that create exactly what they give out.

NO. NO. NO. With every breath, NO. Your power, potency and potentiality should all be the product of your thirst for living. If you measure them by the yardstick of your chronological age, you're boxed in by limitations designed by you. NO. NO. NO. Yes, have joyous birthday parties celebrating your turbulent entrance into the world, your victorious survival to this moment, and then shift into forward. The game is to do, to know your passion and your thirst and then do. Above all, don't consult the clock. It knows nothing of your powers. Time enough when you fall on your face and ask, "What happened?" One day you will

---

*From Aleksandr Nekrich, *Renounce Fear: Memoirs of an Historian* (London: Overseas Publication Interchange).

run out of steam. That's the nature of living things. *That is a given.* *THE TIMING IS NOT.* Keep your hands on the controls until they slip away.

I've done more dumb things in my life than I want to count, but on this matter of aging I've been a canny cat. At forty I faced up to the irrefutable fact that I really didn't like working on Broadway and what I really wanted was to be in the concert field. A lovely gentleman, a great artist and another canny cat, Paul Draper, convinced me that I could tour a solo program. And I did. I don't remember ever saying to myself, "But Daniel, you're forty years old. A solo program? Shouldn't you start thinking of another way of making it other than performing?" Actually, I came to life at forty. On Broadway I had seen so many beautiful, daring gestures and ideas fold under the iron law of show business; everything had to be a smash, go over big. Everybody had their fingers in the artistic pie and some of those fingers were not very clean. When I found myself on the concert stage doing my solos, for the first time in my life, I knew that if I messed up it was my fault only. And if I did a glory, it was mine. I began to dance better than ever.

Later, when I was really out on my own, after the demise of the Tamiris-Nagrin Dance Company, for a little while I did get into making some rough calculations as to when I would retire —possibly at age fifty-two, but at the latest, fifty-five. Then, I forgot to take note of time and at fifty I went to work on the evening-length solo *The Peloponnesian War,* a two-hour marathon, performing it over fifty times in New York City as well as touring it nationwide. From the ages of fifty-three to fifty-seven, I directed and danced in the improvisational company I mentioned earlier, the WORKGROUP. At fifty-seven I went back to the solo form, constantly creating new works and along the way, at sixty-one, ripping up a knee cartilage. In the same year, I adapted *The Fall,* a novel by Albert Camus, for the stage. It was a monologue—a two-hour monologue. At this time of life, aren't we supposed to start losing our memories according to that calendar? Not knowing any better, I only responded to my love for this devastating work of art by Camus, even though I had not done much straight acting work over the years. I just assume everything is hard to do, so that can't possibly be a sufficient reason for not memorizing forty-two pages of text.

I fall in love with an idea and *whoosh,* there's a contract. It has

The Heart-Mind of the Dancer

to be done. At this writing, my last full concert was in 1984. I was sixty-seven. Viewing the videotapes of the concert, I was shot up. Didn't like what I saw. The joke: The feedback was the opposite. Hard-nosed people insisted it was fine.

All of this must sound like boasting. Of course it is, but actually it isn't. I'm only describing a possibility—a possibility that has been realized by a sufficient number of dancers to demolish the myth that turning forty is the cue to start looking for an alternative way. *It is not a given.* The myth is powerful and not bending to it calls for a powerful assertion of the will to do and some luck.

CHAPTER VII

BACKUP

This chapter is primarily addressed to a very specific group of people: young dance students who have lined up their lives to become professional performers and/or choreographers. Precisely put, they are planning to cover all the necessaries *and* the goodies they will be wanting, *by dancing*. Facing the limited work opportunities available in both concert and commercial dance demands some hard-headed realism.

Before pursuing this, let us regard those young dancers who expect to carry on their professional work within educational structures. If their plans succeed, they will have designed their lives with a built-in backup. Teachers of dance, be they working in private dance studios, colleges, universities or secondary schools,* can and often do, in addition to teaching, pursue their performing and choreographic careers. A few even manage tours. True, they pay a price and so do their friends. They never seem to have enough time to do their "own work" and they never cease to complain about it. Running a private dance studio is a difficult, time-consuming gamble which sometimes rewards all that effort

---

*More and more, we are seeing secondary schools employing teachers of dance, full time. There are even some elementary schools employing dance specialists. We are a growing business!

with considerable economic security. Employment in an educational institution gives the security of a weekly paycheck, lower medical insurance, tax benefits and a pension. All obviously have to be paid for, with time—time devoted to teaching and/or administration.*

I know this too well, for as I write this, I am finally, for the first time in my life, in the position of having a steady job. I am a professor of dance at Arizona State University and, like all my teaching colleagues from coast to coast and up and down the educational ladder, I continually bug my friends about how difficult it is to find the time to do "my work": writing this and several other books on dance. I love the teaching work. In almost every class I experience a "high" wherein I will suddenly come to and realize I have been teaching. My most serious weakness as a teacher is that I never know what time it is, continually getting lost in the excitement of the moment. Still, there is this matter of "my work." Perhaps writing this paragraph will help me deal better with the bumpy contradictions of my three loves: the love of teaching, the love of "my work" and the appreciation of that security fence, the regular paycheck.

Now, to return to the young people to whom this chapter is addressed, those of you who plan to make your living by dancing and/or choreographing. Just as teachers have to face up to the price they must pay for their security, you will have to face the reality that in our country *anyone working in the arts faces the high probability of periods of unemployment of short or long duration.* There are a few young people who, because of a staggering talent, the position in which they find themselves and luck, fall right into employment and never need to do work-work. For many dancers this is not the case.

Some dancers, from the very moment they arrive in the big city—New York, Los Angeles, San Francisco, Chicago and even Seattle or Minneapolis—have made the most serious error of all: NO backup. There are two parts to a solid backup. The most obvious is arriving with enough money to cover *all* costs for a minimum of three months. Without a substantial kitty, every decision is bent by the most immediate necessities, and the dancer

---

*Also, one should note that working in academia, the level of talent with which one interacts is usually lower than can be found in the big urban centers and further, the cultural experiences available are generally less sophisticated and more dated.

is trapped in a hateful apartment and forced to grab any available job. Less obvious is what should be obvious: Not only are the easily available jobs low paying, but aside from the craft of dancing, *most young dancers have no skill beyond miserably paid work.* The naïvely optimistic belief that one can get by by waiting on tables in any but the expensive restaurants or working at semiskilled office work runs one into a deadly trap. For work like that, nothing less than a full eight-hour day, five to six days a week, will keep you alive in the big city, or anywhere for that matter.

I wonder how many young artists have come to the big city full of hope and genuine talent with no backup, spent a few harrowing months or even years and finally fled with bitterness and the sour taste of defeat. Too many, I am afraid. There's no way a dancer can grow or even maintain his/her craft while being drained by forty hours a week of work-work. There's no way one can feel good about oneself and live in an awful home or a frightening area.

Thus, the second part of the backup is having a skill that can earn enough money to get by, while doing twenty hours or less of work per week. Six things make up the ideal backup skill:

1. It should be work that interests, excites and challenges you.

2. You should have a talent for this line of work.

3. It should be a skill you can learn part time in less than two years.

4. Ideally, it should allow for flexible hours.

5. It should be work that is in demand in the city or area where you plan to make your big splash.

6. *It should earn a minimum of three times, and preferably four times, the minimum wage.*

In all this talk about earning a living in and out of dancing, I have been ignoring two specific areas of work where age and a youthful appearance are critical: classical ballet and commercial theatre. The classical ballet makes many demands on dancers, but certainly one of the most important is physical virtuosity. Dancers, who have virtuosity at the core of their talent, may very well begin to have difficulty as the years roll by. As talent, skill, taste and performance resonance grow richer with the years, there is some diminishment of physical powers with age. A dancer, ballet or modern, whose talent is limited to virtuosity will be in trouble earlier than a dancer who is more richly textured as a performer. Modern dance, having less emphasis upon physical virtuosity than ballet, can actually be enriched by the presence of older dancers in the ensemble as well as in lead roles. Not so with ballet; here, with the exception of a few character roles, the inhabitants of the balletic mythos are all young, beautiful and skinny. Modern dance more readily finds powerful human metaphors in mature adult figures. More of this later.

Conclusion: In the ballet world, the extraordinary star dancers have a greater expectation of extended survival than the ensemble dancers. There, the corps has to be youthful. Similarly, in the commercial theatre, be it Broadway, film, TV, commercials or industrial shows, a premium is placed upon young performers, or rather *young-looking* performers. An older person does not have a chance in most dance auditions for ensemble work in the commercial theatre, even if the dancer *looks* young onstage with makeup. The auditioners will discount that because of what they see under the harsh lights of the rehearsal hall or the bare audition stage.

There is a hard rule here: Dancers who wish to survive in the commercial arena must from the beginning enrich their talent with training in acting and singing. With these as a backup, the experience of appearing in shows and becoming known in the business, it is not at all improbable that many roles would open up, thus extending careers long past the faded bloom of youth.

There is afoot a movement to prepare dancers for that time when they can no longer dance and/or earn a living dancing. The following paragraph appeared in the arts publication called *FYI* (*For Your Information*), Winter 1986:

> For dancers in New York City in the throes of transition, there is the Career Transition Project, a pilot program administered through the Actors Fund. With money from Actors Equity Foundation, the American Federation of Television and Radio Artists, the American Guild of Musical Artists, and the Motion Picture Players Welfare Fund, the Career Transition Project is providing concrete services for dancers who have stopped dancing, including psychological

counseling, career counseling, the development of internships, and even small grants for courses or projects instrumental to making a successful career change. For more information, contact Diane Nichols, Career Transition Project, 1501 Broadway, New York, NY 10036 (212) 221-7300.

It is good to know that there are people concerned about what happens to us. Of course, the entire premise of this book is that too many of us retire from dancing too soon, for the wrong reasons. Having a profitable backup skill may very well come in handy if for one grim reason or another you have to quit our lovely, mad profession.

In Chapter XI of this book, More, there is a list of skills that command three times the minimum wage—or more (see pp. 313–320).

CHAPTER VIII

TRICKS

Tricks of the trade. These are the little lifesavers we invent for ourselves as we duck and weave past the rough spots in our work. If we're lucky, we meet an old-timer who says, "Silly, not like that!" and we learn a new way.

As I began to organize this chapter, I noted a total of twelve tricks, six of which are about feet. No surprise. It's that part of us that is constantly impacting upon the world. We're on them every minute we dance, unless we happen to be stretched out on the floor or lifted high in the air by a noble cavalier. Worse yet, when we finish dancing, we spend much of the rest of the day on them. Our feet are our icebreakers.*

Warm Feet

This super-simple trick is a development of an injunction from G.B.S. A generation ago, that would have been sufficient to communicate the name of George Bernard Shaw. He was the intellectual hero and wit of my youth. Part of his fame was his longevity. He lived to ninety-four and his pronouncements were all carefully quoted. One in particular made a strong impression on me. He

---

*See the results of the survey in Chapter XI (p. 277) for the awful frequency of injuries to the feet.

insisted that keeping feet warm and dry throughout the winter was essential to health and a long life. Hating the cold, I took to that. For years now, I have worn two pairs of socks from the moment the weather turns cold.

The inner sock can be thin nylon and the outer a light wool mixture, and when you arrive at the studio to strip down for work, you will have what G.B.S. said you must have for health and a long life. In addition, it's easier to get going.

Toe Grips

This is my personal invention. Very early in my work with Helen Tamiris, I was rehearsing her *Liberty Song*. Stepping up on a high half-toe piqué preliminary to a bow in attitude, I felt a stab of pain in the left metatarsal. As the pain persisted, I learned I had a stone bruise, but when a hard growth sprang up at that spot, forcing me to go to a podiatrist every few months to have it dug out, I became a bit desperate.

One day, I passed the original home of Murray Space Shoes on West Fifty-sixth Street in New York City. Their shoes were both ugly and reputed to be the best in the world, particularly for ailing feet. I went in. The salesman explained that every customer had a plaster-cast impression made of the sole of each foot and from them, a pair of inner soles were made as an exact copy. The theory being that in this manner every part of the foot had a surface to work against for support.* It sounded great, until I learned the price, which was at least five times more than the going rate for a good pair of shoes. That settled that. Walking away from the store, the idea of the entire foot having a surface on which to act, unlike most shoes, where the inner soles are essentially flat, kept cooking in my mind. At the time, in order to protect the sensitivity of the ball of my foot, I wore metatarsal pads in my street shoes and even in my rehearsal shoes. Suddenly I saw it. If the toes could curl over something that would fit under the second joint, every downward pressure of the toes would, like a lever, lift the metatarsal a bit, taking some of the weight off it. On the way home, I stopped off at a drugstore and bought some lamb's wool (the fluffy kind, not the yellow combed stuff).

---

*Recently I read somewhere that this kind of support and the high arches on some running shoes frustrate and insufficiently exploit the natural spring action of the arch of the foot impacting upon the ground.

Tricks

At home I made a roll of it as thick as a cigar and tucked it under the second, third and fourth toes and looped the ends lightly together. Walking on it seemed to make an immediate difference.

Summing up, not only did it relieve the pressure, making it unnecessary to use metatarsal pads, but, best of all, I never grew another growth and never returned to the podiatrist for that awful gouging. The lamb's wool, in very short order, felts up and takes on the exact shape of the underside of the curl of the toes. I let the looped ends fold over each other on top of the foot, felt into each other and they stay put. After a while I would add a bit to the toe grip as it compressed to a smaller size. For years I used it for all my dancing, including performances. A small army of metatarsal sufferers suffer no longer, having learned from me to make their own toe grips.

Even though I am a modern dancer, I rarely dance barefoot: thus never tried to use the toe grips while working barefoot. I imagine they could be taped in place.

One of the miracles of dance is that there isn't more metatarsal stress and damage than there is. When you consider that most of us weigh a hundred pounds or more and that in full relevé the entire weight of the body goes down into the head of the metatarsal bones, which are tied to only a couple of inches of toes set at right angles to the full length of our body, it is unnerving. Full relevé is a daily practice and yet most of us survive it. The toe grips should help anyone through a healing if and when that area gets roughed up.

Cracked Feet

For a time in my beginning, I gloried in the toughness of the soles of my feet and showed off by occasionally grinding out a lit cigarette (quickly, of course). When I began to work on Broadway, I was fitted out by some of the best shoemakers in the world. Bare feet became less attractive. Shoed, crazy turns and slides could be done with impunity. By the time I got to *Touch and Go*, a charming and forgotten revue by Jean and Walter Kerr, my feet were going soft. Tamiris had devised two dances for Pearl Lang and myself, both calling for bare feet. (Modern dance is torn down the middle by a schism that will never heal. On the one side are arrayed the DRY FOOTS and on the other, stand the WET FEETS. Much as I adore and admire Pearl Lang, our feet are forever at opposite poles.)

HOW TO DANCE FOREVER

In *Touch and Go*, between cracked skin and dry feet slipping on battleship linoleum (the old stuff), I was deep in the heart of one of those rough spots. One morning, directly after the shower, trying to soften the new calluses and cracks of my feet, I worked some petroleum jelly into them. That night the cracks still hurt, but I had traction. For the rest of the run of that show, each morning directly after the shower, I would give my feet this treatment and then slip on an old pair of socks for a bit of time, until the stuff was absorbed. The cracks healed and I stopped slipping. I imagine this trick is only for us DRY FOOTS.

Patrick Suzeau's Monkey's Paw

Watching Patrick Suzeau dance is a privilege, as is watching him teach, which he did here at Arizona State University a few years ago. Among his gems was a true trick: a removable taping to protect the balls of the feet. This should prove particularly valuable for soft-skinned ballet dancers when visited by a modern choreographer who expects them to dance barefoot. Of course, many modern dancers on occasion suffer from chronic cracking and torn feet.

The tape used should be the athletic stretchy kind.

Daniel's Alternative

This is not only an alternative to Patrick Suzeau's Monkey's Paw but an alternative to shoes and/or bare feet. Incidentally, it is also another of my inventions. I seem to specialize in inventions that cannot be patented, a tragically flawed talent.

The ideal foundation for this "alternative" is not easy to come by: a pair of heavy wool socks. All one seems to be able to find these days is a mixture of wool and synthetic. Try army surplus stores for the real thing. If you have the luck to find all-wool socks, get a slightly larger size than you need and wash them in hot water to shrink them to your size or a bit smaller. The stronger the grip, the better it will act as a shoe, for that is what you are about to make. A cotton sweat sock won't work, having too loose a weave, thus permitting the foot to move about within it too freely.

Purchase a tube of the heavy rubber cement runners use to mend their worn shoes. One good product is called Shoe Goo.

1. Tape should be stretched but not tight. Have full weight on the foot, since it becomes wider, before wrapping around once.

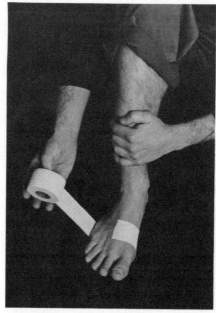

2. The second time around, get closer to the toes.

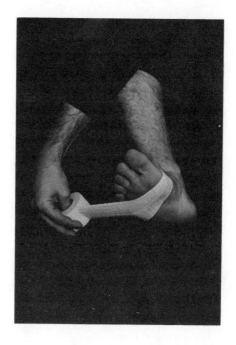

3. The third time around, go in a curve next to the toes.

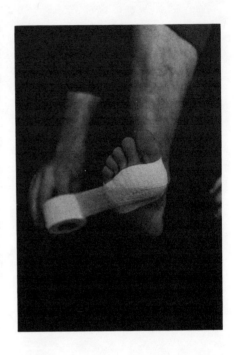

4. Cut at the spot where you started.

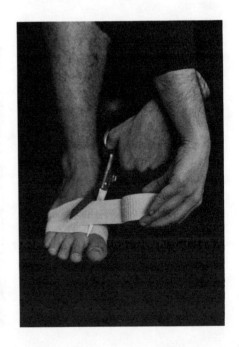

5. Start a new piece of tape lengthwise, ½ an inch beyond the bottom of the tape. Tape should *not* be stretched. Cut it when you have doubled the distance from starting point to big toe.

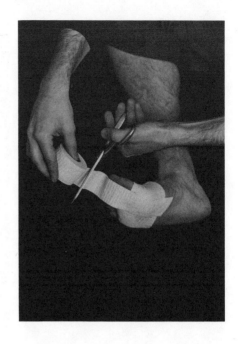

6. Split tape so that the first flap can go between the big toe and second toe, the second flap between the second and third toes.

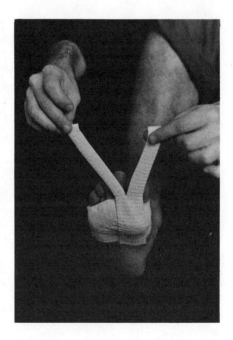

7. Point your foot, making sure you do not stretch tape. Pinch it thin between toes.

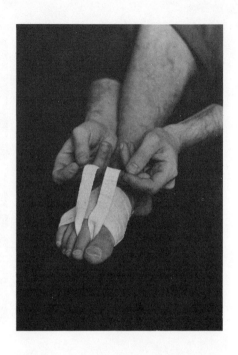

8. Start another piece of tape lengthwise, overlapping the first piece by ⅛ of an inch. The length should be the same as the first piece.

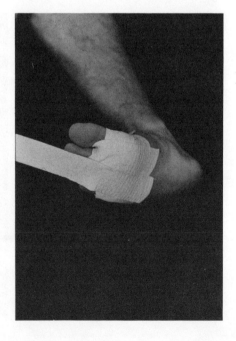

9. Split the tape, placing one side between the third and fourth toe, the other between the fourth and fifth toe. Again point the foot, without stretching the tape and cut the excess of ½ an inch beyond the tape in width.

Patrick at work making his monkey's paw.

10. Curl the tape in width so that you can flip the extra ½ inch under.

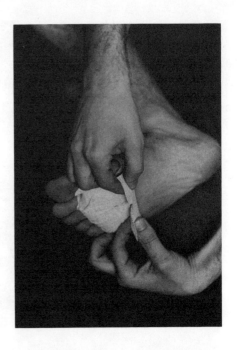

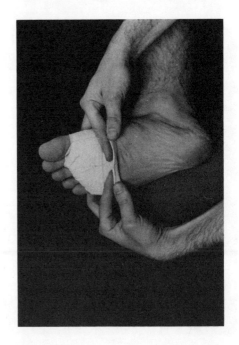

11. Do the same thing on the top of the foot.

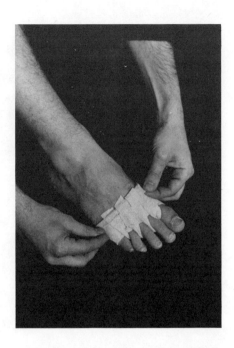

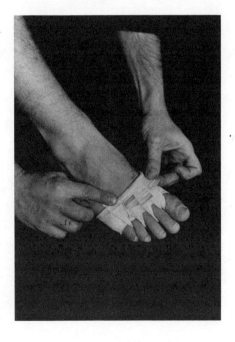

12. Put on stage makeup and it will be almost invisible in performance.

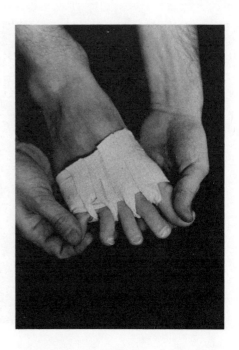

13. To remove, pull inside out.

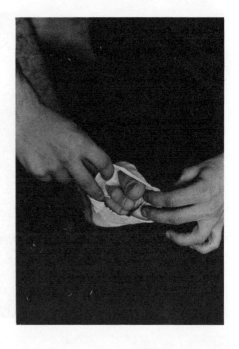

14. Flip it again back to normal shape. It can be used over and over again, like a shoe, until it wears out. If the floor is too slippery, you can put rosin on the tape; if too sticky, use talc.

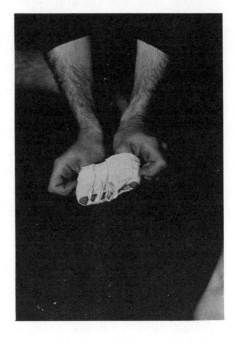

HOW TO DANCE FOREVER

Spread out newspapers and don old gloves to protect your hands from unnecessary mess and, using a thin flat stick or a disposable plastic knife, spread the stuff evenly on what would be the soles of the socks. Give them at least one day to dry. You now have made a warm dance shoe, *with traction!*

So many times I have seen dancers trying, for one reason or another, to dance in socks. It rarely works because we slip in socks. I find Daniel's Alternative works best when worn over another pair of socks, preferably a cotton sweat sock. The combination reduces the sliding about of the foot inside the sock. You now literally have a shoe in which you can dance. It has warmth, traction, it permits turns and *it launders!* After about the eighth washing, you may lose some of the traction and find it necessary to give the sole another coat of rubber cement. This is probably the least expensive dance shoe you can have.

Changing Shoes

A good way to get through the week is to have a variety of shoes with different heel heights. In this way, the angle of stress on the ankle joint is never quite the same from day to day or from morning to afternoon work. The usual recommendation for an unhappy Achilles tendon and posttibial tendinitis is a heel lift. Considering all the force and violent stretching our work demands of the back of the lower leg, when we are not dancing, a modest heel lift is much to be preferred over flat, no-heel or low-heel shoes or sandals. Even if you have the best designed arch in the world, a shoe with an arch support is an act of kindness to that exquisite bridge that serves you so well in the dance studio or on the stage. Also, badly fatigued feet can profit from elastic bandaging during long rehearsals.

Along these lines comes the suggestion of Sybil Huskey, a colleague here in the Dance Department of Arizona State University. A lovely dancer with feet as beautiful as they are strong, she is one of those who turn other dancers green as she hovers on one foot at ease and at length in full relevé. "I think that the wearing of Scandinavian clogs since 1965 has greatly increased my foot-muscle power. I have, since then, worn clogs a minimum of three days a week. The few times I've not done that, my arches suffer dramatically. I never go anywhere without my wooden feet keepers. Feet must work in order to remain inside the clogs."

Tricks

Twist Your Ankle

In the complex sequence of stretches that you perform before you begin the "hard" dancing, you might include twisting your ankle. Twist it precisely in that inward torsion that produces most ankle sprains. The reasoning: If a sudden, violent twist occurs, the limber ankle will tip over and back with little or no damage. With a tight, unyielding ankle, the unconscious nervous system controlling your muscular response, particularly in those swift bad moments, *will know that you are not limber there* and not release the muscles, thus adding to the rigidity and the amount of serious damage. Stretching, of course, lengthens and relaxes muscles that should never be rigid.

The Slimline Kneepad

Another of my not-for-profit inventions. I designed it for myself, since some of my work involves knee spins and falls. It eludes notice when pants are worn and I wear them for every performance.

Its construction is simple: Choose a knee girdle or supporter that fits comfortably, i.e., not tightly. Unfortunately, the best, which fit with the least number of wrinkles, are the most expensive kind. They are made of surgical elastic and are found only in those frightening stores that sell trusses, crutches and braces. What you'll pick up in sporting-goods stores or pharmacies will work so-so and not last very long. Now buy uncombed lamb's wool. Not the long, silky yellow stuff but the clumpy stuff that comes in cloudy sheets. Spread one sheet out for each knee, spreading out each piece until it covers all the bony surfaces. Thickness? Squeezing should bring it to about an eighth of an inch. Then, locate a torn old pair of panty hose (why be extravagant?). Sew up a flat envelope of the panty-hose material, enclosing the sheet of lamb's wool, and then tack the enveloped lamb's wool to the inside of the knee girdle. The result is not bulky and takes up most of the shocks. Tacking in ten to twelve spots should be sufficient to hold it in place and still make it easy to remove when you want to wash the knee girdle. Don't ever wash the lamb's wool. It will shrink to half its size, turning to tough felt.

While on the subject of lamb's wool, if you're working on dance material that requires falls, particularly unfamiliar or difficult ones, a few wads of well-placed lamb's wool will protect you. When I become aware that one part of my body is beginning to take a beating and is on its way to becoming tender or even bruised, I slip one of these sheets of lamb's wool inside my work clothes and, if necessary, tape it into place. Nothing wrecks coordination more easily than pain. A tender spot will force you to avoid it, even though the correct way to do that fall is to roll precisely over that spot.

Getting Out of Bed

Getting through a life of dancing without some back trouble is rare, probably just as rare as getting through any kind of life without that problem. Coping with my major back injury was the beginning of a new awareness of how to work. For one thing, I learned how to get out of bed: *don't*. At least, not right away.

For anyone with a temporary or chronic back condition, those first few moments out of bed are precarious. I think many back spasms occur then. Suggestion: On waking, before leaving the bed, swing the feet over the edge of the bed, to hang down or rest on the floor. First, rock the torso from left to right at least eight times in an easy tempo, using your hands to support you. You can either keep the shoulders level as you sway from side to side or let the shoulder girdle tilt in the direction of the sway or a combination of both. Second, reach far to the left with the right hand while supporting yourself with the left hand. Alternate hands, reach the left hand far to the right while supporting with the right. Do this eight times. Third, rock the body far forward and back, using your hands for support if needed. Do this four to eight times. Do *nothing* that strains or is uncomfortable or painful. Fourth, make a really wide circle with the tilting body, supported by the hands, at least four times clockwise and four times counterclockwise.

Now repeat the entire sequence, but keep your shoulder girdle *directly over your pelvis the entire time.* Thus, first rock sideways from buttock to buttock with shoulders rocking in opposition but over the hips. Second, twist left and try to touch the bed with both hands behind and close to your back, and then reverse that action. Third, rock the pelvis forward and back under the non-moving shoulder girdle. Fourth, rotate the pelvis in a clockwise direction, not moving the shoulders, at least four times, and then reverse at least four times.*

What is the reasoning behind this? As noted earlier, with backs, rising is usually the most difficult, and sometimes the most vulnerable, moment. In fact, the very first move, sitting up, is commonly done from flat on the back, moving straight up and forward, difficult at that hour and a frequent cause of spasms. Much better to reach the far arm across the chest, letting the body double up as it follows the reaching hand to roll over on its side, and with that same arm push down to sit up.

Sleeping, involving little motion, creates little circulation. The blood and other body fluids collect in pockets created by gravity, having little reference to function and movement. Thus, most humans are stiff upon rising. The blood is in all the wrong places. The unrehearsed waking stretches of pussycats and people have but one purpose—to recirculate the blood throughout the muscles. At first when I had the injury, I never got out of bed without fifteen minutes of the heating pad. But then I thought, "I'm heating more skin than muscle and it's muscle that's injured, and furthermore, nothing warms a muscle better than using it." This gentle series of exercises does exactly that and takes but two to three minutes.

The Secret Science and Art of Napping

As a matter of daily practice, napping is my meditation, mind wash, renewer and general all-around tranquilizer. Those of us who know this trick of slipping off quickly and returning just as quickly have a goody. At this moment I can see Gary Harris, the sound and light artist with whom I have worked for many years, stretched out on a gymnasium floor. He had asked to be awakened in ten minutes and was out immediately. Working through the night before and right up to curtain time, which was but thirty minutes away, he was vigorously at it the moment we woke him.

You too can become a napper. The secret? Don't try. My pro-

---

*In all this business of giving exercise sequences, whether by me or *anyone else*, there is the pretentiously omniscient air of giving a precise number of repetitions as if they had been cut in stone on that mountain of the burning bush, long long ago. Nonsense. They are what can be called educated guesses, often given by knowledgeable people but still only guesses which should be modified by each person according to their instincts and physical condition.

cedure: Before anything, be certain that you have a reliable alarm set to go off in ten minutes. I have learned not to trust people to wake me on time. They never seem to believe that ten minutes is enough and, probably out of love and kindness, let me sleep a little longer, just what I do not need. The longer I nap after the ten minutes, the dopier I get. There are a few kitchen gadgets, multiple timers, that will ring for a full minute unless you turn them off. They cost, but the naps deliver.

Now get comfortable and warm. (It does not work for me when I'm chilly.) I center what I do around breathing, slow breathing. The specific focus doesn't matter so long as it is slow, repetitive and with a little challenge in it. Simple mental games such as addressing sequences of muscles with gentle messages of relaxation, numbered sequences of breathing (backward, by threes, in tens, etc.), silently repeating some syllables, all fill the mind with undemanding and quieting activity. Try this and that until one feels right. If an intrusive or disturbing thought looms up, witness it but don't deal with it. Most important of all, don't try to sleep; put all your effort into your ever-so-slightly-complex mind game. You may not fall asleep but the odds are you will gain a freshet of energy.

Looking As Young As You Are, or Even Younger

The ineluctable mark of youth is smooth skin, but there are vigorous, youthful people who give the impression of being considerably older than they are. With the best of intentions, they wrecked their own skin.

There are but two rules for a good skin. Both are negative, inexpensive and probably unpopular.

1. Obey the dictum of the English beauties and Southern belles: *stay out of the sun.* If it's outside you must be, cover up and wear a hat, whether you're a boy, girl, woman or man. A suntan is the panic reaction of the body attempting to block, to the best of its ability, the repetition of a potentially lethal invasion.

2. Regard soap as a dangerous necessity—all soap, no matter how good, how expensive and whatever the pH value. Soap should never touch any part of your body more than once a day, except for the palms of your hands at eating time or when leaving the bathroom. A little dirt during the day? Water and a washcloth or

a paper towel will do all that is needed. Need another shower after a workout? Great, but no soap. Water is the greatest solvent in the world.

In Your Practice Bag

In my early youth, for a few misguided years, I was an enthusiast of a book series about Pee Wee Harris in the Boy Scouts. Pee Wee Harris made a religion out of the Scout's motto, "Be prepared!" He was prepared for everything; a little fellow, burdened by every possible piece of hiking equipment. I too, when I leave home, tend to take it with me. I load down my practice bag *à la* Pee Wee Harris. Regardless, every practice bag could well have a few items:

1. A pair of kneepads. You never know when the choreographer will demand a knee spin. Also, a couple of wads of lamb's wool, just in case a rough fall creeps into the choreography.

2. Trail mix and/or fresh fruit.* I think it is an error to go for long periods of time without eating. Longevity and health statistics favor people who eat frequently.

3. Eight to ten feet of latex tubing, at least ⅜ inch in diameter, and a ⅛-inch wall is the equivalent of a portable gym. Except for those dancers who do extensive partnering work, we do little to tone and strengthen our arms and shoulder girdle. Our technique does almost nothing in this respect. With imagination, ingenuity and some wall hooks you can give almost any set of muscles a workout. Russian wrestlers have been seen in airports patiently and persistently tugging away at a short doubled length of tubing. Surgical-supply stores carry many varieties. An eight-foot length weighs all of five ounces. A Nautilus machine weighs how much?

In Your Refrigerator

By now almost everyone must know the neat acronym RICE— meaning Rest, Ice, Compression and Elevation—as the first sequence of treatments for musculoskeletal injuries. Suggestion: Buy some small paper cups and some tongue depressors (say "Ah!"). Fill a couple of cups with water, adding a tongue depressor to

---

*But please note that trail mix has many nuts, nuts have a lot of fat and fat has a lot of calories.

each one. Put them in your freezer. If you return home with some well-earned ache or strain, five to ten minutes of ice massage becomes a simple matter: Just loosen the ice from the cup under running water and, with the stick firmly embedded, you have perfect control to treat the area troubling you without freezing your fingers.

There seems to be little question these days that ice immediately following trauma reduces swelling, giving the torn capillaries time to close up and stop bleeding. Abatement of pain, freedom of motion and, most important, healing, all wait upon reduction of swelling. The real problem is that when there's need for ice on the job, in rehearsal, in the class, or in performance, more often than not it's not available or there is considerable delay and hassle to find some. Small freezer chests are not terribly expensive and would be an ideal piece of equipment for every dance studio and gymnasium. Failing that, there should be available those temporary stopgaps—plastic bags with an inner compartment that when compressed strongly and suddenly releases a chemical mix that is very cold. They're not as good as ice but should be on hand when ice is too difficult to come by. I've used them and they do work.

A Note to the Reader

For obvious reasons, I would receive enormous satisfaction if this book were to achieve enough popularity to ensure its going into a second edition. My fantasy is that almost every one of you dancers out there will, after reading this chapter, realize you too are the inventor of a not-for-profit "trick" you just know other dancers could use *and you will mail it to me*! The second edition of *How to Dance Forever* might have a much longer chapter on tricks, with yours included.

CHAPTER IX

THE SURVIVORS SPEAK

Some of my colleagues are living proof of the premise of this book. They are the beautiful survivors still gracing our stages, exemplars of the long-distance run in dance. They have consented to add their thoughts to this book and I am indeed grateful.

Murray Louis

Mr. Louis is a modern dancer whose artistic lineage extends from Mary Wigman and Hanya Holm through to Alwin Nikolais, with whom he has been associated from the inception of his career. He is internationally recognized as a fine choreographer, the director of one of the most successful touring dance companies in the world, and one of our very best dancers. He has just touched sixty and is performing beautifully.

"The idea of age never entered my head until quite recently. One day on tour, my company was playing a musical game. It had to do with songs which included water of some nature in the lyrics. When it came to my turn I would sing parts of songs I always remembered as being very popular. After a while the dancers asked me to sing more of each song. They had never heard most of them.

" 'Well,' I thought. 'This certainly represents a generation gap, and generation gaps mean old and young.' Prior to that it was mostly injuries that made me conscious of how long I'd been using my legs for speed, air work, balance and strength. Injuries I could handle. Arthroscopic surgery on both knees gave me back my legs. Anything less than that was part of the game.

"Maturity to an artist is a very luscious time of life. So many things mingle to create all sorts of delicious memories. The past means nothing unless it is relative to the future, and the future itself can be scary if there is no experience to jack you up.

"Sometimes I do find myself saying, 'Listen, kid, a person your age shouldn't be doing things like this,' and then I laugh, because there I am doing it, and doing many of those things better than I had ever done them before.

"Age has to do with spirit, and of all the blessings for which I've given thanks, it has been for my young spirit. Spirit has always given my legs their spring and my back its resiliency.

"Artistry grows, and to be a performing artist it stands to reason it can only grow with performing. Musicians and actors are never questioned about their age. In the minds of audiences generally, dancers are never supposed to grow up. They are portraits of eternal youth. Well, we all know how *eternal* youth is, and that the depth a young person has to draw from is indeed a shallow pool.

"Today there are not as many mature dancers as there were in my day. (Oldster talking.) I saw many of the greats who created my profession, and for the love of me I cannot remember any of them leaping or flinging themselves about. What I remember most was their power of presence. Their power to take me into their art. I remember their richness of gesture and how they made me tremble.

"Age? You're talking to the wrong guy. I've still so much growing to do. So much living to live, and besides, I've got to get this fucking new solo choreographed for my season in New York this April. Let me alone."

Annabelle Gamson

Annabelle Gamson's strongest early influence was study and performance of Isadora Duncan's dance with Julia Levine. From sixteen on, she worked as a professional with a succession of powerful teachers and choreographers: Katherine Dunham, Jerome Robbins, Michael Kidd, Anna Soko-

low, Helene Platova and Agnes De Mille, for whom she did the Cowgirl in Rodeo *on a European tour with the American Ballet Theatre. In 1974, she premiered a solo program featuring the dances of Isadora Duncan. This work and the recreation of solos by Mary Wigman earned her an international reputation and the gratitude of audiences everywhere. She is in her own right a fine choreographer and, at fifty-nine, she is choreographing and performing with her new company, Dance Solos.*

"The key to survival for me has been to maintain the integrity of my artistic spirit. There is more to dancing than the dancing body. In 1923, Isadora Duncan wrote to a critic on the *Journal Éclair:*

> Monsieur Merejkowski writes on the subject of my art that my tired legs amused the public at the Trocadero. To this I can only reply that I have never sought to amuse the public, my one desire being to make them feel what I myself am feeling. And sometimes I have succeeded. But my legs are the least of my means for, being neither an acrobat nor a dancer, I have the pretentions of being an artiste. And even were I legless, I might still create my art.

Kazuo Ohno

Kazuo Ohno was born in 1906 in Japan. At the age of thirty, while working as a physical-education instructor in a Tokyo high school, he began to study modern dance with a teacher who had worked with Mary Wigman and Harald Kreutzberg. He is one of the two artists who are credited with creating the distinctive Japanese contribution to modern dance, butoh. *Richard Philp in* Dance Magazine *in April 1986 wrote of Ohno's performance at the Joyce Theatre in the fall of 1985: ". . . I was hardly aware of his age." Ohno was seventy-nine at the time.*

"I am now preparing for my new performance in Tokyo next February. A year and a half have already passed since I started working on it. This period has contained all of my seventy-eight years, and in fact I often reflect on the time that lies beyond those actual years. But when the moment arrives for me to dance onstage, I want to throw away all those thoughts that I have collected and touch the desires that are inside me, as completely as possible, in a simple presence and spirit of life. I hope that I can in some way answer all the people who have helped me in my life."

HOW TO DANCE FOREVER

Barton Mumaw

Barton Mumaw became a member of the Denishawn dancers in 1931. He was the leading dancer with Ted Shawn's Men Dancers during their seven tours of the United States, England, Canada and Cuba from 1933 to 1940. After serving in World War II for three years, he appeared in solo concerts and Broadway musicals. He has revived Shawn's dances for the Alvin Ailey Company, Richard Cragun and other distinguished dancers.

"I stopped dancing when I was sixty-nine—my last performance was at Jacob's Pillow. . . . You ask me to write something to young people about what it takes to keep going 'and dance beautifully.' . . . The first thing to know is if, as in any career, nothing else will satisfy you. This, you alone can know and you are blessed or damned, as the case may be, to follow your desire no matter where it may lead you, and it will be up to you to 'keep going,' as you put it, Danny, in whatever manner you can devise, 'and dance beautifully.' Many dancers have danced gracefully into old age through good health, keeping the body in condition, and by not attempting movement beyond their power. I was able to see performances of both Ruth St. Denis and Ted Shawn in their last years . . . he danced well into his sixties in dances which he could still perform well, and at seventy-five danced for the last time *St. Francis*, for which his restricted movement, the modest robe and no theatrical makeup created a poignant and moving farewell to an enthralled audience. Ruth St. Denis danced into her eighties on special occasions and celebrations exerting the same audience response that had been hers throughout her life."

Paul Draper

A college dropout hoping to express himself without studying, Paul ran through a series of odd jobs until he met a fellow teacher at Arthur Murray's who could do a "time-step." Paul was hooked, made some dances, got a few jobs and then decided he ought to really learn to dance and enrolled at the School of American Ballet, where his teachers included Vladimiroff and Balanchine. His great innovation was a harmonious mix of ballet, tap and classical music as well as jazz. His concert tours have never been anything but successful. In later years, he achieved renown as a teacher, becoming the Andrew Mellon Professor in the Drama Department of Carnegie-Mellon University. At my own Sixtieth Birthday Gala Concert, Paul, at the age of sixty-seven, stole the show from me.

The Survivors Speak

"I understand that you want to know how to make a living by dancing until the day you die. It isn't easy because I'm already having a hard time and I'm only 77. To begin with, you have to know pretty early on that you really want to dance. If your aim is to become a famous dancer and be a success, you're wishing for a noun and nouns never last as long as verbs. So make certain that dancing is what you love to do and try to dance as well as you can. This means not only that you study and rehearse every day, but also that you become aware of the art, the whole beautiful art, and try to become a piece of it. You become a piece of the art by making a difference in the life of anyone who sees you.

"Having done this, you still have to make a living. You can wait on tables; you can sell advertising (I did both) or you can convince someone to sponsor you; the state or an individual. It is unlikely you can do this for your whole life. It is, I think, not only unlikely but, in a certain sense, immoral. The performing artists: dancers, singers, actors, musicians, do their work before an audience *right now*. Their work is immediate and so is the judgment of it. At some point you are going to have to convince an audience that you are worth spending money to see.

"Well and good, but what happens when the legs don't move as speedily as they did and the behind stays closer to the floor? What happens is that you either give up appearing onstage and show other people what you know, or you make what you can do have more meaning, more of your self. Take a chance! It is, I'm sure you know, very easy to hide behind technical virtuosity and never reveal yourself at all. If you haven't been doing this then you haven't been dancing much anyway. An artist must indeed have some awareness of the human condition and is obligated to disclose it. The ever-present conflict between what you know and what you do generates the heat of your being.

"So if you stay in shape, stay hot, and remember that both success and failure are fickle jades, you stand a pretty good chance of becoming a human being. If you can do this, then surviving, by any definition, becomes academic because, of course, a human being can do anything and lives forever and ever."

CHAPTER X

THE YOUTH CONSPIRACY

DENNIS THE MENACE

"WELL, WHAT'S IT GONNA BE TONIGHT, DAD? FUZZY BEARS,
CUTE LITTLE BUNNIES OR SOMETHING I CAN REALLY SINK
MY TEETH INTO?"

Can it be that there is more relevance, probing, philosophy and sensitivity to the envelope of our lives in one
Sunday comic section than in an entire dance season? Amid the
laughter, the mockery and the funny noses, they manage to touch
on our deepest fears and hopes. While I was doing the final edit
on this book, in April 1987, I came across this *Dennis the Menace*
cartoon, and in the wake of my laughter, an article sleeping in
my files snapped into focus. An unexpected perspective on this
entire problem of aging in dance opened up.

HOW TO DANCE FOREVER

Jack Anderson is a dance critic for *The New York Times* with whom I have disagreed on many occasions, but on March 23, 1986, he wrote a piece entitled "Older Dancers Should Have a Place in the Theater," wherein he raised a point I had never thought of:

> . . . Just as older and younger people coexist in life, so they should be able to coexist on stage . . . dancing can communicate on many levels in many ways. . . . If dancers can rid themselves of their illusions of youthfulness, and if dancegoers are willing to admit that dancers can be human beings as well as gods or angels, then dance may at least sometimes be an art for all ages.

It was a year ago when I filed this since it was directly related to the concern of this book. It took the acerbic *Dennis the Menace* to call it up in memory and to highlight what I can only call a conspiracy that has been going on for a thousand years; a conspiracy of dancers, choreographers, patrons, audiences and Western society to relegate dance to the role of the good-time girl of the arts, with youth almost exclusively at the center. Thank you, Dennis, and of course you, Jack.

The "conspiracy" starts with the Romans. The Greeks used dance for the gravest of occasions as well as for celebratory lightness. Statesmen and military generals danced in public on solemn occasions. In their great theatre art, dance was woven into the fabric of the action equally with words and music. The opening of Euripides' last play, *The Bacchae*,* has this scene:

Enter Tiresias.†

Tiresias: ". . . Call out Cadmus from the halls—"

Enter Cadmus.‡

Cadmus: ". . . Where must we go to dance, in which direction turn our feet and set our gray heads tossing? . . . I should not tire, all night or all day long, of striking the earth with the thyrsus. We have joyfully forgotten that we are old!"

Tiresias: ". . . I too feel like a stripling and shall undertake the dances."

---

*Euripides, *The Bacchae*, trans. Geoffrey S. Kirk (Englewood Cliffs, NJ: Prentice-Hall, Inc., 1970).
†Tiresias is the blind prophet who plays a prominent role in the Orestes trilogy.
‡Cadmus is the old king of Thebes.

The Youth Conspiracy

Cadmus: "And shall we be the only men in the land to dance
for the bacchic god?"
Tiresias: "Yes, for only we are sane—the rest are mad. . . .
Will it be said that I have no shame for old age since I
intend to crown my head with ivy and to dance? But
the god has made no distinction, whether it is the young
who must dance or the older man, but he wishes to
have honors equally from all, counting no one apart in
his desire to be magnified."

Ancient Rome changed this attitude toward dance. In the early
days of their power, anything Greek was chic and their young
people were tutored in dance and the other arts by Greek artists
and scholars. But when the democracy fell and the Empire was
established, the appreciation of art became the thing, and the
doing—the making of art—was left to slaves and imported Greeks.
For a Roman to dance came to be considered effete and degen-
erate. As the power of Rome spread throughout the ancient world,
a terrible sickness overtook it. Rome elevated bestiality to a form
of civilization and dance was its garnish. Dance became purely
entertainment, ranging from the staggering skill of the pantomime
artists to literal pornography and filler for the horrors of the bloody
games. Is it any wonder that when the Church assumed power
in Rome it turned away from dance with a revulsion so fierce that
professional and public dance forms disappeared for a thousand
years?* Finally, the doors were opened again by the Renaissance
princes and what prances in? Spectacle and entertainment.

The art of Giotto, Dante, Masaccio, Michelangelo, Monteverdi,
though coexisting with this rebirth of dance, was anything but
spectacle and entertainment. They were serious—serious artists.
From then to the present, much of dance has been lightweight
fluff performed ideally by lovely, skillful young people.

No matter whether it is "classical," modern, contemporary,
avant garde, punk, new or postmodern, most dance is *about* young
people. A while ago, I heard a then brand-new darling of the
dance lecturing and afterward was moved to write him this question:

*In medieval times, some rare church services used bits of reserved proces-
sional dances.

HOW TO DANCE FOREVER

It is now more than 20 years since the Judson gang appeared on the scene. How is it that with but three exceptions, they and the generation that evolved from and with them, not one has ever touched upon the tragic in their work?

Inventive? Virtuoistic? Cerebral? Humorous? Quirky? Dancey? Yes, all of these but not a single work (and I am talking about the talented ones) that is weighted with concern or pain? The three exceptions—Meredith Monk, Kai Takei and Phoebe Neville—all worked outside that group. When you consider what was happening in the world in that span of years, 1963 to the present, it is an interesting note or is it?

As things stand now, here in America there seems to be little indication that what I describe above will change. It seems to be a flip time despite the evening news. Obviously, this throws me but that's me. What about you?

Just learned of your good news—a Guggenheim Fellowship! Congratulations.*

By now it should be apparent that I'm making two points at the same time; two points that are actually one. Western culture doesn't expect or *want* weighty content in dance, and the dance stages are completely dominated by the image and presence of youth. Each factor explains and justifies the other.

Not that this tradition was not attacked head-on by the American and German giants who created the modern dance. Their line of descent is alive today but is thinning. They had weight and their repertoire could accept and needed mature figures— mature metaphors of our existence. A scant few ballet choreographers come to grips with complex and challenging themes. As for traditional ballet, almost all the dancing roles, principal and ensemble, are young. The few older figures tend to dodder or walk or scowl or camp or sit on thrones. Witness the Ugly Sisters in *Cinderella*, Drosselmeyer in *The Nutcracker*, the father who frowns mightily in *The Prodigal Son*† and Dr. Coppelius in you know what. Only von Rothbart in *Swan Lake* dances, and usually with more posturing than dance.

Recently, when I was a member of a committee adjudicating a competitive video screening for a foundation grant in Boston, one work electrified us. In the midst of a group of young dancers, a

*Still no answer, but, then, I'm not waiting.
†How I would have loved to have seen his rage, love and compassion danced.

couple in their sixties dressed for a social event came waltzing on. The stage became brilliantly alive with the tension set up by the metaphoric distance between old and young people dancing on the same stage!

Essentially, this book addresses dancers and their teachers, but perhaps the aim is all wrong. Perhaps the choreographers should be the target. Do literature, opera, theatre, poetry, drama, painting and sculpture have youth always at their center? Whom do the choreographers place center stage? The mature? The old? Almost never.

If they did, the problem of this book would never have arisen because most humans aim for the door, not for the wall. Confronted by the forty-year barrier, most dancers feel forced to turn their energy elsewhere. If they knew, on the contrary, that there were roles for dancers in their fifties or sixties, *they would be there, ready and fully capable to work—to dance up that proverbial storm.*

Take a look at a few sports for a comparison. Who were the early boxing champions? The Irish, then Jews, then Italians and now blacks. Back in the Depression some of the greatest basketball players were Jews at the City College of New York. For them the doors were open to boxing and basketball. Being black doesn't mean you're a natural-born basketball player. It does mean that in every slum and the most run-down schools there are the ubiquitous concrete courts and an available basketball, *and somewhere down the road there is the possibility of a college scholarship and farther away is a door wide open to blacks as professionals.*

In dance, it is a given that the protagonists are young. It's a given that we must *appear* to be young. If you're a dancer and you're no longer in your twenties, you must pretend to be in your twenties, and that's as good a definition of the pathetic as any. For years I refused to give my age to anyone. Turning forty for us is equivalent to failing.

I myself am intellectually a victim of this treachery of the *givens.* After all, I have been thinking, lecturing and writing about this matter of survival for at least fifteen years. In all that time, the argument and point of this chapter never occurred to me. Even when I read the article by Jack Anderson a year ago, I did not make the connection. It was only while I was shuffling through all the untapped research material as I was working on the final revision prior to publication that the *Dennis* cartoon cracked open the given of the lopsided preeminence of youth in dance.

HOW TO DANCE FOREVER

Even I, who pretend to be a "serious choreographer," out of more than seventy-five works have created only four figures that could be considered as "on in years." As things stand today, most dancers might very well think of retiring when they hit forty because there is an insufficient repertory that *needs* dancers past the bloom of youth, let alone old dancers.

Saying it once more: If mature dancers knew they had a future and would be needed, needed just as a certain type of man is needed to play King Lear, it would never occur to them that they were on the way out at forty-plus. Nothing can make anyone old (meaning weak, sick, failing, inadequate—what have you) faster than the conviction that she/he is not only no longer needed. There is the honor roll of those dancers who resisted this fate, plowed ahead in spite of that traditional forty-year barricade, aimed straight for the wall, cutting through it to shape their own door.

Nothing here is meant as an attack upon youth, which has a clear skin, almost unlimited reservoirs of vitality, lots of hair, virtuosity to spare and the fragile aura of romance. However, one must in all objectivity observe that being young is a condition bordering on banality. For all of their beauty, what the hell do they know? Not all that much. Now, don't any of you aesthetes and aficionados glorify that "innocence" and dare to denigrate knowledge. Of course, that is exactly how you feel about dance and dancers. You want the art and the artists to be illiterate, pulsating, beautiful animals. To be sure, the young do know what the mature and the old do not know, and by all means let our artists probe their special insight and experience, but please don't make them the metaphor for all of us. *Don't define "life" in terms of youth.*

Strangely enough, Jack Anderson did not address the choreographers. Well, let's:

Dear Talented Choreographers,

Why don't you open the door to the world since ". . . older and younger people coexist in life, so they should be able to coexist on stage . . ."? If you do this only because you think you should—trouble. Guaranteed failure. If you *want* and need to go through that door and don't—too bad. If you do because you must, will there be resistance? . . . from patrons? . . . from audiences? . . . from critics? Probably. Come on, be brave and give us ". . . something we can sink our teeth into."

The Youth Conspiracy

What is the point of our art if it does not reflect the lives we live? What would you think of an art that phased out almost everyone over forty from the center of interest in the theatre? in opera? in novels? in painting? in films? *in dance?*

Sincerely,

Daniel

Does one ever stop? A reasonable question. At a recent dance performance, during intermission, in the presence of several people, a young man asked me, "Daniel, when are you going to retire?" I replied, "Probably never. I have an agenda that will take at least another three hundred years to accomplish." I'm sure he had his reasons for putting that query to me, but the question remains: Does one ever stop?

When I first began to attend dance concerts, on occasion I would see an older dancer performing—with difficulty. I noticed two things: how labored and ineffectual were attempts at elevation, and how the shoulders heaved and the arms seemed to flail about as if to compensate for the failing legs. One time, when I was writing dance reviews for *The Campus*, the undergraduate newspaper of the City College of New York, I verbally lacerated an important dance figure who to my eyes was not dancing as well as her company. I attributed it to her age. I had been dancing less than a year, but the fact supplied me with no humbleness.

Someplace else in this book I claim that most successful performers do not let vanity obscure their self-judgment, which is usually ruthless. If at any time for whatever reason weight, conditioning, inner turmoil, injury or age cut at the quality of their work so that the artistic intention is blurred, slurred or denied— that's it. They stop. A few have the bad taste *and the vanity* to continue. Too bad. On the other hand, Charles Weidman in later years couldn't do much of what he did earlier, *but with whatever he had left, he was still magic,* and I consider myself privileged to have seen him dance in his tiny studio a few months before he died at age seventy-four.

Most fine artists know that at any stage they never really express their vision completely. Young, they reach for the impossible and for a rare moment or two almost graze it. Mature, they may be getting closer to the bone of their intention in spite of weaker technical resources. There are strengths at either end of the spectrum of time, and we the audience need all of it. Most artists know when to stop. The real problem is how to ensure that they remain productive for as long as possible. Artists may be our most precious resource, not to be dumped merely because of a blind-sided youth fetish.

CHAPTER XI

MORE

ON HELEN TAMIRIS

Young, she found interpretive dancing in a settlement house on the Lower East Side of New York. As World War I ended, she joined the ballet of the Metropolitan Opera House. A few years of that was followed by dancing in Broadway revues, tours on the movie-vaudeville circuit and nightclub appearances. Dissatisfied with all the dance training and dance culture she had experienced, she went into the studio and a year and a half later emerged to give her first solo concert in 1927, one year after Martha Graham's debut and a year before that of Doris Humphrey and Charles Weidman. The language of her body, infused with the energy of her time; the contemporary music, Debussy, Gershwin, Negro spirituals; her themes, human and immediate; all were the hallmarks of what came to be known as the modern dance. In her lifetime, five names were always credited with the creation of modern dance in America: Graham, Humphrey, Weidman, Holm and Tamiris. As a dancer she was a breathtaking panther and as a choreographer she was always probing and searching for new forms to express her central concern for human dignity.

After World War II, she turned to work, with great success, in the field of musical comedy, choreographing Broadway shows and a few Hollywood musical films. Finally, in 1960, she returned to the concert field to form the Tamiris-Nagrin Dance Company.

HOW TO DANCE FOREVER

In addition to her astonishing beauty and power as a dancer, and her innovative choreography, she had a brilliant mind capable of searching analysis, exquisitely clear exposition and some of the best teaching I've ever observed. We were married and together for over twenty years.

THE SURVEY OF
HEALERS AND TREATMENTS

Notes on Methods and Procedures

In the spring of 1985, a questionnaire was sent out to six hundred professional dancers. They were asked to list their major injuries, the healers and treatments they experienced and how helpful these were. It was felt that for too long dancers have relied on advice from a narrow circle of fellow dancers or the limits of personal experience. The survey was designed to give a wider sense of what is happening in this crucial matter of healers and treatments. How well it succeeded you can judge shortly.

The research was carried on with the generous cooperation and advice of Dr. Morris Axelrod, director of the Survey Research Laboratory at Arizona State University. The services and skill of two doctoral candidates, Ms. Rose Ohm and Ms. Shang-Luan Yan, made the practical work of devising the questionnaire and tabulating the results possible. Analysis and interpretations were my responsibility.

For our purposes, there was a good resource at hand. Each year, *Dancemagazine* publishes a comprehensive listing of dancers who have established their presence as soloists, guest artists, choreographers and teachers. The dancers were chosen from three lists in the 1985 issue of the *Dancemagazine Annual:* Guest Artists, Solo Dance Attractions, and Choreographers/Master Teachers and Lecturers. The first two lists were short and so we used every name. From the third, which contained one thousand names, we selected every fifth name, giving us a total of six hundred, a manageable number for our research. Only dancers living and working in the United States were included. Medical methods and treatments in other countries as well as living and working conditions abroad are probably different enough to introduce many more variables than we could conceivably examine.

Since the names of ensemble dancers do not generally appear in the *Dancemagazine Annual*, an additional mailing of two hundred

HOW TO DANCE FOREVER

questionnaires went to the corps dancers of ten highly active dance companies: the San Francisco Ballet, American Ballet Theatre and the companies of Alvin Ailey, Eleo Pomare, Alwin Nikolais, Murray Louis, Ririe-Woodbury, Bella Lewitzky, Trisha Brown and the José Limón Company.

This made a total of 800 questionnaires mailed out. We received 178 replies; 22.3 percent is not a sensational response, but it happens to be tipped precisely in the direction needed to answer the questions concerning us most in this inquiry. Not only are they intensely active as a group but they are largely dancers who have worked long years as principal dancers, guest artists and solo dancers; in other words, survivors.

There are gaps in this survey. *Dancemagazine* has no separate listing of dancers who work on Broadway, in TV, in films or in industrial shows. Though there is a college listing, lacking individual names we did no mailing to academe. Even though dancers from all of these categories responded, there is no certainty that the proportions represented in the survey parallel the way dancers are actually spread out in the profession.

For any survey to have validity, it should receive responses from a true cross section of the group that is to be described. We are a nation of more than 240 million. Characteristically, the professional pollsters interview fewer than 2,000 people (.00008 percent of the whole), and then we read in the newspapers a profile of national opinion, saying without equivocation and apparently complete conviction that 51.9 percent of the population is going to vote for Rambo as the next president. TV and the newspapers usually ignore the polltakers' notes about the margin of error.

The 1980 census, also on the basis of a sample, claimed that there were 13,194 professional dancers in the United States. Our sample of 178 responses was .01 percent of that total, a bit larger than the pollsters' .00008 percent, no?

Because of the limitations of this survey, one cannot make any firm generalization or conclusion about the *entire* field of dancers in America. Whatever picture is drawn here by the statistics that have been gathered and analyzed is true of the 178 people who answered the questionnaire. With that limitation in mind, one may ask of what use it is. It amounts to this: All of us at one time or another have chosen healers and treatments on the basis of the recommendations of our narrow circle of friends and professional colleagues. The wisest and best use of the information in this chapter is to regard these 178

The Survey of Healers and Treatments

people and what they say as a wider circle of professional colleagues. Weighing their experiences against yours should give you some new thoughts about how to deal with healers and treatments.

Step one is to let you view the questionnaire.

Text of the Questionnaire

Surviving as a Dancer Project

This questionnaire is designed to provide information on how dancers like yourself have dealt with healers and treatments of dance injuries. Strict confidentiality will be maintained to protect your identity and any information you share will be used for statistical and analytical purposes only.

Please return the completed questionnaire to us by May 6, 1985, at the following address, or use the enclosed envelope for your convenience: Survey Research Laboratory, Arizona State University, Tempe, Arizona 85287.

The first series of questions refers to your past and present status as a professional dancer. For this study, "professional dancer" refers to an individual whose main income or livelihood is obtained from dancing.

1. For how many <u>years</u> have you been dancing or have danced professionally?

    _____ YEARS

2. What is/was your primary status as a dancer? Are/were you: (CHECK ALL THAT APPLY)

    ( ) A SOLO PERFORMER
    ( ) GUEST ARTIST
    ( ) PRINCIPAL DANCER
    ( ) DANCE COMPANY/ENSEMBLE MEMBER
    ( ) CHOREOGRAPHER
    ( ) TEACHER/PROFESSOR OF DANCE
    ( ) OTHER (SPECIFY: _____)*

*Upon tabulation, there were found to be a significant number of directors, therefore a DIRECTOR category was added.

HOW TO DANCE FOREVER

3. What is/was your major area of employment? (CHECK <u>ONE</u> THAT REPRESENTS YOUR MOST RECENT AREA OF EMPLOYMENT)*

( ) BALLET COMPANY
( ) MODERN DANCE COMPANY
( ) COLLEGE/UNIVERSITY
( ) PRIVATE DANCE SCHOOL
( ) NIGHTCLUB
( ) TELEVISION
( ) SOLO DANCE ATTRACTION/GUEST ARTIST
( ) OTHER (SPECIFY: _____)†

4. Which of the following dance styles best describe your skill or skills?

( ) BALLET
( ) MODERN
( ) JAZZ
( ) TAP
( ) SPANISH
( ) AFRICAN/AFRO-AMERICAN
( ) EAST INDIAN
( ) OTHER (SPECIFY: _____)‡

5. To your best recollection, approximately how many <u>major</u> physical injuries have you experienced throughout your dance career?

_____ NUMBER OF <u>MAJOR</u> PHYSICAL INJURIES
_____ NONE. HAVE NEVER EXPERIENCED MAJOR PHYSICAL INJURIES. (<u>Skip to Q. 7.</u>)

QUESTION #6 REFERS TO MAJOR PHYSICAL INJURIES THAT YOU MAY HAVE EXPERIENCED: TYPES OF TREATMENT RECEIVED AND HEALER OR MEDICAL PRACTITIONER CONSULTED, AND YOUR COMMENTS ABOUT RECOVERY.

TO MAKE IT EASIER TO ANSWER THE QUESTIONS, A GUIDE IS PROVIDED AT THE BOTTOM OF THE PAGES. THE GUIDE CON-

*Asking respondents to "CHECK ONE" proved to be unrealistic, and the dancers (realists) often checked more than one since many had more than one area of employment.
†There were a sufficient number of responses to add the category of BROADWAY/FILM/INDUSTRIAL SHOWS.
‡The significant number of resonses added a FOLK category.

The Survey of Healers and Treatments

TAINS POSSIBLE ANSWERS. HOWEVER, YOUR RESPONSES MAY NOT NECESSARILY BE IN THE GUIDE.

BEGIN WITH THE <u>MOST RECENT</u> MAJOR PHYSICAL INJURY YOU EXPERIENCED AND COMPLETE THE INFORMATION REQUESTED REGARDING EACH INJURY. IF NECESSARY, FEEL FREE TO ADD ADDITIONAL SHEETS TO COMPLETE THE INFORMATION.*

6. Beginning with your most recent physical injury, answer each question horizontally across the page. Refer to the guide below the chart for possible answers (THIS IS ONLY A GUIDE AND DOES NOT NECESSARILY INCLUDE ALL YOUR RESPONSES).

   a. Date of injury (Mo./Yr.)
   b. Type of injury
   c. Type of medical practitioner or healer consulted
   d. How would you rate the healer or medical practitioner?
      ( ) VSat.
      ( ) Sat.
      ( ) Fair
      ( ) Unsat.
      ( ) VUnsat.
   e. Type of treatment received for this injury
   f. Would you recommend the healer or medical practitioner to others?
      ( ) Yes, w/res.
      ( ) Yes, w/out res.
      ( ) No, will not rec.
      ( ) Not sure/Und.
   g. How many <u>weeks</u> did it take to recover from this injury?
   h. How satisfied are you with the results of the treatment?
      ( ) VSat.
      ( ) Sat.
      ( ) Fair
      ( ) Unsat.
      ( ) VUnsat.

<u>ANSWER GUIDE TO Q. #6</u>:

<u>COLUMN a</u>: Self-explanatory

*Because of statistical limitations, only the first four injuries were tabulated.

HOW TO DANCE FOREVER

COLUMN b: Examples of Injuries
　　Dislocated vertebrae
　　Torn knee cartilage
　　Fallen metatarsal
　　Achilles tendinitis
　　Herniated disk
　　Etc.

COLUMN c: Examples of Healers or Medical Practitioners
　　General practitioner
　　General surgeon
　　Orthopedic surgeon
　　Chiropractor
　　Acupuncturist
　　Physical therapist
　　Etc.

COLUMNS d & h: Rating Scale
　　1. Very satisfactory
　　2. Satisfactory
　　3. Fair
　　4. Unsatisfactory
　　5. Very unsatisfactory

COLUMN e: Examples of Treatment
　　Rest
　　Surgery
　　Laser
　　Ultrasound
　　Diathermy
　　Etc.

COLUMN f: Would you recommend?
　　1. Yes, with reservations
　　2. Yes, without reservations
　　3. No, will not recommend
　　4. Not sure/undecided

COLUMN g: Self-explanatory

NOTE: IF NECESSARY, FEEL FREE TO ADD ADDITIONAL SHEETS TO COMPLETE THE INFORMATION.

The Survey of Healers and Treatments

7. Estimate how many hours per week you now spend on each of the following activities. If an activity does not apply to you, check "NONE" on the space provided.

ACTIVITY	NUMBER OF HOURS SPENT PER WEEK		
a. Rehearsals/ Preparation time	_____	( )	NONE
b. Actual performance	_____	( )	NONE
c. Teaching classes	_____	( )	NONE
d. Taking classes (whether for self-improvement or re-quired by employer)	_____	( )	NONE
e. Other dance activity/activi-ties not mentioned above (SPECIFY:* _____)	_____	( )	NONE
f. TOTAL WEEKLY HOURS SPENT ON DANCE RE-LATED ACTIVITIES (Add 7a to e)	_____		

8. In your career, whose dance movement do you or did you generally perform?

( ) MY OWN CHOREOGRAPHED MOVEMENTS
( ) A CHOREOGRAPHER'S (NOT MY OWN)
( ) BOTH MY OWN AND ANOTHER'S

9. Have you toured in the past five years?

( ) YES   (Answer Q. 10)
( ) NO   (Skip to Q. 11)

10. Assuming that one week's performance means 3 or more performances in one week, estimate how many weeks you performed in the following years?

_____ 1984
_____ 1983

*Only physical activities, such as classes, performances, teaching, and/or choreographing were totaled. Administrative work was excluded in our figures.

HOW TO DANCE FOREVER

_____ 1982
_____ 1981
_____ 1980

11. How old were you when you began intensive dance training—that is, spending approximately 4 or more hours on dance lessons per week?

_____ YEARS OLD

12. If you studied tap dance for two years or more, at what age did you start?*

_____ YEARS OLD WHEN I STARTED
_____ STUDIED TAP DANCE BUT FOR LESS THAN 2 YEARS
_____ NEVER TOOK TAP DANCING

13. At what age do you expect or plan to retire from professional performing?

_____ YEARS OLD
_____ NO PLANS FOR RETIRING
_____ ALREADY RETIRED (How old were you when you retired?) _____ YEARS

14. How old are you now?

( ) 18 to 29
( ) 30 to 39
( ) 40 to 49
( ) 50 to 59
( ) 60 to 69
( ) 70 and above

15. What is your present annual income?

( ) Below $15,000
( ) $15,000 to $29,999
( ) $30,000 to $39,999
( ) $40,000 and above

*This question is checking on a theory of mine, that people who had a substantial amount of tap training at an early age would have fewer injuries than other dancers because tap demands subtle, multiple and swift weight changes.

The Survey of Healers and Treatments

16. Are you:

    ( ) MALE
    ( ) FEMALE

17. What is your racial, nationality or ethnic background?

    _____

18. Do you have any additional comments about your survival as a professional dancer and/or any other comments about this study?

    _____
    _____
    _____

THANK YOU FOR YOUR COOPERATION. IF YOU WISH TO RE-CEIVE A SUMMARY OF RESEARCH FINDINGS REGARDING THIS PROJECT, PLEASE SEND A NOTE TO: Daniel Nagrin, Department of Dance, Arizona State University, Tempe, AZ 85287.

The Results

Was our sample a true cross section of the dance profession in America? It might be, but only an extensive and well-funded research project could begin to answer that question with any degree of certainty. There is an interesting exercise open to the reader, particularly if you are a dancer: You can compare what you read here with your impression of the field as a whole.

Who were the people who did answer this questionnaire? By breaking down the answers to each question, giving the *count*, *percentage proportions* and the *injury profile* of each group, we get an idea of who the 178 were. This injury profile is expressed in each case in the last column, which is labeled *AVG.*, meaning *AVERAGE*—the average number of injuries per person. At first look, there may appear to be very little difference among the figures you find in this column. However, even in the first table of figures below, a bit of arithmetic reveals an enormous difference between the first two figures in that last column. An average of 1.2 injuries as opposed to 2.0 injuries for the next group is not simply 0.8 less, *but 60 percent less*. Reading that last column with this perspective in mind is going to reveal some startling differences among dancers. Each set of figures is followed by an analysis and commentary.

HOW TO DANCE FOREVER

1. For how many years have you been dancing or danced professionally?

YEARS	COUNT	(%)	INJURIES	AVG.
10 OR LESS	46	(25.8)	57	1.2
11–20	75	(42.1)	150	2.0
21–30	32	(18.0)	63	2.0
31–40	18	(10.1)	25	1.4
41 OR MORE	7	(3.9)	11	1.6
	178	(100.0)	306	1.7

The largest group danced professionally from 11 to 20 years. If you add to this the 10 years OR LESS group, most of the sample, 67.9 percent, is probably below the age of 40. I'm basing this on the assumption that most dancers start their professional work in their early twenties.* Also notice that the number of those in the 21–30 group, all of whom are likely to be over 40, *is less than half of the 11–20 years of dancing group*. What a falling off. This is that mythical cutoff point for dancers. After 40 we're supposed to look for other work. With our sample, it's no myth.

The last two columns list the number of major injuries noted by each group and the *average number of injuries experienced by each group*. It appears that those who danced the least and the most had the smallest number of injuries. Those who have been dancing between 11 and 30 years had the brutal average of two major injuries per person. One explanation for the low average of the 25 dancers who danced for more than 31 years could be that the unfortunates with a high number of major injuries left the profession early. The 46 youngsters, having danced fewer than 11 years professionally, have the unsurprising average of only 1.4 injuries per person. In the entire sample there were 45 who had never had a major injury.

2. What is/was your primary status as a dancer?

GROUP	COUNT	(%)	INJURIES	AVG.
SOLO PERFORMER	104	(15.8)	179	1.7
GUEST PERFORMER	78	(11.9)	139	1.8

*Definition for a statistic: An assumption divided by a premise, squared.

The Survey of Healers and Treatments

GROUP	COUNT	(%)	INJURIES	AVG.
PRINCIPAL PERFORMER	87	(13.2)	151	1.7
COMPANY MEMBER	115	(17.5)	212	1.8
CHOREOGRAPHER	122	(18.5)	221	1.8
TEACHER	129	(19.6)	232	1.8
DIRECTOR	23	(3.5)	40	1.7
TOTALS*	658	(100.0)	1,174	

As expected, in terms of status, the sample is clearly lopsided, partly because many dancers have played multiple roles in the profession. Also, I doubt whether ensemble, company and chorus dancers make up only 17.5 percent of the dance profession. Still, the remainder, 82.5 percent, have borne the brunt of the rigors of our work for more years than the company members, who are most probably the younger group. It would follow that they have more of the information we are looking for. Chalk one up for the survey.

In terms of injuries, there seems to be no significant difference in the entire list. In point of fact, the average number of injuries for the entire group was 1.7.

3. What is/was your major area of employment?

AREA OF EMPLOYMENT	COUNT	(%)	INJURIES	AVG.
BALLET COMPANY	46	(20.1)	83	1.8
MODERN COMPANY	61	(26.6)	116	1.9
COLLEGE/UNIVERSITY	36	(15.7)	76	2.1
PRIVATE DANCE SCHOOL	31	(13.5)	50	1.6
NIGHTCLUB	6	(2.6)	17	2.8
TELEVISION	10	(4.4)	22	2.2
SOLO DANCE ATTRACTION/ GUEST ARTIST	26	(11.4)	39	1.5
BROADWAY/FILM/ INDUSTRIAL SHOWS	13	(5.7)	23	1.8
TOTALS†	229	(100.0)	426	

*Though there were 178 in the sample, many checked more than one category. This explains the large totals. Actually, a total of 306 injuries were reported, but if one person reporting two major injuries was a solo performer, a choreographer and a teacher, the 2 injuries were recorded 3 times.

†Again, the 178 dancers worked in more than one field; thus the total of 229.

HOW TO DANCE FOREVER

Here again, we have multiple answers and lopsided figures. If we combine NIGHTCLUB, TELEVISION and BROADWAY/FILM/IN-DUSTRIAL SHOWS, we get a total of 12.7 percent from the commercial fields, while combining BALLET and MODERN gives us 46.7 percent from the concert field, an improbable proportion and an unfortunate gap in this survey. As noted earlier, the *Dance Magazine Annual* from which we drew our names has little focus on the commercial field and none on dancers of the ensemble. All other categories, BALLET, MODERN, UNIVERSITY and PRIVATE DANCE SCHOOLS, are substantially represented, though probably not in actual proportions. I haven't the faintest idea whether there are more professional modern dancers than ballet. Does anyone?*

That dancers working in nightclubs have the highest injury rate is not surprising. The hours are evil, there are two and three shows nightly, the floors are slicked for the patrons to do *their* dancing, and the sensationalist demands make hazardous stunts de rigueur. TV dance almost always is performed on concrete floors, which are exactly what the equipment needs to roll about smoothly and exactly what dancers do not need.

The MODERN and BALLET averages are neither low nor significantly different from each other. But, irony of ironies, a much lower injury average occurs among those in this sample who are teaching in PRIVATE DANCE SCHOOLS. It is a given among most professionals, college and university teachers in particular, that bad, bad teaching is the rule in private dance schools. This may be, but these teachers are doing better physically than the dancers employed in colleges and universities, who have one of the higher average number of injuries per person in the sample.

4. Which of the following dance styles best describe your skill(s)?

SKILL	COUNT	(%)	INJURIES	AVG.
BALLET	80	(28.2)	143	1.8
MODERN	115	(40.5)	201	1.7
JAZZ	39	(13.7)	69	1.8
TAP	16	(5.6)	28	1.8
SPANISH	9	(3.2)[†]	16	1.8
AFRICAN/AFRO-AMERICAN	2	(0.7)[†]	7	3.5

*See Chapter V, Questions Asking to Be Researched, p. 152.
† = Too few statistically to discuss.

The Survey of Healers and Treatments

SKILL	COUNT	(%)	INJURIES	AVG.
EAST INDIAN	6	(2.1)*	13	2.1
FOLK	17	(6.0)	35	2.0
TOTALS	284	(100.0)	512	

Here again, MODERN has a larger representation than all the other styles. Difficult to tell what it means. Is it an accurate reflection of the profession? Do more dancers have modern as an additional skill than any other? Are modern dancers more likely to take the trouble to answer questionnaires than other dancers? Am I the bending factor because my name was attached to the questionnaire and is probably better known in the modern dance community than in any other? Undoubtedly this proportion will affect the figures.

The injury profile is fairly even for four of the skills, and then there is a jump. The high AFRICAN/AFRO-AMERICAN injury figures should be ignored because too few are represented to make any reliable assumptions. The FOLK dancers in the sample had a comparatively high average number of injuries. I can't begin to speculate why that should be so.

5. Number of major injuries (for the entire sample)

MAJOR INJURIES	# OF DANCERS	INJURY COUNT
NONE	45	00
ONE	36	36
TWO	44	88
THREE	30	90
FOUR†	23	92
TOTAL	178	306

Though 45 dancers, 25 percent, reported no injuries at all, the gross total was 306 major injuries, an average of 1.7 per person. Will knowledge and the sharing of knowledge reduce that figure?

* = Too few statistically to discuss.

†In our tabulations we ignored any injuries over four because of the limitations of labor, time and available funds.

HOW TO DANCE FOREVER

6. Injury by body part: ranked by frequency of reported injuries

BODY PART	COUNT	%
BACK	61	20.3
KNEE	58	19.3
ANKLE	49	16.3
FEET	39	13.0
SHIN AND CALF	27	9.0
THIGH	19	6.3
SHOULDER/ARM/HAND	13	4.3
HIPS AND PELVIS	11	3.7
NECK	6	2.0
NEURAL PRESSURE AND/OR DAMAGE	5	1.7
ABDOMEN	4	1.3
RIB CAGE	2	0.7
OSTEOPOROSIS	1	0.3
ARTHRITIS	1	0.3

It's obvious that we are in trouble from the waist down. Breast-beating and mea culpa are expected here. It's true that bad alignment, bad placement and poor teaching are causes of many of our woes, but some things should be faced. If we had four legs on the ground with the spine suspended in between, we'd all have considerably less back trouble, dancers *and* civilians. The moment we reared up off our knuckles to balance on only two feet, we asked for it. All the stresses and thrusts of the body intersect at that juncture of the spine and the pelvis. Between that and the entire weight of the upper torso resting on the sacrum, the locus of every torsion and every lifting action, the lower back bears the brunt of most intense physical action. Intense physical action is what we do for a living.

The knee is another matter. It's a poor engineering solution of a tricky problem. If the body weight were divided among four legs, equine style, knees would be happier. Two legs supporting it all, plus quick changes of direction and vulnerable deep flexions, mean danger.

These results are quite different from Dr. Garrick's (see page 88). In his study, 29 percent of the dancers were treated for knee injuries and only 10 percent for spinal injuries. In our survey, backs were 20.3 percent and knees 19.3 percent. Three possibilities for the discrepancy: Since his group was much larger than our sample, his results may be more accurate; and his group was younger and in-

The Survey of Healers and Treatments

cluded nonprofessionals. These factors could radically affect the differences.

As for the feet, if you combine FEET and ANKLE injuries, you get the greatest number of injuries, 28.8 percent. Add SHIN and CALF and the total is 37.6 percent, certainly showing this to be the dominant location of trouble for us. Why not? They bear all the weight and receive the hits of almost every motion and travel.

Knowing all this, it behooves us to go for strength, freedom of motion and correct working methods and, no matter how hard we work, to set aside time for recovery, not only from injury but from the day's work. The body is a great healer, if given the opportunity.

7. How many hours per week do you dance, including teaching?

HOURS DANCED PER WEEK		COUNT	(%)	INJURIES	AVG.
NONE		4	(2.3)	10	2.5
1–17	(FEW)*	23	(13.4)	35	1.5
18–23	(MODERATE)	16	(9.3)	26	1.6
24–37	(MANY)	57	(33.1)	94	1.6
38 PLUS	(VERY MANY)	72	(41.9)	129	1.8
TOTALS		172	(100.0)	294	

Hard workers in this sample. If you add the last two groups, MANY and VERY MANY, you get 75 percent putting in from half a day to a full day of dancing through the week. The injury profile indicates that the longer the hours worked, the greater the chance of injury. Perhaps dancing more than, say, 36 hours per week, or 6 hours a day in a 6-day week, is not correctly described as VERY MANY but should be labeled TOO MANY. The worst average to be found in this entire survey is among NONE (2.5), the group that answered that they no longer danced, which may of course be the reason they no

---

*In the process of participating in the creation and design of this questionnaire, I have come to realize how often in statistics one is forced to make reasonable but arbitrary divisions and categories. Who said 1–17 hours a week is FEW? I did. I will never again look at a set of statistics as absolutes. Not for one moment should you, the reader, regard what you read here as immutable. At best, it's an arrow pointing in the right direction. That is as far as anyone can go with statistics. One must never be misled by the apparent precision of "18.9%" or any other figure. All statistics are "maybes" and, at best, "probables," sometimes stated with misleading precision.

HOW TO DANCE FOREVER

longer dance. However, out of a sample of 178, a group of 4 is too small statistically to discuss seriously.

8. In your career, whose dance movement do you or did you generally perform?

WHOSE MOVEMENT	COUNT	(%)	INJURIES	AVG.
MY OWN	26	(14.8)	45	1.7
A CHOREOGRAPHER'S	57	(32.4)	90	1.6
BOTH	93	(52.8)	165	1.8
TOTAL	176	(100.0)	300	

Earlier, in Chapter III, Danger, I speculated that dancers like myself, who spend the major part of their careers performing movements created by themselves for themselves, might have a built-in survival factor, while at the opposite pole, those who mainly performed what was given to them by choreographers would have a harder time physically over the long run. The figures are so close that nothing is really definitively indicated. There's a statistically weak arrow that says I'm wrong. The lowest injury rate here was for those who danced primarily what was choreographed for them.

9. Have you toured in the past five years?

TOURED	COUNT	(%)	INJURIES	AVG.
YES	139	(78.1)	250	1.8
NO	39	(21.9)	51	1.3

Not surprising. An average injury rate of 1.8 is 40 percent worse than the 1.3 average for the nontourers. Traveling squoonched up in airline or bus seats for too many hours wrecks the body. Strange and/or hard stages, long working hours, erratic eating, all contribute negatively to one of the best and most exciting aspects of our life, going out on the road.

10. How many weeks performed in the last five years?

NUMBER OF WEEKS		COUNT	(%)	INJURIES	AVG.
NONE		29	(17.0)	36	1.2
1–4	(FEW)	29	(17.0)	65	2.2

The Survey of Healers and Treatments

NUMBER OF WEEKS		COUNT (%)		INJURIES	AVG.
5–14	(MODERATE)	66	(38.6)	109	1.7
15–24	(MANY)	25	(14.6)	35	1.4
25 OR MORE	(VERY MANY)	22	(12.9)	47	2.1

The only clear pattern here is that performing is more dangerous than not performing. It is my dream and certainly every dancer's that this should not be so. In fact, one of the reasons for writing this book is that I hope to add a bit to pushing down those statistics for injuries—in every category. Among the performers, I can see neither logic nor a pattern. FEW and VERY MANY had the worst records, while MANY had the best.

11. Age started intensive dance training?

AGE		COUNT	(%)	INJURIES	AVG.
14 OR LESS	(EARLY)	90	(51.1)	162	1.8
15–18	(YOUNG)	50	(28.4)	77	1.5
19–24	(MATURE)	33	(18.8)	58	1.8
25 PLUS	("OLD")*	3	(1.7)	1	0.3
TOTALS[†]		176	(100.0)	298	

In terms of freedom from injury, according to this sample, the happiest group did not start at an EARLY age, but rather between the ages of 15 and 18 (YOUNG). "OLD," though the fewest, is much too small a sample upon which to draw any assumptions.

12. Age started tap training?[‡]

AGE		COUNT	(%)	INJURIES	AVG.
14 OR LESS	(EARLY)	38	(27.9)	70	1.8
15–18	(YOUNG)	3	(2.2)	6	2.0
19–24	(MATURE)	2	(1.5)	4	2.0
LESS THAN 2 YEARS		34	(25.0)	62	1.8
NEVER		59	(43.4)	83	1.4

*Starting to study dance as a profession at 25 or later is starting old.
[†]These totals vary from table to table because some questions were not answered by some of the respondents, thus there were fewer cases to tabulate.
[‡]All the totals are off (less) because this question was either not answered clearly or not at all by many of the respondents. Perhaps it was too complex or not well put.

AGE	COUNT	(%)	INJURIES	AVG.
TOTALS	136	(100.0)	225	

This question and its results are in pursuit of a pet theory of mine. Theories, as every scientist knows, are potentially threats to truth. We tend to prove what we believe. Who wants to be wrong? My theory: I have always been in awe of the swift and subtle weight-shifting of tap dancers. With such coordination acquired at an early age, is it possible that tap people have fewer injuries than other dancers?

The 59 who *never* studied tap had an average injury rate of 1.4 per person, *35 percent lower than the tappers*. Even more surprising is to look at the proportion of those who had no major injury at all. Of the nontappers, 37.3 percent had no injuries, while the figure for the tappers was only 23.6 percent with no injuries. Tapping, for this group at least, turned out to be hazardous. So much for my theory, but it proves, at least to my satisfaction, that I can discover what I do not believe.

13. Age plan to retire?

AGE PLAN TO RETIRE	COUNT	INJURIES	AVG.
18–29	1	2	2.0
30–39	18	27	1.5
40–49	15	33	2.2
50–59	5	10	2.0
NO PLANS	112	170	1.5
RETIRED	18	32	1.8
TOTALS	169	274	

13A. Age retired?

NOT RETIRED	156
RETIRED AT AGE:	
18–29	1
30–39	12
40–49	4
50–59	1
TOTAL	18

The Survey of Healers and Treatments

AVERAGE AGE OF THOSE LISTING THEMSELVES AS RETIRED: 37.5!

This entire question about retiring was neither well put nor well defined. Two of the respondents, though very active as teachers and choreographers, thought of themselves as retired because they were no longer performing. We have no way of knowing whether others who said they're retired thought similarly. The survey regarded all teachers and choreographers as active since most of them make dance demands upon their bodies, though not on a performance level. It is a fault of this survey that these words were not more precisely defined.

14. Age now?

AGE NOW	COUNT	(%)	INJURIES	AVG.
18–29	31	(17.4)	42	1.4
30–39	76	(42.7)	146	1.9
40–49	42	(23.6)	67	1.6
50–59	19	(10.7)	34	1.8
60–69	8	(4.5)	10	1.3
70 PLUS	2	(1.1)	2	1.0
TOTALS	178	(100.0)	301	

This is unmistakably a mature group. The great majority are over 30 (82.6 percent), and 39.9 percent are over 40. Roughly, the average age is about 39.* The injury profile shows the youngest and the almost oldest (60–69) with the lowest averages. The highest average is in the 30–39 group, leading us to believe that the high dropout rate after 40 is probably due to a heavy accumulation of injuries.

15. Annual income?

INCOME	COUNT	(%)	INJURIES	AVG.
BELOW $15,000	75	(42.4)	128	1.7
$15,000–$29,999	61	(34.5)	107	1.8
$30,000–$39,999	22	(12.4)	29	1.3
$40,000 AND ABOVE	19	(10.7)	36	1.9
TOTALS	177	(100.0)	300	

*When I first conceived of this survey, it was precisely dancers of this age that I wanted to hear from because they would have "been through it all."

HOW TO DANCE FOREVER

This isn't much compared to doctors' salaries. There are far, far too many in that lowest bracket. A rough computation from the above figures says that the average salary of our sample is $21,000.* The injury curve seems to prove nothing, except perhaps to say that earned income and the number of injuries are not a clear function of each other: The highest average of injuries goes to the biggest money earners and the lowest to the next biggest money earners. The BELOW $15,000 and the $15,000–$29,999 were in the middle.

16. Sex?

SEX	COUNT	(%)	INJURIES	AVG.
MALE	68	(38.4)	99	1.5
FEMALE	109	(61.6)	202	1.9
TOTALS	177	(100.0)	301	

Do more women answer questionnaires than men? Probably most dancers are women, but the proportion indicated above may not reflect the actuality. The shocker in this report is how much more the women suffered from injuries than the men. Of 68 males there were 99 major injuries, an average of 1.5 per man, but 109 women suffered 202 injuries, an average of 1.9 per female dancer, *almost 30 percent more than the men*. Even considering those who had no injuries at all, the women did unhappily by comparison. Of the men, 21 had no major injuries out of 68 cases (31 percent), while the poor ladies had 23 with no injuries out of 109 (only 21 percent). Going to the opposite extreme, 7 men had a total of 4 major injuries, or 10 percent, while 15 women reported 4 major injuries, or 14 percent. What's going on here? In Chapter V, Questions Asking to Be Researched, researching this problem has been suggested as crucially necessary. If there is substance to the figures in this survey, something is seriously wrong and needs tracking down.

I'll make a guess: *Too many female dancers are cursed with the injunction that they have no professional future unless they are bone thin. The New England Journal of Medicine* (May 2, 1986, p. 1,348) reported in calm, precise terms what to me is a horror. The authors, examining 75 female professional ballet dancers, discovered a high

---

The American Almanac of Jobs and Salaries, by John W. Wright, plays it safe by saying, "The estimated annual range is $15,000 to $29,000." Our figure seems to be in the ballpark.

incidence of delayed menarche, secondary amenorrhea, irregular menstrual periods, scoliosis and, incredibly, 46 of them (61 percent) *had bone fractures*. The investigators' assumption was that rigorous dieting to conform to the thin image of the classical ballet dancer, particularly at an early age, causes hormonal imbalances and calcium deficiencies.

17. Race?

RACE	COUNT	%
AFRICAN	10	5.7
AMERICAN INDIAN	2	1.1
ASIAN	7	4.0
CAUCASIAN	153	87.9
OCEANIAN	2	1.1
TOTALS	174	100.0

I suspect these figures. I doubt they accurately reflect the racial composition of our profession here in the United States, and by that token, the entire survey is off in this respect. Further, since the number of dancers in this sample other than CAUCASIAN are too few for any statistical validity, injury comparisons would be meaningless.

18. Do you have any additional comments about your survival as a professional dancer and/or any other comments about this study?

More than half the respondents answered this question. Every one gave me pause for reflection. (They begin on p. 297.)

The Heart of the Matter

Now that we have a sense of who the 178 dancers were, we can ask what they did with their 306 injuries.

1. To whom did they turn?

2. How did they rate them as healers?

3. What treatments did they experience?

4. How were these evaluated?

HOW TO DANCE FOREVER

There are five more statistical tables in this chapter. I hope you have the interest, the patience and the frame of mind to study them. As the title to this section claims, they contain the heart of the matter. You will probably observe some things that I do not mention, either because they are not in the eye of my interests or because I didn't notice them.

THE HEALERS

Here, there are two versions of the same information. The first table is ranked by the number of healers consulted by the dancers in our sample, the highest number coming first. The second table is ranked in order of approval, i.e., those with the highest SATISFACTORY rating coming at the head of the list and the lowest at the bottom.

HEALER RANKED BY FREQUENCY OF CONSULTATION

HEALER	COUNT	(%)	SAT.	FAIR	UNSAT.
ORTHOPEDIC SURGEON	148	36.7	60.8	17.5	21.7*
CHIROPRACTOR	68	16.9	70.2	16.4	13.4
PHYSICAL THERAPIST	64	15.9	74.2	12.9	12.9
GENERAL PRACTITIONER	39	9.7	47.4	26.3	26.3
NO ONE OR SELF	23	5.7	50.0	20.0	30.0
KINESIOLOGIST	12	3.0	100.0	0.0	0.0
ACUPUNCTURIST	11	2.7	50.0	20.0	30.0
OSTEOPATH	11	2.7	72.7	9.1	18.2
PODIATRIST	8	2.0	62.5	37.5	0.0
LICENSED MASSEUR/MASSEUSE	8	2.0	100.0	0.0	0.0
.... †
ROLFER	5	1.2	75.0	25.0	0.0
SHIATSU AND ACUPRESSURE	3	0.7	66.7	33.3	0.0
NEUROSURGEON	2	0.5	100.0	0.0	0.0
NUTRITIONIST	1	0.2	100.0	0.0	0.0
AVERAGE	403		65.1	17.0	17.9

*In presenting these figures, I decided to reduce the five categories of VERY SATISFACTORY, SATISFACTORY, FAIR, UNSATISFACTORY and VERY UNSATIS-FACTORY to three: SATISFACTORY, FAIR and UNSATISFACTORY. Five categories seemed too complicated to discuss and three gives the essence of the situation.

†Below the dotted line are samples too small to consider alone in evaluations.

The Survey of Healers and Treatments

HEALER RANKED BY SATISFACTORY RATING

HEALER	COUNT	(%)	SAT.	FAIR	UNSAT.
NEUROSURGEON	2	0.5	100.0	0.0	0.0
NUTRITIONIST	1	0.2	100.0	0.0	0.0
KINESIOLOGIST	12	3.0	100.0	0.0	0.0
LICENSED MASSEUR/MASSEUSE	8	2.0	100.0	0.0	0.0
ROLFER	5	1.2	75.0	25.0	0.0
PHYSICAL THERAPIST	64	15.5	74.2	12.9	12.9
OSTEOPATH	11	2.7	72.7	9.1	18.2
CHIROPRACTOR	68	16.0	70.2	16.4	13.4
SHIATSU AND ACUPRESSURE	3	0.7	66.7	33.3	0.0
PODIATRIST	8	2.0	62.5	37.5	0.0
ORTHOPEDIC SURGEON	148	36.7	60.8	17.5	21.7
NO ONE OR SELF	23	5.7	50.0	20.0	30.0
ACUPUNCTURIST	11	2.7	50.0	20.0	30.0
GENERAL PRACTITIONER	39	9.7	47.4	26.3	26.3
AVERAGE	403		65.1	17.0	17.9

Quantitatively, the 4 healers used the most were ORTHOPEDIC SURGEONS, CHIROPRACTORS, PHYSICAL THERAPISTS, and GENERAL PRACTITIONERS. Qualitatively, KINESIOLOGISTS, LICENSED MASSAGE people, PHYSICAL THERAPISTS and OSTEOPATHS led the list with the most positive responses. Negatively, the worst responses were reserved for GENERAL PRACTITIONERS, ACUPUNCTURISTS, NO ONE OR SELF and ORTHOPEDIC SURGEONS.

Again it would appear that a pet theory of mine is just that. In Chapter IV, Healers and Treatments, I put in a big plug for self-treatment. I should have separated "NO ONE" and "SELF-TREATMENT" since they are not the same, and substituted "NO TREATMENT" for "NO ONE." This would have been clearer.

Perhaps I should qualify my support of self-treatment. The questionnaire only asked questions about *major* injuries, and these probably require attention buttressed by more skill and knowledge than most of us have. Yet those hallowed gods of medicine, the orthopedic surgeons, who are consulted more than any other healers, rate with the lowest. Still, it is only fair to point out that this unimposing score of the orthopedic surgeons, 60.8 percent satisfaction rating could be laid partly to the probability that most of us go to them when we are in very serious trouble with problems not easily healed, even by the best. Having said that, it may be that many of the traditional solutions

HOW TO DANCE FOREVER

that come so easily to them, such as rest, steroids, antiinflammatories and, scariest of all, surgery, could all stand some rethinking.

The low score for ACUPUNCTURISTS could be laid to the fact that this ancient form of medicine is far from the land of its creation. How many who practice it have learned it in depth and from authentic sources? On the basis of this rating, I would not for one moment put down a healing tradition that has a four-thousand-year history, though I would be doubly careful in my choice of an acupuncturist.

The most shockingly low score of all is given to GENERAL PRACTI-TIONERS—47.4 percent! Their stock-in-trade for our problems is to prescribe drugs and rest and/or advise us to stop dancing, any one of which may be correct in a particular case but not as a universal panacea for the complexities of the neuromuscular and/or the musculoskeletal systems. These doctors tend toward cautious solutions that may not come to grips with the problems we face. At the opposite pole are the KINESIOLOGISTS and the BODY RETRAINERS. They receive the highest rating of all, as will be seen in the next table of figures. In the middle are the OSTEOPATHS and the CHIROPRAC-TORS, having a 72.7 percent and a 70.2 percent SATISFACTORY rating, respectively. Many dancers use them—20 percent of all the consultations in this sample. In my earlier comments I was somewhat negative about the matter of manipulation as a form of treatment over a sustained period of time, and yet 7 out of 10 approvals, though not fabulous, indicates that a significant number of dancers felt this form of treatment served them well.

The average response to all of the healers, 60.1 percent SATIS-FACTORY, is, at best, a deplorably low figure and explains much of the bitterness manifested not only in my text but in the comments of the dancers who answered the last question with a paragraph of their own.

THE TREATMENTS

Again there are two versions of the same table. The first is ranked by frequency of treatments and the second by the rate of approval.

TREATMENTS IN ORDER OF FREQUENCY

TREATMENT	COUNT	(%)	SAT.	FAIR	UNSAT.
REST	92	16.4	64.0	15.1	20.9
MANIPULATION	55	9.9	77.4	11.3	11.3
ULTRASOUND	51	9.1	72.0	22.0	6.0
SURGERY	45	8.0	69.1	2.4	28.6

The Survey of Healers and Treatments

TREATMENTS IN ORDER OF FREQUENCY

TREATMENT	COUNT	(%)	SAT.	FAIR	UNSAT.
EXERCISE AND CONDITIONING	37	6.6	73.0	16.2	10.8
PHYSICAL THERAPY	34	6.0	74.2	9.7	16.1
SUPPORTS	28	5.0	74.1	22.2	3.1
MASSAGE	28	5.0	76.0	24.0	0.0
ICE	25	4.4	75.0	16.7	8.3
NOTHING	17	3.0	20.0	0.0	80.0
CAST	16	2.8	75.0	25.0	0.0
STEROIDS	15	2.7	40.0	33.3	26.7
BODY RETRAINING	15	2.7	100.0	0.0	0.0
ANTI-INFLAMMATORIES	15	2.7	35.7	28.6	35.7
ELECTRICAL STIMULATION	12	2.1	66.7	25.0	8.3
ACUPUNCTURE	12	2.1	58.3	16.7	25.0
. . . .*					
SALT BATH/SOAKING	9	1.6	87.5	12.5	0.0
HEAT	8	1.4	71.4	0.0	28.6
TRACTION	8	1.4	62.5	12.5	25.0
ROLFING	7	1.2	66.7	16.7	16.7
DIET	5	0.9	100.0	0.0	0.0
DIATHERMY	5	0.9	80.0	20.0	0.0
WEIGHTS	3	0.5	100.0	0.0	0.0
FRICTION MASSAGE	3	0.5	100.0	0.0	0.0
SHIATSU AND ACUPRESSURE	3	0.5	100.0	0.0	0.0
ALEXANDER	3	0.5	100.0	0.0	0.0
PILATES	2	0.4	100.0	0.0	0.0
LASER	2	0.4	100.0	0.0	0.0
FELDENKRAIS	2	0.4	100.0	0.0	0.0
VITAMIN THERAPY	2	0.4	100.0	0.0	0.0
HYDROTHERAPY	2	0.4	100.0	0.0	0.0
ORTHOTICS	1	0.2	0.0	0.0	100.0
AVERAGE	562		69.9	14.6	15.5

TREATMENTS IN ORDER OF SATISFACTORY RATING

TREATMENT	COUNT	(%)	SAT.	FAIR	UNSAT.
VITAMIN THERAPY	2	0.4	100.0	0.0	0.0
HYDROTHERAPY	2	0.4	100.0	0.0	0.0
DIET	5	0.9	100.0	0.0	0.0
WEIGHTS	3	0.5	100.0	0.0	0.0

*Below the dotted line are samples too small to consider alone in evaluations.

HOW TO DANCE FOREVER

TREATMENTS IN ORDER OF SATISFACTORY RATING

TREATMENT	COUNT	(%)	SAT.	FAIR	UNSAT.
FRICTION MASSAGE	3	0.5	100.0	0.0	0.0
SHIATSU AND ACUPRESSURE	3	0.5	100.0	0.0	0.0
ALEXANDER	3	0.5	100.0	0.0	0.0
FELDENKRAIS	2	0.4	100.0	0.0	0.0
PILATES	2	0.4	100.0	0.0	0.0
BODY RETRAINING	15	2.7	100.0	0.0	0.0
LASER	2	0.4	100.0	0.0	0.0
SALT BATH/SOAKING	9	1.6	87.5	12.5	0.0
DIATHERMY	5	0.9	80.0	20.0	0.0
MANIPULATION	55	9.9	77.4	11.3	11.3
MASSAGE	28	5.0	76.0	24.0	0.0
ICE	25	4.4	75.0	16.7	8.3
CAST	16	2.8	75.0	25.0	0.0
PHYSICAL THERAPY	34	6.0	74.2	9.7	16.1
SUPPORTS	28	5.0	74.1	22.2	3.1
EXERCISE AND CONDITIONING	37	6.6	73.0	16.2	10.8
ULTRASOUND	51	9.1	72.0	22.0	6.0
HEAT	8	1.4	71.4	0.0	28.6
SURGERY	45	8.0	69.1	2.4	28.6
ELECTRICAL STIMULATION	12	2.1	66.7	25.0	8.3
ROLFING*	7	1.2	66.7	16.7	16.7
REST	92	16.4	64.0	15.1	20.9
TRACTION	8	1.4	62.5	12.5	25.0
ACUPUNCTURE	12	2.1	58.3	16.7	25.0
STEROIDS	15	2.7	40.0	33.3	26.7
ANTI-INFLAMMATORIES	15	2.7	35.7	28.6	35.7
NOTHING	17	3.0	20.0	0.0	80.0
ORTHOTICS	1	0.2	0.0	0.0	100.0
TOTALS	562		69.9	14.6	15.5

The complexity of what we are staring at is enormous. Hard conclusions are dumb, and yet there are tentative insights that can, for the present at least, enter into our thinking and future research. In the first table it is easier to see which treatments dominate. *It also*

*Re Rolfing: There is an inconsistency. In the Healer table, Rolfers rated modestly high, 75 percent. Here, in the Treatment table, they rate a low 66.7 percent. A pretty safe theory will cover that problem: It is not impossible for people to be inconsistent, admiring the rolfer and not the treatment!

The Survey of Healers and Treatments

tells us which figures should not enter into serious consideration. In a sample of 562 treatments, anything fewer than 10 treatments of a particular nature are not to be weighted very heavily in any assumptions. On the other hand, many of the treatments listed can and should be grouped together.

Examples: In the table above, PHYSICAL THERAPY is one form of treatment and yet it often involves 12 others that are also on the list (HYDROTHERAPY, WEIGHTS, FRICTION MASSAGE, PILATES, LASER TREATMENTS, DIATHERMY, MASSAGE, ICE, EXERCISE AND CONDITIONING, ULTRASOUND TREATMENTS, HEAT and ELECTRICAL STIMULATION). PHYSICAL THERAPY alone received a SATISFACTORY rating of 74.2 percent. Ganging it with all the other forms of treatment that are generally received from physical therapists, we get a combined SATISFACTORY rate of 75.3 percent, statistically the same figure.

Using this same regrouping procedure, we come up with something that does deserve attention. In the treatments cited by the dancers, BODY RETRAINING was experienced by 15 dancers as a healing method and *rated 100.0 percent!* Now, if we recognize that WEIGHTS, ALEXANDER, FELDENKRAIS, PILATES, EXERCISE AND CONDITIONING, and ROLFING* should also be considered as forms of BODY RETRAINING, we get a total of 69 such treatments, or 12.2 percent of the dancers having had BODY RETRAINING, rather than 15 cases or 2.7 percent. The SATISFACTORY rating is now 90.8 percent, and higher than any other.[†] In the previous tables, on Healers, KINESIOLOGISTS, with 12 consultations, received a 100 percent rating from the dancer patients. These are body retrainers. The group as a whole—therapeutic practitioners schooled in Feldenkrais, Alexander, Bartenieff, Pilates, Rolfing and kinesiologists—deserves our attention.

High up in the middle rating of 70 percent or more is precisely that form treatment of which I am so suspicious: MANIPULATION, with a SATISFACTORY rating of 77.4 percent in a large total of 55 cases.

On the negative side, there is disturbing information here, not

*If we make the distinction between the treatments that the therapist administers to patients and those where the therapist helps patients do the healing act *themselves,* Rolfing falls in the space between. The Rolfer *does* something to the patient, but the effect is, in their words, to repattern the carriage and motions of the body. Thus, its goal is body retraining.

†For the statistically minded, note that this percentage was arrived at by multiplying each percentage with the number giving that particular rating.

HOW TO DANCE FOREVER

merely because of so many UNSATISFACTORY ratings but because so many cases are involved in some very common types of treatment. SATISFACTORY ratings of lower than 70 percent, starting from the bottom of the list, are: NOTHING (17 cases), ANTIINFLAMMATORIES (15), STEROIDS (15), ACUPUNCTURE (12), REST (92), ELECTRICAL STIMULATION (12) and SURGERY (45)—a total of 208, or 37 percent! Worrisome.

If we make another linkage, of those forms of treatment commonly practiced by orthopedic surgeons, we have SURGERY (45), TRACTION (8), CAST (16), SUPPORTS (28), STEROIDS (15) and ANTI-INFLAMMATORIES (15). This represents 127 treatments out of a total of 562, or 22.6 percent. The total weighted SATISFACTORY rating for treatments associated with orthopedic surgeons is anything but satisfactory—63.1 percent. Again, one must recognize that though the questionnaire asks only about major injuries, we generally go to orthopedic surgeons when we have major, major injuries. These are probably harder to heal and the results are less likely to draw a satisfied resolution.

Still, among the lowest scores are the drugs so easily prescribed by general practitioners and orthopedic surgeons—STEROIDS, which include cortisone, and ANTI-INFLAMMATORIES. Again ACUPUNCTURE takes a beating, and again I ask, How many in America really know how to administer it?

One final statistical note to answer the question of how well or badly we are doing physically, as a profession. The best answer we can give at the moment is to ask how well or badly these 178 dancers are doing physically.

TOTAL NUMBER OF YEARS ALL 178
    HAVE DANCED .... 3,355 years
                                (An average of 18.8 years)

TOTAL NUMBER OF YEARS ALL SPENT
    RECOVERING FROM MAJOR INJURIES .... 105 years (3.1%)
                            (Not bad, until the next figure appears)

TOTAL NUMBER OF CHRONIC INJURIES............... 49 (27.5%)

TOTAL NUMBER WITH *NO* MAJOR INJURIES ....:........45 (25%)

The Survey of Healers and Treatments

I'm sure we all congratulate those fortunate one out of four who are injury-free and feel compassion for those others who carry on in spite of one or more chronic injuries. Their vaunted heroism and love of the life of dance is not overrated.

Answers to Question 18

18. Do you have any additional comments about your survival as a professional dancer and/or any other comments about this study?

In all, 116 dancers chose to answer this question. I found the cumulative effect of these statements moving, disturbing and, most of all, they made me proud to be a dancer. In a way, they compete with this book, since they add up to a primer for "surviving against the odds." All the answers are here, unedited, with but a few spelling and punctuation corrections. The breaks in numbering sequence occur because some chose not to answer question 18. My name occurs a few times and so does that of a few others whose teaching and methods were held up as playing critically positive roles in survival. All other names were deleted.

005   I have always believed never specialize. I studied acting, video production, mime, etc. I plan to keep on dancing till I can't, till my body says no!, *but* to stay active in theatre some way. Also, dancers are lasting on stage!

006   Too much emphasis on "prestige" dancers and companies grabbing up money grants (N.Y.C. Ballet, etc.) no $ available to less prestigious dancers (financial survival).

007   Dancing, in my case classical dancing, is a strenuously physical endeavor, and although I had 8 yrs. of Junior Olympic training in sports, only through correct and aggressive training in the Balanchine style have I avoided *any* injury.

010   AGMA medical coverage greatly facilitated treatments, as well as connection with the N.Y.C. Ballet. It was not my income that paid for treatments. The study seems angled toward some (undefined) but particular view or context. Survival as a dancer means surmounting more than physical injuries.

HOW TO DANCE FOREVER

012   I have managed to avoid major injuries by being extremely careful about always warming up carefully for any activities. Of course, it's getting more difficult as the years add up. I also don't take more than 1 week per year off without daily class. It becomes too hard to get back in shape if more time than that elapses.

014   Do not recommend orthopedic surgeons for dance related injuries relating to muscles, nerves, tendons, ligaments—only for major breaks and fractures. Highly recommend good masseurs and chiropractors.

015   It is hard and there are aches and pains but nothing due to injury. I hope the results prove to be of help. Good luck!!!

016   I find that bad training in my early years was the main problem for many pulled muscles, etc. Bad placement, since corrected I have very few problems. P.S. I have had many pulled muscles and I find natural healers that combine massage and physical therapy the most satisfactory.

017   Retired from ballet companies in 1979—now dance is a partial career for me; I am also an actor and singer; sometimes choreographer.

021   I find it especially difficult in the United States for American men to find employment in the principal ranking in the major U.S. companies. Also if you weren't able to come up through the company's school it's more difficult to get into that company, but those rules go clear out the window if you are a foreign dancer in this country. A double standard.

022   I believe that the vast majority of injuries are a result of consistently incorrect working habits and that the problem is to find what one is doing wrong and how to correct it. I'm suspicious of shallow surveys.* I suspect you're not asking the right questions or enough questions to get any really pertinent information.

025   Dancers are the last of the true American Pioneers—we are the Divine Crazies—some of us survive in the field.

*So am I.

The Survey of Healers and Treatments

026   I believe one must make opportunity and know what one can do. I work to prevent injury and give glory to God for my health and the privilege to dance. Thank you!

028   Brains and quality: 90% of the places I now perform I opened to the field of Mid Eastern dance in order to increase knowledge of the public and employment opportunities for myself and other qualified professionals.

030   Each person is an individual—no one should use a Dr.'s evaluation as their guide—dancers have to know their own bodies well enough to become their own healers. Self-healing is the most effective therapy of all.

032   If you want to survive in this profession develop as many skills as possible that allow versatility.

033   My initial injury occurred at the start of my performing career and caused me to specialize in less strenuous dance forms and the more academic aspects of dance. I free-lance, therefore some months are very hectic and others quite lazy.

034   Since life means *dance* to a dedicated dancer, we often prove a doctor's prediction wrong. With sheer willpower and the discipline we have learned through dance we survive and land like a cat after a fall! My surgeon told me during the operation that I will never dance again!!!

036   Dance—for me—led me to choreography then to directing. It's an incredible background to come from.

038   After my knee injury I became a model and concentrated on choreography then straight theatre directing—it was difficult to be accepted as a director of plays after having been a choreographer—eventually it was fine. I still choreograph when I direct a musical.

039   My schedule as a choreographer is more erratic than questions 7 and 10 can indicate. In 1983, my main income was not from dance; in 1984 it was. 1985 remains to be seen. I believe myself more vulnerable to injury when I am able to dance less, rather than the other way around.

HOW TO DANCE FOREVER

041   Being well rounded in training—a good performer, and following directions with a healthy attitude. Keeping an open mind and taking care of myself. If they want me as a choreographer—I'm there, a soloist, or in the chorus—just call and I'll be there.

042   Sometimes the emotional stress involved is as real and painful as the physical when pursuing a professional dance career. The two types of stress are often inseparable, one affecting the other.

045   Absolutely important to my recovery was the brilliant healing that I received from the Netherlands Dance Theatre masseur—his belief gave me courage and his decision that it was important to keep dancing and performing throughout the injury (I never completely stopped) made my recovery complete almost within a month.

046   I felt being a professional dancer for 15 years helped my physical survival in our culture.

050   I'm married and my husband's secure income allows me to take risks I might not otherwise take. The NEA and NYSCA have assisted my survival with grants. I started my own company because I could not find full-time employment in my expertise at the time.

052   Lucky for me I can lead, teach folk dancing and call squares and rounds.

054   A dancer who wishes to have a long career must train his body organically. He must find a teacher who gives good results. This is the only gauge as to the quality of teaching.

055   My survival as a dancer has (mentally and physically) been the result of excellent training—wonderful teachers who cared that I was always properly placed, working correctly without gripping or straining the body. I also add that they were very *positive*, communicating a love for dancing, and that it was thought to be a great accomplishment to dance well.

057   I think a better sampling of questions could be found. Survival in this business is more than just avoiding injuries and having a fair income (those kinds of statistics can prove anything).*

*I agree wholeheartedly with this criticism. The survey, separated from the book, does give a limited perspective to this matter of survival.

The Survey of Healers and Treatments

059   The hamstring injury was not constantly worked on until 1984 because of continuous use and lack of money to pursue treatment. I never earned income from performing until 1984. Although I was performing for 11 years prior I finally made a decision to be committed to dance and the responsibility of being a company that can be granted for other activities beside performing.*

060   I've been lucky! I also never really was a dancer per se—I studied to choreograph and am a director/choreographer.

061   I have had my share of sprained ankles and bad backs (congenital spondylolisthesis) but nothing I would call major. My husband is a physician and top quality medical care has always been available. I would see the survival issue as relating more to emotional, interpersonal, and spiritual questions than to purely physical health. How do you combine dance and family, the trivialization of dance as art form, the need for success in the face of aging, the need to relate dance to questions of ultimate meaning? I am attempting to deal with these questions through study of theology and working in liturgical and religious dance performances. My husband supports me and 4 kids at over $40,000 level.

062   Bad—ignorant teaching is a major cause of today's dancer injuries, as well as poor rehearsal habits, self-indulgent layering of excessive clothes for class and rehearsal—and an enormous lack of "in tune with" (common sense) of the dancer's body on his/her own part.

063   When I danced professionally—in the early 60's the only place to make a decent living as a dancer was on Broadway—or Las Vegas—my background as a dancer was the Las Vegas shows as a director/choreographer—it's been musical comedy.

065   Nutrition counseling—increase carbohydrates —started in 1984 —stop high protein weight maintenance approach—good results— constant work with mov't therapist/kinesiologist to reduce injury occurrence. Excellent survey—glad you are doing this study!

066   A good education helps think in terms of options for survival and functioning in the "real" world.

*Verbatim and not quite clear.

HOW TO DANCE FOREVER

067 Think it is important to be aware of the possibility of other types of work in case injuries prevent active participation in dance. My recent injury made me realize I am lucky to also have ability as a travel agent.

069 Even though I no longer perform (on stage) or take a daily class, I feel that I have never stopped dancing due to the daily work in the field.

070 I have been very very fortunate at having ballroom dance find me. I never planned for the wonderful success I've enjoyed—and that is greatly the result of my partner, [name deleted].

072 I have had minor injuries but feel that good training at an early age is the best injury prevention, also a healthy attitude and really enjoying one's work is helpful. By the way, my training has been and still is Balanchine.

075 The destruction of the NEA Dance touring program in 1978 curtailed my performing more than my advancing age.

076 Question 7 varies due to performance or non-performance time. The hours are a mean! Survival is determined through utter faith that all things are possible with God's help! A spiritual teaching has been my greatest help in surviving the pangs and pains of our world! A world that has brought me, however, utter joy and sheer ecstasy! One I am proud and happy to be a part of and a contributor to as an artist!

077 I've discovered that surviving means slowing down. Dancing has become a way of life for me. The process and creation of works of art is my work. I wish to be successful and recognized for my work—but I will not kill myself for that. I love my work and will not jeopardize a long career, a healthy career, for fame. Dancers in this country put too much pressure (or buy into too much pressure) on themselves.

078 The effect of racism in the realm of creativity and job opportunities needs to be explored. The range of a career for a person of color in America is stilted by the economic advantage the majority

populous receives from exclusive access. The lack of a true dance union, support system and "respectful" status of gainful employment affects everyone.

079   I have used the discipline to expand to commericals, industrials, video tape, print, ads, anything short of skulduggery to make money—

080   I love it! Good placement and learning to release unnecessary tension will allow me to keep performing another 10 years, I hope.

083   If you do become a professional dancer, build a good, strong, and clean technique. Take class every day, don't mark in rehearsal, but be smart about overdoing. Good diet, take care of your body and save money for retirement.

084   My body for a 29 year old is in great condition. I feel very fortunate. I have put up with my toe (joint was flattened out) injury and will till I stop performing. I have done some barefoot dancing with [name deleted] Ballet and think this may have caused my injury.

085   When asked "Are you still dancing?" I never remember not dancing. I'm still dancing and when I no longer will be able to (which will be Never) I will continue to choreograph. Daniel Nagrin is a great inspiration, and I wish him good fortune.

086   Minor injuries—such as chronic sprains, and problems resultant from major surgery are not included, but these do have bearing on ability to move well. Also, there are the ordinary problems of aging. . . . (Somehow we survive—dancing keeps one younger, healthier . . .)

088   After years of going to doctors, I've discovered that ice therapy is the best anti-inflammatory. That, followed by gentle massage and special strengthening exercises can cure anything. A good healthy high carbohydrate diet also helps to heal faster.

090   I am happy to participate and curious about the outcome. Questions about one's mental state could be useful. Did therapy enter one's training? . . . (psycho) along with physical therapy—etc.—

HOW TO DANCE FOREVER

Sometimes the mind, no I'll take that back—all the time . . . the mind plays the central role in physical trauma—how it occurs and in it's healing.

091   I am very pleased that this survey is being done. "Survival" is not only from injuries, but it ultimately is related to socio, politico, economic forces. I hope that a conference could come out of this— it's time we talked.

092   Our country takes horrid care of their artists. I feel more achievements would be made if artists were paid for their work, as other professions are for their work.

093   Most dancers suffer injuries due to 2 reasons: 1. bad training 2. bad bodies. I have been lucky to have received the best training, but right now I continue to think positive.

097   In both of my injuries, the doctors said long hours and overwork were to blame. I also found that spiritual and emotional states had a direct bearing on the health of my body.

099   Therapy—how to express anger.

100   One important point that needs studying is whether it is good for dancers to continue working through injuries. I for one continued dancing through all my injuries and also have found that there needs to be more research on how dancers should be treated since they use and train their muscles differently. Through my experiences, I have found that most dancers need more help psychologically in coping with society. Most injuries, I think, occur when one's mind is not in full concentration on what one is doing. I know this study is very important but my concern is on the psychology of a dancer.

101   1. Recommend women exercise vigorously and sensibly after childbirth. 2. You might be interested to know how I kept my career going very actively after mastectomy and during chemotherapy.

103   —only that there is now (seemingly) more awareness of the "ephemeral life" that a dance career is. 1. Its short length 2. Its small financial reward (except for a very few) 3. The unreality. *But* that is theatre! and so it goes!

104   It is a peculiar career, when you love it, the injuries don't hurt, when it's time to go on in another facet of your life, they hurt a lot to let you know it's time to change.

106   I do graphic design for my real income—dance income is *spent on dance survival.*

107   It's harder and harder to survive as a professional dancer in the 80's. A relatively few people control the power structure and impose their viewpoints on funding organizations.

108   I have adapted to my various injuries and maintained an active role in dance as a teacher/choreographer. I still perform in non-dance roles, but will never dance as I once did. I do believe that the medical treatment I chose did more to make the injuries worse than better. I believe that healing has so much more to do with our internal dynamics—self-love—patience—understanding—etc. These aware-nesses create an environment in which healing can occur—we heal ourselves. Western medicine has no regard for the complex relation-ship between mind and body. By invading the body for "healing" purposes we create a profound conflict. My various injuries have taken me on a revealing journey into myself and for that I can actually say that I am grateful. Dancing must come from a balanced integrated place. If not, the imbalance expresses itself through injury. Of course I must say "If only I knew that before." But that is precisely why it all happened: Because I didn't.

   #6 Injury dated 8/81.   It is this injury that currently keeps me from dancing. My back goes into spasm if I overextend myself. I have had more treatment than I care to remember: X rays, epidural-blocks, chiropractic, acupuncture, massage, a procedure (can't recall name) in which a substance that actually kills nerve ending was injected into the nerves that feed the facet joints between L5 and S1. The only thing that has helped me regain mobility and a sense of power over my body was a radical physical therapy program developed at a back clinic in Texas. These exercises, done religiously, have made a large difference, but nothing has eliminated the pain completely.

   One other note: The person to whom this questionnaire was sent no longer holds this position. As her replacement I have filled it out—as I believe it is valuable and worthwhile. If I can be of any more assistance—I would be happy to.

HOW TO DANCE FOREVER

109   As a solo artist I spend a lot of time doing office work and self-promotion and P.R. You must be dancer, teacher, choreographer, lecturer, business person to make it in career of dance. (great writer also) I think that is a pain in the butt but that's the reality of the situation.

110   Very glad you are doing this study.

111   I'll be turning 30 this year (1985) and I hope this is my last year dancing. I love this profession very much but after 11 years in the business I've had it. I'm tired of all the rejection, humiliation and working my elbow off for so little money. Unfortunately I become totally entranced the minute I get on stage in front of an audience. I have it in my blood, no doubt, and although I think the business is so unfair, I love it with all my heart.

114   Survival is also a state of mind—a dancer needs a "spiritual" sense of self—how to continue in pain—work thru pain—when not to work and how to get backing, and to be "in tune" with responsibilities in maintaining physical, mental and emotional health of body and artistic spirit.

116   I still feel that, in general, dancers are grossly underpaid—especially when you consider the time and expense spent on training to achieve the expertise of a professional. Living expenses, dance-wear, classes, are so costly that the average dancer cannot afford medical insurance or proper treatment when injured.

118   In 1981 I stopped producing works in the U.S. with my own assembled company because I found costs disproportionately high and seeking government funding too time-consuming to warrant the minimal funding received. Some of my activity since then has been outside of the USA.

119   Thank you for sending me this inquiry. It is interesting. I'm sorry if I don't fit your questions well enough. But I am an unusual case. My R knee still is weak, and it grieves me a great deal. But I do my best, anyway. I cannot possibly afford to take the problem to a doctor. He would probably say "You need to rest it." Survival for an Indian dancer is very difficult. Indian Dance is not at all popular

now and it is a terrific struggle to keep going—to try to get performances and to try to manage in an ever more antagonistic
environment—and to wonder if I can continue with all the problems
of no money, no appreciation, no encouragement, no help, etc.

I have a secretarial typing service which brings me an additional
small income for a lot of troubles and some work, and not much
money.*

121   The spirit helps the body survive great physical exhaustion—
but keeping the spirit alive is a delicate task in itself.

122   Although I have had no *major* physical injuries, I was Rolfed
in spring 1975 to help correct structural misalignment and hip pressure, and the results were very satisfactory. I continue to seek out
preventive and holistic body care whenever necessary. Comment:
The title "Surviving as a Dancer" suggests to me more of a *financial*
concern rather than a physical one, and I hope the project relates to
this aspect along with the body-mind-spirit base.

123   To survive this extremely physical way of life, the dancer, in
this case myself, has made sure the *instrument* is kept highly tuned
at all times—this means daily classes, enough rest and a proper
diet—"We have only one body in this life time to live in—so we
must respect its needs and see to it."

124   Survival as a dancer depends on two things—quality of training
and the reasonable nature of demands on self and by others.

126   My survival from injuries only succeeded because I found a
good physical therapist and could manage to pay them.

127   Survival as a pro dancer means for me to be a businessman
nowadays. Yoga has helped keep me away from injuries, as does
massage and remaining in class.

128   Luck and not pushing my body too hard, not forcing and plenty
of rest.

*The questionnaire released a floodgate for this dancer. I did cut a very long
letter, which discussed a prolonged eye infection attributed to makeup.

HOW TO DANCE FOREVER

129   I feel better now at 31 years of age than I ever have. I am not as flexible as I was but I dance smarter and have expanded my range both physically and spiritually—I feel healthy most of the time.

130   Economics have prevented the fulfillment of my true potential.

132   Longevity has made me successful! (If you hang around long enough)

135   Dancing is the best, easiest and least part of it. The hard part is financial struggle, teaching, publicity, organization etc.—the "survival" part.

138   The study of music and exposure to as much dance as possible lead to a better understand of the art of dance. This might help the younger generation to not be isolated to one thing.

139   In looking at my responses in this survey, I realize how much more important for me the work period is than the time spent on performing. I do feel, though, that I started teaching too young, and that has limited my performing opportunities.

140   This is an awfully simplistic study—for example, no consideration for emotional injuries to dancers, their physical effects . . . but I guess you have to start somewhere! You might be interested in the work being initiated in Canada by the New Dancers Transition Center—based in Toronto.

141   Dance even with a Ph.D. in Dance and related Arts does not feed me. I am an R.N. and *nursing* and good investments make my living—at 79 I'm still relief night nurse.

501*   It's definitely rough. I wish more monetary gratitude was given to the dancer rather than applause and receptions.

502   Question 7 (a–f) is not specific enough. When a dancer is on tour, you can't take 2 classes a day, but you spend a great deal of time rehearsing in the theatre w/a "warm-up" class beforehand. Also,

*The last two hundred questionnaires were mailed a month later and numbering started with 500 for coding purposes.

The Survey of Healers and Treatments

with all the traveling by bus (usual means of transportation), your schedule becomes a bit hectic with sometimes only 5–6 hours of sleep a night. Performances are done on tour which occurs maybe 20–30 weeks out of the year.

504　It's difficult to say exactly how much I've toured and performed with this 3 shows = 1 week format. I included performances in NYC and divided tours that included many shows per week into more weeks. Also, medically, I've had *many* minor injuries treated extremely well by a chiropractor. Perhaps she is the reason they have all been minor.

505　1. One problem in surviving in my particular work situation is having to take company classes and warm-ups. The director feels that the policy is necessary to provide training and to protect against injury, but the dancers would rather take care of their own needs at least part of the time. They/we feel we can warm ourselves more effectively in individual work-outs.
　　2. Needless to say, hard floors are a killer on tour.
　　3. Thanks for doing this project.

507　This is the lowest paying hardest working field in the Arts. Fame means little more than a subsistence income.

508　Survival is difficult, especially with the cost of studio space eating up ½ a week's salary; unemployment insurance is a very big help—I found several of the questions too vague which thus forced me to answer in the same manner.

509　A good "healer," mine is a chiropractor, is *essential*.

510　This is a very well organized survey. I have been relatively lucky in not having sustained more injuries. Particularly when you consider the various demands on the body which touring presents in performance. During this time, you are not always able to warm up sufficiently for all performances.

511　The minor (relatively) injuries I've had (patellar tendinitis, pinched nerve in cervical vertebrae, etc.) have responded well to good orthopedic care, physical therapy, and rest. I've been lucky to work with Bella Lewitzky, she cares about the bodies of her dancers. I'm not afraid of my job if I have an injury. So far that is.

512   Would not been able to continue without Alexander work or other types of body work. Taking classes only does not help. Since as a dancer you need to thank (think?)* yourself. Economic status is a hindrance in that work.

513   I have avoided much unnecessary stress and prolonged recovery periods because I have taken responsibilities for my recovery—my background in anatomy, physiology, kinesiology and dance has made me my best healer—I train for 2 hours daily w/myself.

514   Workmen's Compensation has taken care of work-related injuries and muscle spasms.

515   Thank you. We do need help with *our* injuries as they have in sports.

516   Dear Danny
          Do you really want me to fill this in? I have had so many crazy injuries that it will throw your statistics off track.
                    Love,
                    [name deleted]

    As I say Danny—you may not want to use this. If they had been operating on knees properly when I injured my knee all of the rest might not have happened. Who knows—I'm still working hard and just can't seem to take my fingers out of it—

518   Have had no major injuries due to carefulness, common sense plus luck.

519   Regarding the injury section—it makes a difference whether or not the injury occurred at home or on the road. At home the doctors and therapists you trust and that know you are available. On the road, you take your chances and scheduling usually does not permit getting real treatment.

*Not quite legible.

The Survey of Healers and Treatments

521   I see great potential in many directions for a study such as this, though I was disappointed the questions weren't more in depth. My personal survival has, with my new affiliation w/a large modern company, for the 1st time become possible solely financially in doing what my life is dedicated to. I wish like all dancing artists that this were more "commonplace" and not a phenomena. I have waitressed up to this point: directly antithetical to a dancers' maintenance needs.

522   That when I did receive an injury, to be diligent about therapy, keeping a positive attitude, and be aware of others who go through the same traumas, encouragement.

523   You have only touched on the bare physical facts, many feel that a great number of injuries are a result of emotional distress, in my opinion there is a lot of truth to this belief. However, if a dancer is injured, the injury must immediately be taken care of. I ice 1–4 parts of my body almost every night. I find this simple maintenance a major factor in being able to work through many injuries. The importance of ice cannot be overemphasized.

525   You have to want to do it badly enough.

526   I survived this long in the dance world because I am a positive person who loves to *dance*!!!

527   Zen Attitude = No Injuries

529   I thought it was important to include minor physical injury as well as major injuries especially since I had very satisfactory results from seeking medical care. I would encourage all dancers to seek help and advice from medical circles before trusting less informed sources.

530   Daniel, as stated in the questionnaire, all conventional and not so conventional methods of dealing with severe back injury were discarded one by one. It also was not a matter of money for I went to the best in the dance field.
   It is frightening to see the power these "Dance Doctors" have over educated performers. Dancers who work years to educate their bodies and mind suddenly say—here I am—*you* make me better.
   In short I feel very lucky to have stumbled upon a Dance Movement

HOW TO DANCE FOREVER

Therapist trained in "Connective Tissue Massage Therapy" and the work of Irmgard Bartenieff. It has been a slow healing process and one of body re-education, but positive at every step and one that without I'm sure I would not be dancing.

Thank you.

531   I believe that this study will change and bring a more accessible treatment for dancers in need. Our financial state being very low, there is a necessity to educate and bring awareness concerning our discipline, physical demands and hope for a better care system.

533   A lot of my energy has been devoted to pain management as a dancer. I always have something wrong with my body. I sense this is due to a combination of genetic weaknesses and a tendency to ignore early warning pain which goes away quickly in the heat of pursuing goals. Sometimes achieving the goal is worth paying the price and sometimes it isn't. Also, survival as a dancer isn't necessarily desirable. People like [names deleted] have all tortured us with their "survival" on stage. They all missed reasonable retirement age by a decade or two.

534   There's no regularity in performing schedule for a self-producing, modern dancer, the daily maintenance is the only regular factor.

535   Delighted you're doing the study—was working in France April–May–June hence delay in responding. I survive with much much help (housing—low rent—no clothes—low production costs, etc.) from family, friends, and require little.

536   Sorry I'm sending this so late—I just recently found it. I would like to say, though, that life for an injured dancer is extremely hard. Many people are encouraged to dance with an injury—latter resulting in permanent physical damage. To take care of the injury usually means being left behind, or left out for a long long time, sometimes even being fired. I've seen many dancers "punished" for being injured.

ON BACKUP

Profitable Work-Work Skills

NOTE: The federal minimum wage is $3.35 an hour.

CODE: **Figures in bold are from New York State publications or researched April 1987 in New York City.**

Figures underlined were researched here in Arizona and apply locally.

- −*= less than twice minimum wage ($3.35 to $6.70)

- * = more than twice minimum ($6.70) but less than three times minimum ($10.05)

- ** = more than three times minimum (more than $10.05)

- *** = $20.00 or more an hour

* **	auto mechanics **5–10+** 10–13
** ***	foreign-car servicing (tough to break into, competing with those who have spent as many years doing this as you have in the studio). Top money to those with Type A diploma = 5 years' experience, minimum. A two-month course can get you work.
***	free-lance (minor repairs)
**	gas station
* ***	bartender (depending upon shift and location)
	body retraining as therapy:
***	Alexander (training 3 years daily, very competitive in N.Y.C.)
***	Ben Benjamin Muscular Therapy (training 3 years part time, located in Cambridge, MA)

HOW TO DANCE FOREVER

***   Feldenkrais (training 9 weeks per year for 4 years)
— * **   pilates (training period . . . ?)

**   bookkeeper

        bricklayer
***   craftsman (nonunion, small jobs only)
-*   laborer

        cabinetmaker
***   free-lance
**   shop

— * *   caring for children, bedridden or old people (poor pay, but
        sometimes you can get free lodging for this service)

* **   carpenter (jobs usually go all day for days at a time)

— *   cashiers

* ***   ceramic tile setter <u>8–12</u>

        computer programmer (Can be anyone who takes a 6-month
        course and earns $27,000 a year to esoteric hotshots earn-
        ing $60,000 a year. Most are full time. Free-lance, part
        time are rare.)

        construction work 6–20 (in New York almost all union and
        full time) Hazardous work.
*   helpers 6–8 <u>4.25</u>
**   journeymen 15
**   master 18–20
          (union membership can take 3–4 years)
**   skilled nonunion 10–12

***   cutting hair ± 25/head free-lance (Professionally this is prob-
        ably out, since most states require a diploma from a beauty
        school, which entails two years of full-time study.)

*   designer, cloth **9.00 Av (surplus N.Y.C. 1985)**

On Backup

? designer, clothing **(shortage N.Y.C. 1985)**

* designer, graphics **9.50 Av (shortage N.Y.C. 1985)**

* ** driving instructor **12.50**

* *** electrician **6–15 +**

* ** exercise instructor
(Aerobics can be more lucrative if you have a following.)

* hotel clerk **9.50 Av**

*** horseshoeing ± 35

* ** housecleaning **(T.A., New York acquaintance, gets 25 for 3 hours but he does it in 1.5 hours which equals 16.66 an hour. (Few openings N.Y.C. 1985)**

house painter (usually full-day work and can be dangerous)
* ** interior
** exterior

legal: *see* office work

makeup artist
** *** free-lance
** stores

* marble installer 5–10

** *** massage 17–21

mechanic
** bicycle 4.75 to 9
*** free-lance (hard to find)
motor bike 7.50 (part time is rare)

modeling
* art 6

HOW TO DANCE FOREVER

***	commercial <u>50–100</u>
***	fashion
***	in-store modeling and sample dispensing
***	robotics (A new wrinkle. Models pretend to be moving mannequins in store windows and have been attracting large crowds.)
***	runway and show <u>100–125</u>

(Aside from looks, height [5'9" at least], slenderness, this work requires a substantial investment in photographs, clothes and the initial hustle to locate an agency.)

* **   music and/or percussion for dance classes <u>9</u>

***   music lessons, private <u>7</u>

*   night auditor **9 +**

office work: In the hierarchy of pay, office temporary work pays better than a steady job, but by its nature is less reliable. Work for law firms and Wall Street pays better than other forms of business. Listed here are the most probable rates for legal and/or Wall Street temp work. Deduct for other kinds of employment.

**   **legal temporary jobs**

word processor	**14–19**
wp w/steno	**16–19**
typist w/steno	**12–18**
typist w/o steno	**10–15**
proofreader	**12–16**

*   pattern maker **21.50**

photography

* **	dark-room technician 7–9
* ***	photo researcher for textbook and trade publishers 25–30
***	photo retouching
***	weddings

On Backup

***   physical therapist
(Best to forget this since it is really a single-minded full-time profession demanding 2 years full-time training.)

***   piano or harpsichord tuning (if you have a perfect ear; apprenticeship can last 4 years)

* ***   plumber

** ***   program analysts (Troubleshooter, either in-house or hired out by the retailer. Know programs/hardware well enough to solve problems. Part-time and temp work possible.)

        publishing house part-time work
* **   proofreader
**   copy editor
** ***   photo researcher (interesting and unusual work, finding appropriate photographs for new books that are either inexpensive or in the public domain)
**   translators **(usually a minimum of 15 an hour)**
**   word processor **(12–15 an hour)**

* **   secretary **5–10 +**

* **   securities clerk **9 +**

**   shorthand reporter <u>11.25</u> Av

***   stage managing (almost all union)

        stage technician/lighting/sound/etc.
*   nonunion
***   union (difficult to enter and little or no part time) (I mention these only because many dancers who have a reasonable degree of skill in stage craft get involved with this work when they have no paying dance work. In my limited experience there is a dangerous pitfall here. When technical stage work gets under way, it is all-encompassing; going on for unspeakable hours, sometimes for weeks on end, and if on tour, for months on end, *and you can't dance while the job lasts.* In and out of dance does not

HOW TO DANCE FOREVER

work for us. One of the most talented dancers to surface in recent years, a winner of a Guggenheim Fellowship, slipped out of dance under the guise of necessity by becoming a very good stage manager. He wasn't the only one.)

* **   taxi driver

teacher
*   elementary **8 av**
*   **preschool 7.50 av (shortage in N.Y.C. 1985)**
**   secondary **10 av (shortage in N.Y.C. 1985)**
*   substitute (start at 8:30 A.M. go to 3:30 P.M. There seems to be a demand in N.Y.C.; hard work, too many hours, **$70 a day = less than $10 an hr**)

* ***   **theatrical costume house work**

fabric painter	**15–20**
knitter	**7.50–10**
sewer	**7.50–10**
shopper	**7.50–8.50**

*   translators <u>high tech .04 to .06 per word</u>

videographer
***   for dance
***   for weddings, legal testimony, re-creations of accidents, job interviews
(It may be possible to acquire the craft by apprenticing to a skillful person who owns the equipment. Once trained, I am uncertain how well one could make out by renting equipment for each job.)

waiter/waitress
* **   captain **9–15+ (N.Y.C. 1985)**
**   catering services start waiters at 10–12
* **   waiter/waitress (if you take this road, aim for <u>very</u> expensive restaurants)

* **   word processing 6.26 av
(the graveyard shift starts at 8–10, can go to $15)

On Backup

Speaking to a dancer who has managed to keep at it in New York City for the last fifteen years, I learned that expenses for clothing and classes in dance, acting and singing are very heavy. He says he has been able to get by on $7,000 to $8,000 a year by being frugal and living in a rent-controlled apartment. (Rents are generally staggeringly high in New York City.) He must average a net of $135 to $155 a week to manage. This is living very close to the bone.

Statistics from New York City indicate that average weekly earnings there of people employed in the amusement and recreation services were $258.18 in 1978 and $383.48 in 1983. If you do get work in the commercial theatre or TV, you make out modestly well.

From my New York researcher, April 24, 1987:

"Working through this entire list, word processing appears to be the best bet for the combination of good money, flexible hours, available jobs and minimal training—if you have the skill and feel for typing. It usually takes a thirty-hour class and thirty hours of practice to learn a word-processing language.

"Second choice would be legal proofreading. The money isn't quite as good and it's harder to get started. It usually requires a college degree and a very good command of English.

"Then there are those people who for one reason or another can't sit still or bear to work on Wall Street or in the business world in general. Waiting on tables or bartending, the money is sometimes as good, you're moving around, and you're not working in isolation. I'd much rather shoe horses than serve account executives.

"Construction and high-skills work are all union, except for bit jobs. There are some free-lance carpenters out here who make modest livings, but the jobs usually go all day, days at a time. How do you do class? Plus it's not too hard to injure yourself.*

"Body-retraining work and skilled massage would seem to offer the most enriching kind of knowledge, good pay, flexible hours and, best of all, you can be your own boss. Fees range anywhere from $20 to $65+ an hour.† Training time varies widely. The Swedish Institute of Massage licensing course runs a year, three hours a day,

---

*I left New York in 1982. At that time, I had the impression that there were a number of what we called loft plumbers, loft carpenters and loft painters. They literally did work the SoHo, NoHo and TriBeCa lofts, and those who were both skilled and fast charged a goodly fee for their labors.

†Not exercise instructors or health-club attendants, who make $6 to $12 an hour.

HOW TO DANCE FOREVER

five days a week, and costs $4,500 (student loans can cover two thirds of that)."

Perhaps our schools of art, including dance programs, might someday include body retraining instruction. It would be an insurance that could carry dancers through the years and help others, including dancers. As noted in the survey, the dancers who used body retrainers generally had good and helpful experiences.

What Is the Situation When We Do Work?

New York City is the dream city for many ambitious dancers and well it should be for many reasons. Many come and some work. How many? Out of the complex pages of the *Annual Labor Area Report*, New York City, fiscal year 1986, come these statistics.*

DANCERS' ANNUAL AVERAGE JOB OPENINGS
   N.Y.C., 1984 AND 1986

DANCERS' EMPLOYMENT   1984 = 1,402
                                   1986 = 1,502

DANCERS' AVERAGE ANNUAL OPENINGS   196
   (New jobs)

DANCERS' GROWTH 1980–1990   500
   (Anticipated job growth for 10 years)

How many dancers were there bucking for those 1,502 jobs? It does appear grim and yet the statistics that get into these tables probably come from the commercial theatre, the big ballet and modern companies. Dancers working with smaller companies and teaching dance are most likely not in these figures. How many? Hard to tell.

Good Luck!

*Table 47, p. 105.

MEDITATION TECHNIQUES FOR DANCERS

I could accurately be described as a creature designed for stress. I work best under pressure and deadlines. When disaster strikes, when I smack bottom, I seem to discover renewed strength. Still, as a constant rhythm, all through the day and all through any project, I find myself pausing, stopping and turning away. For many years, this was a haphazard, hit-or-miss activity, from eating an apple to reading a bit out of a mystery novel. Then, with the formation of the WORKGROUP, certain meditation procedures surfaced—some from my directorial need to get the work more focused and some coming from the company members and some from the atmosphere of the times (1970–74). The first chapter of this book finished with a discussion on the nature and value of meditation, a most subtle way of bridging the schism and/or the conflict between mind and body. In Chapter IV, Healers and Treatments, the therapeutic possibilities of meditation were noted, particularly in relation to stress.

Here are a few of the meditation techniques that evolved during the growth of the WORKGROUP. Though usable by others, they are designed by dancers for dancers and some of them dance.

Eye Scan

This is the quickest way I know to clear the head and pluck out the needles of stress. Walk around the space in which you find yourself until, like the sorcerer's disciple in Carlos Casteneda's first book, you find the spot that belongs to you—a place in the space where you feel right. In all my touring, I inevitably experience tension when working in a new place. I prowl about like a nervous cat until it becomes familiar. THE EYE SCAN is one way of settling in.

Finding "your spot," sit cross-legged* or however and take a sequence of long deep breaths with the eyes closed. At a moment that will be clear to you, open your eyes to look at the tip of your nose. Yes, just as the yogis do, except you don't stay there. When you've had it with looking cross-eyed at your nose, transfer your gaze to the highest level of your chest that you can see. From this moment on, at whatever pace suits you, your eyes will travel downward along your body to the floor, across the floor to the wall, up it and across the ceiling, stopping only when another move farther back would cause you to fall over backward. Return the head to a level position, close the eyes and breathe easily and evenly until ready to "face the world." The range of focus should be no wider than the space between your eyes. The pace of the travel of the gaze is completely on impulse. For no reason at all, you may pause at one floorboard for a long time, or go past it without pausing, but see *everything* in the path of your traveling gaze.

Spelling out the EYE SCAN in writing sets up an inevitable error and contradiction. To explicate the sequence of the EYE SCAN on this page, I had to *name* where you are to look. On the contrary, it becomes an amazing trip when you allow yourself to look at all that you encounter *without naming what you see.* It can be done for brief intervals and grants the doer an elusive moment in another mind-set.

If sitting on the ground is not to your taste or the floor is too cold, there is the equivalent—standing. Call it the HORIZONTAL SCAN. Find your place/space within the room. Close the eyes and take several slow, deep breaths. Then turn slowly in place a few times, giving yourself the sense of moving in a spiral, narrowing to a point. Pause when you arrive at the "point," and when ready, open the eyes to look at the tip of the nose. You will know exactly how long you have to do that, and then look straight ahead at eye level and in your own tempo, turning in place counterclockwise or clockwise, it matters not, scan the room at eye level looking, just looking, *without*

*Lenox Hill Hospital, in a pamphlet on a meditation technique, gently downgraded the difficult and exotic lotus position as being used in cultures where chairs were scarce.

naming what you see. When you return to the starting point, close the eyes, taking a few breaths to conclude the HORIZONTAL SCAN.

The beauty of the EYE SCAN and the HORIZONTAL SCAN is that they do not take you out of the world but allow you to perform a meditation within the context of your surroundings. You travel loosely through a slice of your present life, just looking. Does that make it easier to deal with the next task? I should hope so.

Some teachers of meditation techniques get uptight about the matter of "distracting thoughts." Usually these are rigid religionists of one kind or another. I like the open-endedness of the technique of Maharishi Mahesh Yogi, the founder of Transcendental Meditation. In his method, no attempt is made to control the appearance or the departure of any thought or image. My version of this is to regard each thought that comes into the mind as a bird flitting into your line of vision. It can stay, leave, light on your shoulder and even enter into your life. You witness what takes place without directing it.

Sound Crystal

This meditation technique is a steal from the idea of the mantra as used by the Transcendental Meditation people. As I understand it, in TM a novice observes a ceremony of thanksgiving and is then given a mantra, a few syllables which are actually Sanskrit sounds. These are secret and known only to the giver and the receiver. In my method no one knows the mantra or SOUND CRYSTAL but the person meditating, and it is re-created afresh each time.

The SOUND CRYSTAL is best done seated with the eyes closed. Clearing the mind with the breath and settling down to an empty moment, create a silence within for a time. In your silence wait for the first sound to well up into your consciousness. When it fills your mouth, repeat it, silently or audibly, whatever it demands, and at whatever tempo occurs. There should be the sense of witnessing rather than of making something happen. This is not unlike the fashion in which scientists "grow" crystals. (A tiny crystal is suspended in a solution supersaturated with more of the same compound. It slowly attracts more of itself to assume its unique configuration.) In this way, allow the first sound to attract and/or create other sounds in tandem until something clicks in you, telling you the SOUND CRYSTAL is completed. What you arrive at may make no sense at all or words may form. Whatever. Either is fine. You continue with this, audibly or silently, until there will be a turn in the road of your energy and you will know that you are finished. Your eyes will open and if it works for you as it has for me, your head, your mind, will seem not only clear but lighter, as if a gentle breeze were blowing through it. In this manner you can have your own private mantra that will not even be known to you until it happens. In fact, you will probably forget it the next day. The SOUND CRYSTAL is your daily mantra. Since there is no attempt to re-create it, anything may emerge. It may even repeat itself the next day in whole or in part. Should a recognizable word or words rise up, resist it/them not. I have performed the SOUND CRYSTAL many times myself and even demonstrated it for improvisation classes, and each time I really take off for a while.

There are four other meditations which by virtue of using movement might be of special interest to dancers:

Valley/Mountain

VALLEY/MOUNTAIN or YIN-YANG BREATHING is for a beginning or a low energy time. It eases the neck and back muscles and opens the lungs. Sitting cross-legged, find the VALLEY place, by allowing the entire torso to sag, the spine to bend, and the head to fall forward. Slowly and gently sway the weight of your body forward and back across the balance center, the sit bones, constantly narrowing the sway on either side of your weightlessness, finally stopping when there is no effort to avoid falling forward or back. This is the VALLEY place.

Allow the ribs to settle down and all of the air to escape from the lungs, but don't force. Find quiet and nothing for a time. As the hunger for air touches you, breathe in slowly, deeply, from the roots of your pelvis, illusioning yourself that the act of inhaling is slowly erecting your spine. A deep breath should bring you half to two-thirds erect, as if you had gone partway up the MOUNTAIN. Pause, as if suspended, and let the air flow out. A second slow, deep breath will straighten and lengthen your spine and bring you to the top of the MOUNTAIN. Without grabbing, float on that intake of air for a long time, as the back assumes a constantly extended line. Stay with images of floating and opening wide. After a time, your energy will rise over a crest, and as the descent starts, let the air flow out easily; let the head fall forward and the spine bend, *always over the balance center*. Half to two thirds of the way back down the MOUNTAIN, emptied of air, pause, suspended, stopping the slow curving fall. Inhale deeply, slowly, and then let the lungs empty out, and let the head and back resume the slow fall all the way down to the

Meditation Techniques for Dancers

Valley place. Arriving, make no immediate attempt to inhale as you fill out the VALLEY. All the muscles that were used to elongate and lift the spine are now experiencing a long, sustained release. The enormous weight of the head becomes more and more evident as the muscles continue to release tension. When the air hunger asserts itself, again start the ascent to the MOUNTAIN. Thus, the VALLEY and MOUNTAIN cycle continues to repeat until you know that it has been done. When you ascend for the last time, you reach the heights and float, ready for a change. This time when the breath at last is released, you become, as it were, a spruce tree atop the MOUNTAIN with outstretched branches which lower with the outflow of air, and the back grows even longer. Inhaling, use the image of roots reaching deep down into the ground through the sit bones. This should also elongate the spine. Exhaling on the heights, using the image of heavy boughs lowering with each air release, will lengthen and relax the neck and upper back muscles.

Schematizing VALLEY/MOUNTAIN by sequence:

1. Starting in the VALLEY, inhale.

2. Pause partway up and exhale.

3. Inhale, continuing the ascent, and float a long time atop the MOUNTAIN.

4. Exhale, starting the descent.

5. Pause partway and inhale.

6. Exhale, continuing the descent, and rest for a while, deep in the VALLEY.

7. Repeat until done, and then:

Ending VALLEY/MOUNTAIN:

1. Exhale, lengthening the spine and letting the shoulders relax and fall away from the neck.
2. Inhale, lengthening the spine, the neck.
3. Repeat this until done.

If at any time an impulse to yawn surfaces, allow it full play and then pick up where you left off.

BREATH RHYTHM, PULSE RHYTHM and the INTERNAL RHYTHM, the last three of the meditations offered here, are danced. They require a body warmed and prepared to dance. All start while standing.

Breath Rhythm

Find your own place in the area. Closing the eyes, clean out a quiet, empty space in your mind. When settled and clear, turn all of your attention to how you are breathing. Observe everything: the depth, the force, the texture, the phrasing, the tempo, the rhythm. When all of these assume a clear configuration, allow it to infuse your entire body with motion. Your motion will be the metaphor of your breath. Your breath becomes the music of your motion.

There is no attempt here to make beautiful or interesting movement. What you do is not the *idea* of breath in general. You only do what you find. There is an obstacle to the innocence and accuracy of such an observation: The act of observing alters what is being observed, as Heisenberg the physicist noted. If this is true of hard little neutrons and quarks, think of that sensitive weather vane of the moment, the human breath. What to do? Do the best you can. How long to do this? The body will tell you when to stop.

Pulse Rhythm

Find your spot, close your eyes, clear your mind and turn your attention to those subtle parts of the body that occasionally sense the action of the pulse: the tip of the nose, the ears, the lips, the fingertips, the base of the throat. If none of these rewards you with an awareness of the pulse, do the obvious and touch the inside of your wrist.

Again, everything you can absorb from this study of your pulse should be noted carefully, even more so than the breath, since once you begin to move, you will not concurrently be able to maintain awareness of the pulse as was possible with the breath. By observing its thrust, timing, texture and force, the impact of its totality will surface. When confident that you can retain this configuration, let it take full possession of the body and its motion. All of your body becomes your pulse beating. In all of this, as best you can, avoid anticipating and/or visualizing what you are going to do. Wait to discover what you will do. In both the BREATH RHYTHM and the PULSE RHYTHM, if your movement does not cover ground, try keeping the eyes closed. For obvious reasons, it helps the meditation process. If the rhythm you find needs to cover space to be articulated, open the eyes.

As an insert, this business of keeping the eyes closed has in itself an exercise of value in an old space as well as a new one. The instructions: *Go on a blind journey of curiosity*, seeking to experience and sense what you would never take note of with your eyes open.

All of these meditations have a sweet paradoxical action. On the one hand, they help for a little while to cast off the multiplicity of sensations, people, demands, pressures, etc., superseding all of that with an open, easy, clear space. On the other hand, unexpected doors, windows and closets open, letting surprises, the forgotten and the new, into that emptiness. Warning: When you're open, there are no guarantees as to what will come through that door or window. It could be disturbing or madly beautiful, which explains as much as anything why some dancers shy away from improvisation. They use control to avoid the unexpected and the unplanned. For me, if it's there, I want to know it. So much for the *blind journey of curiosity*.

Internal Rhythm

This begins exactly like the BREATH and PULSE RHYTHMS. Now you are seeking something not so obviously palpable. In the quiet of the space you create within yourself, try to sense, hear, feel, become aware of a rhythm within you. A rhythm of this moment. In the patterns of your living, you are crisscrossed by dozens of rhythms—of your speech, your walking, your talking, your eating, your sitting, your standing, your comings and goings—and yet all of them contain a curve and a character that are you. You are seeking the rhythm of your persona, the rhythm of your insides. It will be changing all through the day, and yet it has characteristics in common with patterns coursing through you years ago.

For some people, this is never more than elusive. For many, it makes itself felt even more palpably than the BREATH or the PULSE RHYTHMS. If you should try this and find little but silence, change your position and seek further. If that doesn't deliver, forget it.

If you do "hear," feel, sense an INTERNAL RHYTHM, give yourself time to absorb it fully before letting it take over your body. Then, as passively as possible, go with it, not knowing in advance what you will do or what it will look like, and above all not trying to make it beautiful or interesting. *There is no choreography involved in this*, though it is not inconceivable that what comes out may later on

HOW TO DANCE FOREVER

become material for choreography. Usually it takes the body a bit of time to realize the entire internal phrase. The rhythm will tend to come out like a chick cutting through an eggshell until the moment when it emerges complete.

At this point there is a fork in the road. One way is to allow the rhythm and its motions to evolve. You don't change it, but as the repetitions go on, changes and impulses may assert themselves. You *allow* them, but you don't *direct* them. The other road is closer to a true meditation, which usually rests on sustained repetition to reach that strange plateau that so many cultures have sought. In the repetitive INTERNAL RHYTHM, once the rhythm asserts itself there should be no change of any kind, unless the movement becomes painful or hazardous to continue. In such a case, retain the rhythm and modify the movement phrase so that you can continue. How long? In the WORKGROUP, we set an arbitrary ten minutes, which seemed to serve us. In fact, we started almost all our rehearsals with an INTERNAL RHYTHM as a means of cleaning off the mess with which we came into the studio and becoming open to whatever was ahead. The evolving INTERNAL RHYTHM is more interesting to look at, and recognizing that, we opened many of our performances with it. The repetitive INTERNAL RHYTHM, though trying and even boring at times, is a true dancer's meditation. It does for the body what many meditation techniques do for the mind.

One final note: It is not impossible that the rhythm that makes itself felt might be awesome, frightening and even dangerous. To receive it passively might be hurtful, physically or emotionally. My suggestion has been that if/when a rhythm is beyond you, for whatever reason, don't turn away from it completely. Deal with a part of it.

Ironic. This section on meditation was introduced as one way of coping with the stress that is inherent in our work, and here I introduce something that can produce its own kind of turmoil. Where I come from, if there's a fire in the basement, I need to know about it. If a ghost is screaming to be heard in the attic, I'll go upstairs, even though I may end up weeping.

I am all too aware that I open the possibility of uncertainty to the reader by describing several methods of meditation rather than only one. Most authors carve out but one path for the reader. Why one? Because there is always only one; one true path that will be yours for the believing. I cannot do this because I am sure of nothing. I share uncertainty with the ancient Chinese. Couples would commonly have three wedding ceremonies: Confucian, Taoist and Buddhist. Who knew which was right? They all had their points; ergo, three weddings.

Another question presents itself: Why all these meditation techniques when there are already out there age-old, time-tested methods? Out of India, China and Japan come t'ai chi chuan, yoga, Zen Buddhism and Transcendental Meditation. Why all this invention and ingenuity when it has already been done and probably much better?

My predilections drive me to this course of invention, and if that is my experience, I'm certain there are others out there such as I. To be specific, I never cared to go to dance class. Instead, I formulated a technique for myself. I made my own dances. I had a passion for Flamenco dance. It never occurred to me to study it, but I came to see Carmen Amaya with eyes that devoured every gesture, and then the time came when I had the chutzpah and the need to make *Spanish Dance*. Some "heavy" Spanish dancers saw it and said, "Fine. Why not?"

I am continually aware of history and tradition, and yet when the time comes to make something for this moment, I reach into myself and both the history and the tradition are right there in my bones. Inevitably, they enter into whatever I create. I am what I have experienced. In that experience, there is my time as a kid playing handball in the Bronx and arguing politics in the basement cafeteria of the City College of New York—a far cry from the Ganges, Kyōto or Hunan Province. The meditation styles from these far-off places are linked to specific philosophies, parts of which I know, parts of which I admire and most of which are alien to my life and my ways. To absorb deeply and master any one of them involves masters. They tend to teach absolutes with which I have difficulty. I love to learn from people, but I never learned to follow masters. Further, they teach ways evolved one to two thousand years ago in cultures that are not mine. These are cultures which in many respects I admire. I study them. Reading Lao-tze or Chuang-tze is a journey across a jagged landscape of thought, clouded in colored mist and suddenly shot through with blinding light. I return to them again and again over the years.

I am quite aware that many of my colleagues have found sources of strength from these Eastern disciplines that have carried them through rough times. To be very clear, suggesting and describing other meditation techniques does not indicate for one moment a devaluation of these traditional ones that have so strongly caught the interest and imagination of many sophisticated people here in the West. Of course, the hottest items for sophisticated people in the East are blue jeans and rock and roll.

To be honest, I *am* hinting that rich as those ancient rituals may be and as ingenious and useful as mine may be, you might consider creating your own. If there's anything central to what I have taught when I have taught, it's the underlying implication that, in the words of old Walt Whitman, you ". . . contain multitudes." You are the guru you seek, and thus you are beholden to study from yourself, which is another way of giving you faith and confidence in your own creative powers.

ON DANCING AND HAVING A FAMILY
by Michael Engel

Daniel, here is a journal entry I made Jan. 28, shortly after reading your book. It is in response to Chapter VI, The Heart-Mind of the Dancer. I wanted to share it with you because I know you are a caring and an aware man; your experiences as a dancer are full and very inspirational and yet not all mine. There are dancers' experiences as parents that would be good for you to know more of and understand better.

"For me, 'dancers who have managed to have full dance careers and a family' have some very special interrelationships with their craft and their children; experiences that go well beyond imagining how it is not easy to dance and be a parent.

"To have kids and to have a dance career brings a sharpness to one's work in rehearsal and in classes. To take class and pay for child care at the same time gave me an added urgency to what I was learning. To work long hours for little or no pay while paying others to take care of my children instilled a focus and drive that I still have even as parenting gets a little easier. I think in those first years after Sam and Trevor were born, I dug my hands and feet and mind into my craft harder than many of the dancers around me. I had to or that craft would have slipped away from me.

"How does one give oneself a class in a small room with a changing table and a crib in it? Very quietly, slowly, by holding on to the edge of the table, sometime between 9 P.M. and midnight, while hoping that one can take a regular class soon.

"How does one wake up at night three and four times to care for kids and still rise for class, rehearsal, another job? One learns to fall asleep fast after quickly 'waking up,' one learns to need less sleep, one learns to not get uptight if more sleep is wanted or needed.

HOW TO DANCE FOREVER

Beyond that I am not sure how parents do it. I always got and gave good hugs before going out the door the next morning.

"How does a parent-dancer go from class to rehearsal to part-time job to getting or dropping off children? Not lyrically, not classically, not percussively. You just do it. You get the timing in because that is what you have to do. Such is the basic nature of a parent; there are no styles to imitate, only the elements around and in yourself to respond to, to control, to let go of and try something new.

"Some memories of a parent-father-dancer: 'Sammy, I saw Daddy's feet under the curtain!' Yes, the curtain opens and who are the only two sitting front row center, big smiles on their faces? And who are the first two backstage when Daddy is done working? Didn't anyone tell them to sit farther back and not to go backstage so soon? Who do they think they are, the owners of the place?

"No big congratulations for their dad, no uneasy sounding praise. Just them, their energy and a few basic questions and comments. 'Where's the pop machine, Dad?' 'Around the corner.' 'I liked the last piece.' 'Yeah, me too.' 'Where's the pop machine, Dad?' 'Around the corner.'

"Other memories are of dinner just before going to perform. Usually on performance nights I made dinner earlier so I could eat with the boys. Even then I never could get to the theatre by call-time. At first in my career I felt guilty for being at work later than the other dancers. Now I know my limits, my family's limits, and those of my body. I can eat a light dinner with family, go to work, and have enough time for warm-up, makeup and costumes. I compromise here and there, but when I leave for a show, I go with a fullness that goes past my stomach and that I share with the audience.

"Dancers bring a lot of experiences to parenting and parents bring a lot of experiences to dancing. If more dancers realized this, they might not be so cautious about saying yes to new life in them. Saying yes is what a dancer does anytime they start a new piece or perform. Yes, I am ready for the unknown. Today is a good day to change. Yes, it is scary. I will never be the same. Yes, this is just what I want to do, to become. What? I don't know. If I did, I wouldn't be as interested in the journey.

"Choosing children and choosing a dance career are quite similar. Besides both being unknowns, they are hard work. Both require discipline and flexibility or a belief in inconsistency. Both parenting and dancing involve a seeking within for a will and strength to continue without, to continue being sane when all the signs around you

On Dancing and Having a Family

are insane, bedlam and struggle. And in both, one often finds anger and frustration and doubts galore give way to love and certainty about what one is doing.

"Parents and dancers both work with their body-mind also, overcoming habits and old voices that don't work anymore. Both are constant physical partners of others; both know that to not succeed today doesn't mean the end; both struggle against odds like having clean clothes, adequate sleep, warm bodies; and both learn to observe, listen, make mistakes, laugh and go on. Parents and dancers know the power and depth of their crafts.

"Parents know better than many, at an earlier age than most, the value of never being sure, of the absurdity of life, and still cherishing life through thick and thin, and there are such thin, thin, razor-thick times."

VOCAL PROJECTION
(Adapted from the Methods
of Norbert Jacobi)

When asked to speak, the favorite cliché of dancers used to be, "But my medium is movement." The eloquence of Martha Graham, Helen Tamiris, Doris Humphrey, José Limón and others belie that modest remark. Actually, when dancers become choreographers and teachers, their voices become an essential tool of expression. Unfortunately, only rarely do any of them get training in vocal techniques. Unfortunate for two reasons:

1. Dancers, as well as most physically intense and active people, tend to use too much tension and unnecessary force, particularly in the area of the neck and upper thorax, to produce speech. This tends to result in a high-pitched squeezed sound. Listen to a group of football players. Very few baritones. Many squeaky tenors.

2. Though there is much that choreographers and teachers communicate through movement, an enormous amount is conveyed through speech, in long rehearsals and classes and, even worse, trying to speak in large areas when music is being played. Under these conditions, endurance, power, expressiveness and an attractively produced sound are lifesavers. These are not easy achievements. Rarely does one come across a person with a beautifully placed, strong voice who has never studied vocal projection.

While I was working on Broadway, wanting to extend my range in the theatre, I studied acting, during which process I became aware that I had serious vocal limitations. Many serious actors at that time were studying with Norbert Jacobi. I went to him and learned a method that produced a significant change in the power and quality of my vocal production. In the process, I also learned from him an invaluable principle for all teaching and learning. *Find the strong point and work out from there.*

His criticism of most vocal teaching was that each teacher taught from *his/her strong point* and not from that of each individual student. What follows is a rough approximation of what I recall, what I modified over the years and other bits I picked up along the way.

Ideally, all vocal work should be done with a skilled teacher because what you hear as you speak is not really what you sound like. If that resource is available to you, you will not need to read this section. If not, a tape recorder, and a modestly good microphone and sound system will help you hear what you do. A pitch pipe, a Hohner Melodica, a little music synthesizer or a piano will help, though if you have a good ear they're not essential.

Privacy is critical for relaxed, unselfconscious and concentrated work.

SEQUENCE OF VOCAL EXERCISES

1. Walking about, breathe slowly and fully from deep within the trunk of the body, in through the nose and out the mouth, *making no effort anywhere in the throat or mouth*. Do this for the complete circuit of the room.

2. Each sound throughout the ensuing sequence is preceded by an easy, full inhalation, starting from deep within the trunk, and is created when the lifted chest is released, letting the ribs float downward as the air flows out, *without any forcing or pressure, anywhere*. Continuing to walk about as you do the following exercises will give you the confidence to produce sound while moving, which is what you do when you teach. You can vary this with standing in place.

3. Taking an easy but full breath and letting the lightly lifted chest fall, let the air out as a hum, starting from a low note and sliding up to a high note and back down again. Try the same thing starting from high to low to high. Decide which is the most comfortable and stick with that. Odds are there will be a "bump" or a break in the sound as you move from low to high. Try to smooth out the transition, erasing the break. Do about five of these.

Vocal Projection

4. Do Exercise #3 with the mouth open, still working for smooth-ness, going as high and as low as you can *without forcing*, again about five times. You approach your limits, high and low, but never press against them.

5. Hum a note in your midrange, letting the sound pour out as long as there is air flowing out of your lungs *without pushing and without forcing*. Using your ear, or an instrument, repeat the hum at a lower pitch. Continue this humming of a single note, going lower and lower until you approach a level that will demand forcing. Stop and go back up to the midrange note and do the same, but ascending to a higher and higher pitch. If you have the time, progress up and down the scale one note at a time. If not, skip an interval or two. *This is not an exercise in singing or pitch control*. Ideally, you should start at the midrange note where you can most easily produce a rich, strong sound. It is here that a tape recorder can help you. Experiment with directing the vibra-tions produced by the humming toward the nose, the teeth or the top of the head.

6. Repeat Exercise #5 entirely, except that after two seconds of humming, open the mouth and let the sound come pouring out for as long as the breath flows easily out of your lungs *without ever forcing*. The big decision here is what vowel sound to make. Try all of them: may, mat, me, mine, mit, mow, moo. Select the vowel sound that allows you to produce the strongest and richest sound, and stay with that for this exercise until you begin to notice a distinct change for the better in your vocal production. Then begin to experiment with the other vowel sounds. Decide which one is the most difficult for you, and then:

7. Starting with a two-second hum at the pitch in which you are most secure, open the mouth, making your strongest vowel sound. Now close the lips to hum again and, thinking, remembering and feeling the power of the strong vowel, sing out the weak vowel, i.e., you steal from the strong to give to the weak. Then experi-ment with all the other vowels.

8. For men only: Take a couple of minutes to sing any simple tune in falsetto. Mr. Jacobi used to say that a little falsetto exercise sweetens a man's voice...

HOW TO DANCE FOREVER

9. Exercises in articulation: Walk about at an easy tempo and articulate richly, precisely and quickly each of the sound clusters when your left foot hits the ground:
   a. Rhythmically articulate "ba" or "bo" or whatever vowel sound is strongest for you, on every left step, four times.
   b. Keeping the same tempo and without a break, articulate "bab" on every left step, four times.
   c. Keeping the same tempo and without a break, articulate "babab" on every left step, four times.
   d. Keeping the same tempo and without a break, articulate "bababab" on every left step, four times.
   e. Keeping the same tempo and without a break, articulate "babababab" on every left step, four times.
   f. Keeping the same tempo and without a break, articulate "babababababa" on every left step, four times in 6/8 time, i.e. 6 "ba's" for each time the left foot hits the ground.
   g. Keeping the same tempo and without a break, repeat the entire sequence of a. to f., articulating as crisply as you can "pa," "poo" or whatever vowel is strongest for you.
   h. Keeping the same tempo and without a break, repeat the entire sequence of a. to f., articulately as crisply as you can "da."
   i. Keeping the same tempo and without a break, repeat the entire sequence of a. to f., articulating as crisply as you can "ta."
   j. Keeping the same tempo and without a break, repeat the entire sequence of a. to f., articulating as crisply as you can "ga."
   k. Keeping the same tempo and without a break, repeat the entire sequence of a. to f., articulating as crisply as you can "ka." This sequence exercises the major articulation points of the mouth.

10. Through this entire sequence, it is helpful to keep an image of the sound as a generously round column, pouring up and out of the body. Just as it leaves the mouth it is nicked, cut and shaped delicately and precisely as if by an expert carver of totem poles; only in your case, your lips and tongue are the swift and sharp knives and chisels. The fullness of the column of sound is never squeezed. On the contrary, you open everything to let it flow out freely past the carvers.

Vocal Projection

11. When you achieve a fluency and crispness in this sequence of exercises, make experimental changes of the vowel sounds, including the specific exercise of stealing from the strong to support the weak sound.

12. Make a one-time experiment:
    a. Count from one to ten, keeping the center of action in the back of the mouth.
    b. Repeat, keeping the center of action in the middle of the mouth, just under the arch of the roof of the mouth.
    c. Repeat, keeping the center of action exactly where the lips are.
    d. Repeat, illusioning yourself that the center of action is just a bit in front of the mouth. If you can tape-record this experiment, you may hear yourself in this last version, immediately in front of the mouth, sounding like one of those exquisitely articulate British actors who can make guitar music out of the English language. When doing exercises in articulation, aim for the focus of speaking in front of the mouth.

13. Finish off with a jazzy articulation of "boodiga, pootika" at breakneck speed while doing a hoedown.

HOW TO REALLY DANCE FOREVER

It's easy. Get videotaped. You and all of us can finally become history. There are architects, sculptors, painters and potters who have been dust for thousands of years, and yet their creations can inform and shake us today. What do we have of all those beautiful and very dead dancers of centuries past? Until the few bits of notation that survive from the Renaissance, all we had were the "snapshots" of the sculptors and the painters. Then came film, but its expense and complexity has kept it, even today, beyond the reach of most dancers. Contemporary systems of notation are invaluable, but also very expensive and the province of a very few skilled scribes and readers.

Now comes videotape. Simple, nonprofessional cameras can be operated easily, and VCRs abound for viewing. Almost every performance of a new work is taped. Wonderful? Yes and no. Yes, it's a step in the right direction. No, it stinks most of the time. The picture is too small. The focus is too soft. The gradations of light and dark are too few. Technically, the medium is improving each year, but one element remains a serious obstacle in film or video: The rigid, rectangular window too often robs dance of dynamic nuance, spatial relevance and the sweating, exultant imminence of the living dancer.

For all of its obvious limitations, the technology is here to stay, and it does perform some vital functions: dancing forever into history, and the practical note that important decisions in the dance world are being made today on the basis of viewing videotapes.

But most of the time we look awful on videotape. What to do? There's no question that dancers have to become sophisticated enough to take advantage of this technology. Before anything, the dancer has to be absolutely clear as to the purpose of any videotaping. There are several possibilities. One is for archival purposes, for the record. Another is as a tool for teaching the material to new dancers. A third

HOW TO DANCE FOREVER

is literally to market oneself as a performer or choreographer. Each of these is best served by a different kind of videotaping. The last really means creating a new work of art, translating the poem of the living dance into the new poem of the turbulent shadows on the flat screen.

There are nine factors that will inevitably influence how well a particular videotape creates the kind of excitement a choreographer is trying to provoke:

1. EQUIPMENT

2. CAMERA TECHNICIANS AND/OR DIRECTORS

3. THE EYE OF THE CAMERA

4. SOUND

5. LIGHTING

6. COSTUME COLOR

7. THE DANCE SPACE

8. MONEY!

9. SHOOTING DANCE FOR THE RECORD AND/OR AS A LEARNING TAPE

1. EQUIPMENT: I will list a series of setups, starting with the ideal and, of course, the most expensive, and finishing off with the least satisfactory and least expensive.

Setup #1, the ideal: Three cameras and three VCRs. One camera in the center, the camera eye preferably at the dancers' waist level, with the responsibility to do long shots or the master shot, which includes all of the dancers and much of the stage space. The second camera stationed to, say, the left of the house or dance space and low, as close to floor level as possible, a little closer to the stage or dance space, with the responsibility of doing midshots, shooting one, two or three dancers including arms and legs and, wherever strategic, close-ups. The third camera should be positioned at the other side

How to Really Dance Forever

of the house, far enough back to include the entire space and at least three feet above the height of the tallest dancer.* Its responsibility should be full stage shots and medium shots. These positions can and should be varied to suit the needs of particular works.

This setup calls for a postproduction process that requires viewing time, called logging, to pick out the best shots. The choreographer can save money by doing this either alone or with the editor away from an editing studio. The final step demands the use of videotape editing equipment and a skilled editor.

Setup #2: The same as above, except that there is only one VCR for all three cameras and a director who has a switcher, which is a device that records only one camera at a time; thus the editing is done in "real time," that is, while the shooting is going on. To do it well, the director should be able to talk over an intercom to the camera operators, telling them when to zoom in or out or whom to focus upon. This requires a control area, acoustically isolated from the performance space. Personally, I think the use of the switcher is bad because precise and aesthetically valid editing of dance is almost impossible to do well on the wing. Without the intercom, every camera move has to be intensively rehearsed and remembered by the camera operators. This setup would not be a significant saving if a switcher is involved because it is expensive to rent. Still, some money is saved by eliminating the postproduction process of editing. Only titles would be needed.

Setup #3: Two cameras and two VCRs. They should be placed on different sides of the house; one low, about kneecap level, and the other high, about two feet above head level, and both a bit closer to the center than the second and third cameras described in Setup #1. A system or score should be worked out as to who, at each point, is responsible for what the trade calls the master shot and who is responsible for the medium or close-up. *For safety, at all times one camera has to cover the master shot.*

---

*Shooting in a theatre, all the cameras can have zoom lenses, since they can all be far back enough to do their assigned tasks, with the center camera, which is responsible for the master shot, being farthest back to image the entire stage width. In a studio, particularly a dance studio, it may be necessary to equip one camera with a wide-angle lens. Even then, to do a master shot of the entire space, it may be necessary to position this camera from a corner of the space. There are wide-angle zoom lenses, but they are more expensive.

Setup #4: One camera and one VCR. This makes for dullsville. No way out of it. The only way to circumvent this fate is to shoot the dance once as a master shot and then several more times in close-up, midshot, from different angles, heights, and then do the post-production work of editing the different versions to make one flowing coherent whole. There are some cameras that allow for "editing in the camera." This means all edits and transitions are haphazard, making a clumsy version of the dance probable. A single, nonstop, one-camera shot of an entire dance can never be much more than a tape for the record unless you have a genius camera operator who becomes part of the performance process, moving in, out and around the dancers to make a visual poem of the work. Marry her/him before someone else does.

2. CAMERA TECHNICIANS AND/OR DIRECTORS: Though there are many skilled musicians, a good dance accompanist is a rarity. Though there are many skilled video artists and technicians, very few know dance or the obstacles standing in the way of realizing its beauty and power on the video screen. If you find a knowledgeable and sensitive techy, *mazel tov*. In any event, you yourself must acquire a minimal understanding of the technology, have a clear idea of what impact you want for your dance and be able to express that to your video collaborator. Only deal with one who listens and you be sure to listen in turn. There is the potential for mutual enrichment.

Not a few current leading composers and lighting and costume designers took their first professional steps working for dancers. What better place for them to start developing their craft and artistry than with the most difficult art for which to write music, to costume, to light and now to videotape? Who else would hire those young, raw, fresh-out-of-school, untested people except the dancers, whose budgets usually preclude working with established artists and technicians? The challenge here is not only to find young video technicians but *talented* ones who can listen as well as inform.

3. THE EYE OF THE CAMERA, or loosening the rigid constriction of the camera's window: For me, this is the crux of the problem. It is the obstacle that if understood and controlled can make the camera the instrument of an art form, bringing new insights not possible in live stage performance.

The "normal" camera position is eye level, level with the eye of the performer *and with the eye of the camera operator!* Great for stand-up comics, singers and actors because the face is their *center of focus. The normal height for the dance camera should be waist level, equidistant from the head and the feet.* Shooting at eye level, the camera is closer to the head than the feet, and by the nature of perspective and the exaggerations of the lens, the head gets too big and the legs too short. This is a major reason why most performance videotapes are so terrible. In order not to block the view of the audience, the camera is usually placed behind the audience *and elevated above them to exclude their heads from the picture,* or high by virtue of having a raked auditorium floor, or, worst of all, shooting from a balcony, guaranteeing that all the dancers will have a low-slung look with stumps for legs.

A low camera position lengthens the legs, amplifies all leg movements, gives a heroic cast to the dancers' bodies and makes elevation look higher. Any extended or important leaping or jumping sequence needs to be shot from a low position because the film screen and the video monitor both seriously diminish the impact of all aerial work. In the theatre, it is easy to get a low camera position by shooting from the audience floor, with the camera eye as low or even lower than the stage floor. A low position in the studio is difficult. It's awkward for the camera operator to move or dolly. In professional studios that have the old pedestal cameras, the lowest position is over four feet—ghastly. The newest ones are better and can skim the ground or swing up to twelve to thirteen feet in the air. All are terribly expensive to rent and they demand skilled operators to go with them.

The master shot or long shot, which is responsible for not losing *anything,* can still come in close for a medium shot or a close-up *if nothing significant is happening elsewhere.*

The high camera best catches the excitement of movements covering space and is especially important at those moments when the floor pattern is the most significant statement being made choreographically. Ideally, this is a boom that can carry the camera up above the heads of the dancers. Without a boom, there are ladders, scaffolding and balconies.

Long shot? Medium shot? Close-up? How to choose? You make a choice every moment your eyes are open and, yes, even when they are closed. You wake. What time is it? *You focus in and see only the clock.* What kind of a day is it? You look out the window to look at the sky. *That is a long shot.* It's as simple as that. Conceptually, the mind is always looking at a close-up or a medium shot or a long shot, even in your dreams.

HOW TO DANCE FOREVER

Choreographically, there are times when what is happening across the entire space *is what the dance is about*. At other times, the most significant motion might be seen in a hand opening or in the slow turn of a head. Before calling in a videographer, the choreographer should pause to look again at his/her creation with fresh eyes and make a *looking score*. What must be seen and when? When is it wide or medium or a tight focus? The choreographer should be able to convey this "score" to the videographer *and be able to receive creative input from her/him*. After all, she/he comes to the piece with fresh eyes and should be welcomed into the creative process.

Study the taping of sports. *Whenever they can, they bring the camera in tight.* We see Michael Jordan at the foul line, staring down the hoop, his tongue darting out to lick his lips, tighten them and the shot changes to see him shoot for the basket. We see Lendl tug at the shoulders of his shirt, study the strings of his racquet, bounce the ball; the camera pulls back as he serves and another camera cuts in for a long shot to cover the entire court and catch Becker's return. *These close-ups are the most powerful images of which video is capable.* We can identify, come close to, root for or dislike the player. Whatever, we are involved.

Use close-ups whenever you can without losing the big thrust and intention of the choreography. This is all too rarely done in videotaping dance. Not only is it difficult to identify with someone whose face is barely discernible; it is hard even to know what the dance is about when the figures are small and the faces an anonymous blur. *No time is more important than the first thirty seconds after a dancer's initial appearance. Somehow, a close-up must be squeezed into that space of time, otherwise the presence, import and personality of the dancer will be cloaked, fuzzy and anonymous until there is a close-up.* If the nature of the choreography makes early close-ups not practical, think of using them as an introduction or during the titles or as an opening shot that zooms out when the dance begins.

All of this is to contradict the usual horror of choreographers when a hand or a foot or, horrors, a leg is cut out of the frame. If a dance is being shot as a record or as a learning instrument, close-ups are crazy. If the taped version is to convey the poem of the dance, a sequence containing only a hand may be the most poignant moment of all.

Cameras can move. So can dancers. Most camera operators, partly operating out of fear that the choreographer is certain to scream that

How to Really Dance Forever

she/he is not *following* the dancer, will always keep the dancer or dancers *in the middle of the frame, thus in a very real sense the dancers are not moving at all*. They are frozen in the center of the video window like a deer caught on the cross hairs of a hunter's scope. Only if there is a complex set behind the moving figures can the impact of motion in space be experienced by the viewer. The classic climax of many movies is a chase. The speeding car is usually locked in the center of the picture frame, *but the scenery is rushing by, backward*. Every Fred Astaire set was complicated, emphasizing strong verticals while he *was* usually kept in the middle of the frame.

Conclusion: When there is no complex setting with strong verticals, allow the dancer(s) to move within the frame *without needlessly moving the camera*. When the dancer(s) begins to get near enough to the edge of the picture frame so that another inch and we would become aware of the edge, the camera can subtly move, panning or dollying in the direction of the figure's motion, or zoom out, giving room to wide-ranging movements. The beauty of a stage performance is that the audience can always keep a sense of the entire space within the proscenium, and so every spatial venture is felt. The limitation of the video window is that if we see the entire space, the dancer is ineffectually small, and if we come in close enough to see the dancer fully and strongly, we lose awareness of the surrounding space, and so the impact of spatial action is not experienced by us. Allowing movement within the frame becomes the equivalent of movement within the proscenium.

In fact, the harsh rigidity of that rectangular window can be deliberately and effectively exploited by a high camera placement. Say the choreographer brings a dancer far downstage front to make a specific point. For videotaping, in a long, high shot, place the dancer *in the lower third or quarter of the window*. Similarly, if the significant placing of the dancer is far upstage, in a long, high shot keep the dancer in the upper quadrant of the video window. The same applies if being far off to one side is what the moment is about; keeping the dancer close to the side also gives a view of a large chunk of the bare space.

Needless to say, everything gets more difficult as the number of dancers being videotaped increases. Getting them all in makes the dancers too small to have personalities or impact. Shooting only some gives only some of the choreography. It is here that the choreographer and the videographer must begin to choose. When does the eye make

HOW TO DANCE FOREVER

a close-up and when does it take in the entire stage? When is the thrust of the choreography being carried by the group and when is it in the swift turn of a head?

Little can be expected of videographers who see the dance for the first time the day of the shooting. They should come to see the dances ahead of time, exactly like the costume and light designers, and *without cameras*. Then there should be a meeting of minds to see what he/she sees, what the choreographer wants to be seen, and what is the purpose of the tape to be made.

4. SOUND: In filming dance, Hollywood takes great care to include sounds created by dancers with their feet, costumes and/or props. The technical term for this is "foot and dress noises." In fact, one of the reasons Astaire's dances had so much impact is that he learned to "Mickey Mouse" from the cartoons; meaning that every strong physical action was mirrored by an equivalent sound. If he did a sharp "daaa baaa didopdop," rest assured that at the exact same time the orchestra went "daaa baaa didopdop." In addition, his taps underlined every motion.

Almost all dance shot for broadcast TV lacks these foot and dress noises and consequently loses presence, imminence and vitality. It looks unreal in the worst sense of the word. Why? Even in the best TV studios, when taping dance, there is no microphone in the studio. A high-quality audio recording is sent directly into the VCR in sync with the picture being taped and another audio line goes to speakers blasting away in the studio for the dancers to hear, but, to repeat, there is no microphone in the studio. Good quality music on tape, *but no foot and dress noises.*

To date, no one in the TV industry has solved the problem technically and it is not geared to the extravagant budgets of Hollywood musicals. There, the dancers are filmed to prerecorded music blasting away in a studio with no microphone. The foot and dress noises are recorded later and then dubbed in precise sync with the music and the action, an expensive but necessary process. The reason? If they tried to record the foot and dress noises while filming, there would have to be a microphone in the studio, but the dancers must also *hear* the music to which they are dancing. If they could hear the music, so could that microphone. It would be recording music played over loudspeakers in the studio, thus picking up room acoustics, echo and delay from speaker to mike to recorder, all making the final music track several generations away from the original and muddied.

Believing foot and dress noises are necessary, at a video workshop in Marshall University in Huntington, West Virginia, I hit upon a solution: Using my best performance music tape, I had it sent to two places at once—into the VCR, in sync with the picture being taped, and into the studio through a single speaker. Its volume was set just barely loud enough for me to dance to and it was hung behind the camera and behind a hand-held shotgun microphone whose virtue lies in its ability to hear only what it is pointed at, i.e., me. The techy holding the mike, while out of range of the camera, got as close to me as he could. Thus, the mike only heard my noises and nothing of significance from the speaker. A sound technician mixed the levels of the music and the foot and dress noises.

We made a test of this procedure by shooting the identical dance sequence without the foot and dress noises. It was dead in comparison with the new experimental tape.

Of course, most low-budget shoots don't have this problem. They record the music as it blasts in the dance space along with the noises made by the dancers' feet, props and costumes, and get poor-quality sound along with a sense of reality.

The next point is highly debatable and could be pursued as an experiment. In the sophisticated standards of dance today, "Mickey Mousing," or making dance phrases that duplicate the rhythmic contours of the music is considered naïve and undynamic. For work on the stage I subscribe to this thinking, but in the transposition to the screen should this dictum be reconsidered? Would it be wise to take a hint from Fred Astaire and seek out a few strategic spots in the choreography *and modify them for videotaping by moving in consonance with the music rather than counterpointing the rhythmic thrusts of the music?* Just as sound engineers endlessly experiment and tinker to recreate every facet of the experience of live music, so should we eliminate anything in videotaping that diminishes the impact of the living presence of the dancer and find everything that can amplify it on the screen.

5. LIGHTING: The video camera is dumb when it comes to light. Little light or radical contrasts produce terrible results. Some of the best dance lighting moments onstage are with little light or sharp contrast. This creates problems that can, with ingenuity, be solved, but unfortunately most videographers feel safest with lots of light

evenly distributed. For us, light is the palpable geography through which we travel. If the light configuration is uneventful, moving from here to there (which is what we do for a living) *becomes uneventful.*

Do everything possible to have a lot of light available; enough so that it is never necessary to shoot with the lens wide open. Go for contrast when you want it, but be certain that the dark areas are filled in with enough light so that there is no more than a four f-stop difference between the light and the dark areas.*

Expensive theatrical lighting is not necessary. A dozen to eighteen 250-watt reflector floods and spots housed in those cheap clip-on fixtures, strategically located, will do the job. Better still are 250-watt and 500-watt photo floods in those aluminum reflectors on light-weight stands. Just be sure to get professional advice on how much of a load your electrical source can handle.

6. COSTUME COLOR: Any costume that has the same color as the background will in effect make the dancer disappear. Black on black is the road to invisibility. Black curtains, black wings and *black vinyl floors* swallow black costuming and particularly black shoes. A shoe dye to lighten the tone will help. White costuming will distort the figure of the dancer. Substitute light gray or light blue for white to get white on tape. Also red, magenta and fuchsia can be difficult to light. They too flare up. Broadway shows always have a costume parade before the dress rehearsal. For videotaping, the best idea would be a "monitor parade" of the costumes in the setting where the shoot will occur and before the day of taping. This will allow time to make changes needed to retain the definition of the dancers' bodies.

7. THE DANCE SPACE: The obvious is to avoid dancing on con-crete. The best video equipment is found in broadcast studios, which almost always have concrete floors. If you must work on such a dangerous surface, go over the choreography carefully to see whether you can modify falls and aerial work so that you and/or your dancers don't live to remember that day with bitterness. Use kneepads and padding whenever possible, and if the costuming does not permit it, at least use them for rehearsals. Many of the best-equipped studios

---

*If you are unfamiliar with the term f-stop, a photographer friend will clarify it for you in two minutes.

have inadequate space for dancers. Avoid them if you can, and try to have equipment brought to a proper dance space.

8. MONEY: Try to get Public Access Television people interested. Make a deal. Let them air your stuff for nothing if they will do the job for you. Some are more professional than others. Organize a dancers' cooperative to buy or rent equipment and to train and engage the services of video technicians and artists. Weekend rentals are cheaper. Organize a day or a weekend when several of you can rent the same space, crew and equipment at a significant saving. Get to know the community of videographers and particularly the new, talented and creative ones. *They may be looking for you.*

9. SHOOTING DANCE FOR THE RECORD AND/OR AS A LEARNING TAPE: The archival function of videotaping dance may prove to be its most important contribution. For the first time ever, dance can join sculpture, painting, poetry and architecture in having a vivid history. Even more, works that made little impression in their own time may in the future be revived from tape and prove to be masterpieces. We may have creating and ignored among us at this moment a Vincent van Gogh of the dance. Poor Vincent, who sold one painting in his lifetime, painted a field of irises that recently sold for $53.9 million.

Recording dance for archival purposes should actually be no different than for use as a learning tape. One creates an archive not only to let the future know roughly what the dance looked like but also to be able to revive it, if so desired.

The most obvious recording is the long, uninterrupted master shot that leaves nothing out. If this is of a soloist, many details will be evident, since the camera can get closer than with a large group. Even with the solo, if the work has any significant details that do not show up well on the small video screen with its poor resolution and lack of crispness, some moments should be shot once again in close-up. For example, telling hand movements, facial expressions if they are a vital component to the choreography, and also very fast complex movements. These might even be shot at a slower tempo, so that they can be understood and learned.

As for group works, figures upstage who are obscured by dancers downstage should be taped separately. Large ensemble work would profit from having an additional shooting of smaller groupings. It

HOW TO DANCE FOREVER

becomes the responsibility of the choreographer, when the recording is made, to have it played back immediately and note carefully what has been lost and be certain to do all the necessary cover shots. A separate high master shot will preserve for the future all of the intricacies of the spatial patterns.

A good question: Should the entire work be shot once again *from the rear*? Dancers usually learn movement from teachers, choreographers and other dancers by getting behind them.

If this is not done, there are a few useful tricks when learning from videotapes and films by working in front of a mirror. When the dancer is learning from a videotape, place the monitor to one side but *facing the mirror so that it is visible to the dancer*. The dancer only observes the mirrored reflection of the video screen. Now, when the reflected figure moves right, the dancer moves to the right. This is not the situation when looking directly at the monitor. In that case, if the figure on the screen moves to the right, the learner must move left, and though that can be done, it is a complexity that slows down the entire process, particularly when there are extensive turning phrases.

The best learning procedure of all is if you use film with a projector. In this situation, the projector is placed to one side and directed toward a screen or a wall *behind the dancer, who is looking at the mirror in front of her/him*. Here again, if the figure moves right, the dancer moves right, *and, wonderful surprise, if the figure turns to face upstage, the dancer turning upstage is now facing in the same direction and looking at the back of the filmed dancer*. Here too, when the figure moves right, the dancer moves right. All of this works with film because a projector will throw a large enough image to be seen at that distance. Not so with the small video screen, but it would be possible with a video projector.

CONCLUSION

What has been noted here is a bare indication of the complexity and richness that is possible in capturing dance on tape. Heretofore, the dance has been an illiterate art, *with no history*, except for a few centuries of statues, paintings, abstruse notations and memories. Tape is economically feasible, but few of us have been able to bear looking at ourselves in that medium. Usually we and our work have looked awful seen that way. What's the good of a history if it degrades the quality of the art?

When we videotape dance, we are incorporating the limitations *and the strengths* of that medium into our choreography. We dare

How to Really Dance Forever

not simply point the camera at our work. If however, we design the interaction of camera and dance, exploiting the new parameters and special insights of the video medium, we will be making a creative use of its capabilities and come up with what amounts to a new artistic statement.

MORE ON ME. . . . Who Am I and How Do I Get Off Writing This Book?

There is no way that I can write this book without becoming a bit defensive. After all, my life, my rent money and ultimately my credibility are based on dancing. Here in this book I am thrusting my foot into some complex areas wherein I have little reputation and no obvious experience or training. I am venturing to deal with physiology, medicine, kinesiology, statistical research, philosophy and, occasionally, I even tell jokes! A vast amount of territory for a man who has spent most of his life traveling from plié to plié.

A brief bio might be to the point. I was born in New York City in 1917 of Russian-Jewish parents. Two things were important to them: education and health. My mother was called "Clara Healthy" by her friends. A great baker and a fair cook with a perennial interest in the perfect diet, she constantly proselytized her friends and made me conscious of correct eating without coercion or threats. Pop also read much about "good food" and could listen for hours to the hawkers at the New York City beaches selling elixirs guaranteed to cleanse the alimentary canal of all poisons.

I picked up their style. As a youngster and well into my adolescence, I was withdrawn and shy. The only subject that freed me to speak socially was health and/or sickness. Anyone, my age or an adult, complaining of a trouble would get my interest, concern and questions, and then a somber lecture about the trouble and a suggested cure! You see, I've been at this for a long time. This passion was reflected in my reading. Anything about health in newspapers and magazines or on the radio would get my full attention. In school I loved biology. My earliest ambition was to become a child psy-

HOW TO DANCE FOREVER

chologist, and by high school, I was dedicated to becoming a psychiatrist or a psychiatric case worker.*

It was with this ambition that I entered the City College of New York. Along the way, while still in high school, I inadvertently encountered dance. I had developed a ploy to avoid going out and playing in the street. (In New York City that's where you play.) For economic reasons, our family moved about a great deal and I was having a hard time constantly cutting into a new circle of friends in each successive neighborhood. By fourteen or fifteen I gave up and began to take hours and hours to get my homework done, giving myself that excuse not to go out and play. I did, however, have a problem with a torrent of physical energy that was not being consumed by stickball or handball or football, and certainly not by sitting at a desk doing homework.

It became the thing for me occasionally to explode from my seat, turn on the radio and bounce around to the music. Without having a name for it, I was dancing! I'd give anything now to know what I was doing at a time when I had never been to a dance concert nor had a lesson. Suffice to say there were long moments when I would become quite intoxicated with the sheer act of flying over the furniture and the submersion in music. (Even now, I can see the stuffed green armchair passing under my feet as I land on the red carpet.) I would lose my head for a while, come to and resume my insanely detailed version of the homework assignment. Finally, just before graduating from high school, at a party, I saw two young women talking. One of them was balancing precariously in what I later learned was a halfway position into a Graham fall. It looked difficult, dangerous, beautiful and *familiar*. I had done a move like that many times.

"Gittel, what are you doing?" To this day I am awed. Without moving an iota from her hinge, she flicked her head impatiently toward me, "I'm dancing." Before she could turn her head back to her friend, I asked, "Where do you learn it?" "At the New Dance Group." A year later, while finishing my first year at City College, I took my first dance class. It took two years for me to realize I was on fire. I was sitting in the old Gothic library trying to write a review of Louis Wirth's *The Ghetto* for my sociology class and getting nowhere, I sprang up from my seat, sped out to the stair landing where

---

*In retrospect, all of this is about getting well, and, in fact, in 1978, while healing after an operation, I choreographed a thirty-minute solo called *Getting Well*.

More on Me

we could smoke and, lighting up, muttered to myself, "I don't want to write a review of *The Ghetto*, I want to dance it."

Which of us has not heard from our parents, "But dancing is such a hard life." They're so right. A year later, my confrontation with Mom and Pop took place. It ran far into the night. Somewhere past two A.M., after hours of arguments and counterarguments and constant repetitions, my father suddenly interjected, "But, Daniel, you'll be so unhappy." I said, "Pop. Happiness is not the issue. It's what you want to be happy or unhappy about." At this moment, we were standing in the middle of the room and my mother started to say something but my father shot his hand up above our heads and no one spoke. We had been talking and sometimes shouting for over four hours, and now there was silence as my father held that moment. Finally, he lowered his hand and, slowly nodding his head, said quietly, "All right. I'll help you for as long as you need." This, after I had asked for a little help, for one year, while I tried to find out whether or not I had it as a dancer. He never told me what it was he was thinking that brought those words into his mouth. I should have asked. All I know is that he heard me, and by that action honored me.

I changed my degree study to health education and, two years later, graduated in 1940 with a Bachelor of Science in Health Education. In the interim, I learned and have since forgotten all the rules of lacrosse, badminton and a hundred other games, but I also studied with a passion anatomy, kinesiology and the fundamentals of physical examination. That information stuck with me. The degree was to allow me to be a dancer while holding a steady job in a university. I couldn't attend my graduation ceremony because I was on a train at the time to my first dancing job in a summer theatre in the mountains of New York State. It took me another forty-two years to finally land that steady job here at Arizona State University.

A brief chronology covering those years:

1936–40	Dance study mostly in the Graham technique including a one-year scholarship with Martha Graham and one season in Anna Sokolow's company—all this while attending the City College of New York
1940–43	Summer theatres, dancing and acting, two Broadway revues, one nightclub appearance in the Rain-

HOW TO DANCE FOREVER

bow Room in Radio City; joined Helen Tamiris's company as her partner; began study of ballet with Mme. Anderson-Ivantzova, Nenette Charisse and Edward Caton

1944–54	Leading dance roles in four Broadway musicals, two Hollywood films, some TV, working mostly with Helen Tamiris and choreographing and performing solo concert works
1954–56	Choreography for Off Broadway plays
1956–60*	Solo concerts in New York and on tour
1960–63	Co-direct the Tamiris-Nagrin Dance Company
1964–70	Solo concerts in New York and on tour
1969–73	An overlap; began work on performing improvisation, which develops into directing and touring the WORKGROUP
1974–Present	Solo concerts in New York and on tour
1982–Present	Professor of dance at Arizona State University in Tempe

In the interim, through all the years of Broadway, Hollywood, TV, industrial shows, films and finally the concert field, those two years of anatomy and kinesiology were subtly in daily use, guiding me through the hazards of dance. A true child of my parents, at every opportunity I continued to read and study diet and the body. I was amazed at how little my fellow dancers knew about their bodies. Few knew how to feed themselves properly or how to care for their precious equipment, their bodies. I became, to many of my cohorts, their handy local health guru. Somewhere along the way of my touring the university circuit, I added a lecture on "Surviving as a Dancer." It grew into this book.

One final note: Here at Arizona State University, I am in an ideal

*Extensive teaching from this point on

More on Me

place to write this book. I write a remark about the extinct Indians of Tierra del Fuego and immediately phone someone in the Anthropology Department who verifies that they *have* vanished. I need the Chinese ideogram for *hsin*, "heart-mind," and the gracious Professor Eugenia Tu of the Foreign Language Department, teacher of Chinese and an expert calligrapher, sends me a sheet full of her *hsin* ideograms from which to choose. Aside from a massive library, there is a generous and enormous number of experts in all fields to whom I have submitted this manuscript for advice, criticism and the latest developments. Every doubtful point has been cross-checked with the current literature and with experts.

There is an inevitable risk in this matter of speaking out on all manner of things, people and ideas, and yet, I have a reasonable defense. I have been around for a long time and been to many places. Between luck and knowledge, I'm still dancing when the myth says I should have stopped thirty years ago. The sum of this book is merely saying: This is what I saw/see from where I was/am dancing/living. Not for one moment am I certain of a single statement or thought. I am not yet gone and may not be leaving for a long time, but I am on my way out. For whatever it is worth, it is my obligation to speak now. Discard what you find useless and garner what you need.

INDEX

Index

Index

Index